UNBALANCING
ACTS

◆

UNBALANCING
ACTS

◆

Foundations for a Theater

BY RICHARD FOREMAN

EDITED BY KEN JORDAN

FOREWORD BY PETER SELLARS

PANTHEON BOOKS

New York

Copyright © 1992 by Richard Foreman

All rights reserved under International and Pan-American Copyright
Conventions. Published in the United States by Pantheon Books, a
division of Random House, Inc., New York, and simultaneously in
Canada by Random House of Canada Limited, Toronto.

Library of Congress Cataloging-in-Publication Data

Foreman, Richard, 1937–
Unbalancing acts : foundations for a theater / by Richard
Foreman; edited by Ken Jordan; foreword by Peter Sellars.
p.   cm.
Includes the plays: The Cure, Film is evil: radio is good; Symphony of rats;
What did he see?; and Lava.
ISBN 0-679-40454-6
1. Theater. I. Jordan, Ken. II. Title.
PS3556.07225U53   1992
812'.54—dc20   91-52628

BOOK DESIGN BY DEBBIE GLASSERMAN

Manufactured in the United States of America
First Edition

CONTENTS

◆

FOREWORD

◆

A new book by Richard Foreman is an event, but I think
that this book will astonish. His recent plays are moving
in new directions, and for those who may have found his
work abstruse, elusive, or not worth the trouble, this vol-
ume offers a cogent, candid, and penetrating series of essays
and interviews which make the theater of Richard Foreman
seem like the most natural thing in the world. Entertaining,
even. This is the logical and inevitable form that creative,
responsible, *fin-de-siècle* high-to-late capitalist self-reflexive
spectacle *would* take. Foreman's theater is not an exception
or an oddity—it is emblematic, engaged, accurate, and
deeply typical of the times. And Foreman's new writings
are absolutely essential reading for anyone interested in
theater, or indeed, the idea of culture in contemporary
America.

   In a period in which traditional theatrical gestures have
been co-opted as merchandising functions in TV com-
mercials and movies-of-the-week, the basic assumptions
of contemporary theatrical vocabulary are in need of a

serious reconsideration, if not total overhaul. In dealing
with a population that is word-poor, imaged-glutted, un-
derprepared, overinformed, hyperreactive, and desensi-
tized, strong measures are called for.

First and foremost, Richard Foreman is in love with
theater: boffo surprises, strange one-of-a-kind goings-on,
irrational and obsessive behavior, big personalities, bright
lights, the make-up, the illusion, the reality. The man who
is at the front edge of intellectual activity in the American
theater has an incurable sweet tooth, a monstrous craving
for carny tricks, freak-show hokum, disappearing acts,
outlandish transformations, and delirious spectacle. He
also has a lurid streak that is addicted to bad horror, cheap
effects, and tacky music.

But he is, by training and by inclination, a profoundly
introspective human being. And his aesthetic life has been
shaped by prolonged and serious contact with the art
world. Museum and gallery culture informs his choices,
his structural paradigms, his tendency towards the abstract,
his pleasure in cool, well-ordered space.

Foreman's shows create, like old-time theater, a world
unto themselves. Complete satisfaction is an encounter
with the world on *your* terms—now that is paradise. We
all dream of that every day. In the "written/designed/
directed by" world of Richard Foreman he immediately
establishes *his* terms up front, which is why he clearly loves
watching and participating in his own productions from a
presumed position of ultimate control. Who wouldn't?
How many of us have ultimate control over the small
productions that we offer as our lives? Isn't there some
deep satisfaction that could be derived from harnessing
that which is contrary, obstructive, unfathomable, or banal
past the point of recognition and making *entertainment* out
of it?

Foreman's productions are instantly recognizable and distantly comprehensible. The presence of a series of well-established trademarks indicates that we are encountering further installments in a body of work of a distinguished artist. These signature moments are odd, tedious, and off-putting to some, but they are hardly casual gestures on the artist's part. They represent a systematized approach to documenting a very specific reality.

Vicissitudes, violations, and appalling monotony constitute the landscape. The virtuosity is in Foreman's ability to remain accurate to the random and unhinged nature of the human mind within the context of an immense accretion of elaborately wrought detail, offered in torrents of sound, light, imagery, and endless words. In short, he offers something rather more like the actual uninflected experience of life than the usual reductive experience of theater.

There are messages written all over the set. These are productions that speak of the handwriting on the wall and sermons in stones. The lights are flashing because, in our lives, the lights *are* flashing. Are we getting the signals? Are we even squinting, or are we going to shut our eyes until it's all over? Are we able to gaze steadily into the source of brighest light? At what point does it become too painful? On the other hand, we have learned by now that we are also subject to sudden blackouts. What adjustments are necessary or even possible as this becomes a recurring aspect of our experience?

There are various terms that have been coined to deal with these facets of our mental lives: schizophrenia, aphasia, autism, and so on. But it is too simple to treat these elements of experience simply as pathology, in a way that automatically denies their validity, their ubiquity, and their persistence. We have allowed normalcy to be defined

as an extremely narrow band of consciousness. This probably represents wishful thinking rather than a larger attempt to grasp the purpose and structure of our human
and divine impulses.

What do we mean when we refer to visionary states,
ecstatic planes, and the possessions of the spirit? Are these
states to be avoided or aspired to? To be cultivated or to
be quarantined? To be repressed or achieved? Does one's
life's work lead towards or away from this reality?

The theater of Richard Foreman is poised on the edge
of this vaguely understood yearning that haunts our lives.
In the big weather system of competing philosophical in-
quiries, sexual appetites, and religious intimations, Foreman shows us lost souls in furious flight, beating their
wings, gasping for air, swooping, diving, hovering, not
quite daring to land.

He is one of the few fine artists working in the theater
today.

Peter Sellars

ACKNOWLEDGMENTS

♦

The essays in this book represent an effort to make the working premises on which my plays are grounded more accessible to a wider reading public. The material that makes up the essays, the play introductions, and the biographical interview comes from a series of interviews conducted by Ken Jordan over a period of two years. Ken edited the material into its current form, which then underwent revision by author and editor in collaboration. I should add that without Ken's continual prodding and encouragement this book would never have been completed.

I'd also like to thank Ed Friedman and the Poetry Project at Saint Mark's Church for the kind use of their Macintosh computers; Lee Ann Brown, Steven Taylor, Kim Lyons, Mitch Highfill, and Jacqueline Gens for transcribing various interviews and drafts of play texts; Etan Ben-Ami and friends at Dorsei Embassy for their help with computers; Susan Bee and Wanda Phipps for their thoughts on early drafts of the manuscript; Charles Bernstein for his help in getting the project off the ground; and Mel Gussow for inadvertently titling this book, when, in a *New York Times* review of one of my early shows, he described the play as an "unbalancing act."

Finally, I'd like to thank Kate Manheim, not only for her understanding and support of this entire project, but for the more than twenty years of artistic collaboration that helped to mold and develop the theater of which this book speaks.

R.F.

My thanks to Nina Zivančević for the tickets to *Africanis Instructus*, without which my participation in this project would not have been possible.

K.J.

UNBALANCING
ACTS

FOUNDATIONS FOR
A THEATER

♦

My theater has always tried to spotlight the most elusive aspects of the experience of being human. Human beings are to a great extent unknowable to themselves. Passing through each of us is a continual flow of motor and emotional impulses we are taught to give conventional names—"hunger," "lust," "aversion," "attraction." But these labels are neither truthful nor accurate; condensing our wide field of impulses into a few nameable categories suppresses our awareness of the infinity of tones and feeling gradations that are part of the original impulse. As each impulse is shaped in accordance with the limited number of labels available in a society, the sense of contact with their original ambiguous flavor is lost. Perhaps your impulse has a certain flavor that relates it to "hunger" or "lust," but is neither fully one nor the other. Without a name of its own, its unique truth disappears, rechanneled into one of the already named desires.

Among the countless impulses passing through us at any

moment, some surface in a manner that allows us to continue with our lives along the patterns we've inherited from our society. But any moment of true freedom suggests other structures, other textures, around which life could circle. My plays are an attempt to suggest through example that you can break open the interpretations of life that simplify and suppress the infinite range of inner human energies; that life can be lived according to a different rhythm, seen through changed eyes.

What I show on stage is a specific aspect of a chosen moment that suggests how the mind and emotions can juggle, like an acrobat, all we perceive. The strategies I use are meant to release the impulse from the straitjacket tailored for it by our society. Character, empathy, narrative—these are all straitjackets imposed on the impulse so it can be dressed up in a fashion that is familiar, comforting, and reassuring for the spectator. But I want a theater that frustrates our habitual way of seeing, and by so doing, frees the impulse from the objects in our culture to which it is invariably linked. I want to demagnetize impulse from the objects it becomes attached to. We rarely allow ourselves the psychic detachment from habit that would allow us to perceive the impulse as it rises inside us, unconnected to the objects we desire. But it's impulse that's primary, not the object we've been trained to fix it upon. It is the impulse that is your deep truth, not the object that seems to call it forth. The impulse is the vibrating, lively thing that you really are. And that is what I want to return to: the very thing you really are.

◆

Society teaches us to represent our lives to ourselves within the framework of a coherent narrative, but beneath that conditioning we *feel* our lives as a series of multidirectional impulses and collisions. We're trained to see our lives as a series of projects, one following the next along the road of experience, and our "success" depends upon how well we progress from project to project. But traveling this narrow road shuts out a multitude of suggestive impulses and impressions—the ephemeral things that feed our creative insight and spiritual energy. It's as if we were wearing blinders to restrict our emotional field, making us spiritually and psychically uneasy with the normal ambiguity of our everyday experience. So we compensate. We make self-righteous demands that noncontradiction be the basis of our value systems, but that inevitably means the suppression of all sensory richness. It reinforces our denial of the ambiguity inherent in life, which, when suppressed, makes the world seem rigid and frightening.

I like to think of my plays as an hour and a half in which you see the world through a special pair of eyeglasses. These glasses may not block out all narrative coherence, but they magnify so many other aspects of experience that you simply lose interest in trying to hold on to narrative coherence, and instead, allow yourself to become absorbed in the moment-by-moment representation of psychic freedom.

◆

The aim of art, ultimately, is to speak to man's spiritual condition, his relationship with the universe. I have always felt that I'm a closet religious writer—in spite of the aggressive, erotic, playful, and schizoid elements that decorate the surface of my plays—and it is because of my essentially religious concerns that some critics have attacked my plays for not accurately representing what they refer to as "real people" with "real" interpersonal, psychological, humanistic concerns. But once you become truly interested in man's so-called religious dimension, you lose interest in making an art that only recreates the superficial dynamics of the contingent level of being that is daily life. You lose interest in the level of "personality," because you recognize it as a product of the conditioning of the social world. This conditioning interferes with our contact with the deeper ground of being by preoccupying us with the illusions of psychological, goal-oriented involvement. We live our lives focused on those forces of our culture that give rise to certain personality traits that are the warp and woof of daily life. But character and personality are accidents of circumstance. We don't choose the customs of the culture we are born into; we arrive in a culture by chance. Social life may focus our attention on character and its vicissitudes—and that's been the source from which most theatrical form has always come—but in my plays I want to evoke the deeper ground of being, the originating network of impulse, which precedes the circumstantial "I."

◆

No work of art is absolutely truthful about life, but is a strategic maneuver performed on coagulated consciousness. As Picasso said, art is a lie that tells the truth. And it's a lie that tells the truth because it's a chosen, strategic maneuver, which is not the truth. No art could ever be "the truth," because it has to leave out ninety percent of life. But since even life's tiniest detail is an integral part of the interwoven whole, if you're not talking about all of life you're not really talking about the truth—you're talking about a selective distortion. Art is a perspective; all perspectives are lies about the total truth; so art is a lie that, if it is strategically chosen, wakes people up. Art is a lever to affect the mind. The truth of art is in the audience's, the individual's, awakened perceptions. It is not in the work of art.

◆

In my plays I try to separate the impulse from the object that seems to evoke it, and in doing so, clarify the quality of the impulse itself. One strategy I use is to overdetermine each specific, manifest impulse, so that its origin is no longer traceable to a single object that would falsely paint it with its own qualities. For instance, in a scene where the character says, "I have difficulty getting out of the room," I try to offer several reasons why, not just one. I baffle the impulse to leave the room: first, by tying the character's foot to a table; then by putting a wall between him and the door; and finally by blinding him so he cannot see his way out of the room. This strategy overloads the context. It focuses attention on the impulse to leave the room, blocking the spectator's normal tendency to think: I know how he can leave the room—he can walk through the door. If the spectator is offered a clear solution to imagine (exit through the door), his focus will be on the mundane object ("Will he get through the door?") rather than on what is happening to the character's body and soul, or on how the character's life is changed when it is filled with the impulse, "I want to leave the room."

Paradoxically, bafflement can clarify. Bafflement can force you to refocus your vision. It is the same as making the sun so bright you're forced to look away, but as you avert your eyes you see the delicate flower you've never observed before.

◆

There are several ways to isolate the impulse. One is through a strategy of interruption. Suppose an interaction between two characters is suddenly cut short by loud music, and they begin a silly dance. In this case the impulse of the scene is not allowed to fulfill itself; it's deflected. To take the example of the man who wants to leave the room, his impulse to leave might suddenly turn into a movement of the body that has nothing to do with leaving, but which suggests that impulse is still alive, though manifested in an alternate way, which allows you to observe it from a different angle.

Another way of isolating the impulse is to place it in the context of a so-called "double bind." Suppose a character sits at a table and laments to his friend, "I want to get out of the room." His friend opens a door and says, "This is the way to get out of the room." And the first replies angrily, "Why should I leave the room when I am already out of the room?" This diagrams in external dialogue a self-contradictory internal impulse, a paradoxical configuration. "Double bind" is a psychological term coined by Gregory Bateson and his associates in the fifties. In a classic double bind situation a mother asks her son, "Why don't you ever hug me? Don't you love me?" but she says it with her body tense, using a shrill tone of voice that makes it clear to the child that she has no real interest in being hugged. The child is given contradictory signals; that's the double bind. Bateson theorized that such crossed messages are at the root of schizophrenia. While I may not employ this strategy to drive people clinically crazy, I do find it useful to employ externalized double binds in my plays, because the frustration they create demagnetizes the spectator from normal avenues of conceptualization.

How can I frustrate the spectator's expectations, including his tendency to identify with the performance of a powerful actor? How can I frustrate the flow of the action within the play and prevent the inevitable drift into normal, narrative form? How can I frustrate the commonplace drive toward narrative understanding in the spectator that awakens in his consciousness a habitual identification with the goals, values, and mind-sets received from our social and cultural system? To frustrate habit is to uncover ways our impulses might be freed for use in more inventive behavior. So I try to build frustration into the very structure of my performances.

◆

To make theater, all you need is a defined space and things that enter and leave that space. You could even make a play without an actor. A jar could be thrown out into an empty space, and a minute later a stick from offstage could push that jar one inch forward. That would function as theater.

Theater is presence and absence. Someone or something is either onstage, or offstage. The deeply metaphysical concerns of the playwright-poet should include: who is offstage; who is onstage; who will be coming onstage; when they will come onstage; how can an entrance or an exit have real weight. "Offstage" is a term used only in a specifically theatrical context. There is no equivalent term relevant to the consideration of a painting or a poem. Referring to a painting, you might say something is outside the frame, but that does not have the weight of something that takes place "offstage" in the theater. In film, you assume that what you see on the screen is part of a contextual environment that is always present, "onstage," even though only one part of that environment is captured by the camera in an individual shot.

Most people claim that theater requires an audience. I disagree. I can imagine an entire audience walking out of a performance while the play continues to the end, and yet it remains a powerful piece of theater. I can imagine every member of an audience falling asleep and the play continuing to the end, turning into an objectification of the dream of that audience. Art, conceived as a revelatory process, can indeed spin its web in the void. Who knows who is really watching? When a huge audience seems to be watching, it may be only a mass collection of habitual responses planted in the seats of the theater. When nobody seems to be watching, perhaps an invisible god has his eyes on the performance. This may well be a different kind of theater than any that has ever existed. So be it.

◆

I think of myself as an artist who happens to be working in the theater, and I employ an impulsive poetic strategy in writing my plays rather than the calculated narrative strategy playwrights usually use. It was at the time of my first Ontological-Hysteric plays—after functioning for ten years as a "normal" playwright—that I stopped rewriting my texts. I no longer "corrected" what I had written because I thought rewrites would hide the true evidence of what was happening to me in the moment of composition. Anything other than true evidence of psychic reality seemed dishonest to me. Occasionally there'd be lines I found embarrassing, that seemed especially juvenile, and I'd cut them. But when we went into rehearsal I'd miss them. I'd realize those lines were the strongest and most personal—and I had to face up to the fact that they did come from my most genuine instincts. So I would restore them and stage them as the absolute center of the scene. I thought of writing as evidence of my mental and spiritual state. Above all I tried to be honest about myself by keeping my style uncorrected by my well-schooled intelligence.

Kerouac and Ginsberg were saying the same thing, of course, though I hadn't read them at the time.

◆

My interest in writing has always been to escape the constrictions of personality, the socially conditioned self. Since I'm not able to write under the influence of alcohol or drugs, as many writers can and do, I found other ways to drug myself. One way was to allow myself to sink into a kind of semiconscious state, somewhere between wakefulness and sleep, and set whatever came from that state down on the page. When I'm writing an article or a review I'm writing out of a part of myself that's totally self-possessed and critical. It's the same "me" who manifests as the stage director in front of a group of actors, very much in command. But the me who writes the plays is as far from that self as I can get and still be inside my own skin. In a positive sense, it's a dissolute, irresponsible me —drunk with poetry, as Baudelaire or the Sufi masters might say.

◆

I'm constantly jotting down ideas of all kinds into notebooks, memos to myself about things that seem profound or useful. Most of these notes concern ways to organize my consciousness, how to deploy my mental and spiritual apparatus in ways that facilitate the artistic process. For instance, I might have the idea, "Write without thinking," and I'd jot that in my notebook. I'd have hundreds of rules and suggestions of this sort. Later, thumbing through my notebook, I'd see "Write without thinking." Immediately I'd say to myself, "Okay, don't think"—and I'd write something. Maybe I'd write one line of dialogue, or maybe ten lines, but I'd never go back and ask myself, Was this line *really* written without thinking? The instruction would be simply a prod to begin writing.

But I've never adhered one hundred percent to the writing programs I created; they were simply guidelines within which I tried to orient myself. There are people who make art in which every moment of creation is governed by the rules of the game they've decided to play, whereas I always allowed my rules to be disrupted by my own free impulses. If I departed from the rules—that was fine; the writing was the result of a productive conflict between rule and impulse which enriched the final product. The conceptual universe that governs a work of art should always be under attack by personal impulses that break into and interfere with that conceptual universe.

Other times, though, the dialogue would not come as the product of these strategies, but as a response to something I'd be reading. I often underline passages, make notes in the margins of books. For instance, I might write down in the back of a book, "Yes, man has no center." Then I'd quickly jot down whatever came into my mind as a result of focusing on that idea. For instance:

> "Hey, what happened to my shoe?"
> "You don't need shoes to walk, because I don't walk, I'm falling."

Two quick lines of dialogue. Later, that might end up in a play or it might not. For one of my earliest productions, *Evidence*, I staged twenty pages of these fragments, along with the rules and notations that generated them. I think I wanted to prove I was such a good director I could stage virtually anything!

◆

Even as I have come to have more faith in my ability as a writer, I still war with the notion that "good writing" can be a limiting, oppressive, totalitarian factor, because, as Roland Barthes suggested, it limits the free play of truth's energy in a text. Barthes maintained that "good writing" is a manifestation of power exercised by a certain social class, and to be recognized as a "good writer" you must think and perform in accordance with the habits of that class—the exploitative class. Therefore vernacular, undisciplined, or "bad" writing has the potential to express important ideas that "good" writing cannot touch; ideas that exist, for instance, in the unconscious. Of course, such bad writing isn't normally imagined to include the efforts of educated writers who specifically choose to write "badly," which would be my case. At times I chose to write woodenly, to convey the heaviness of the word as the coagulation of habit. I'd pour out sentences that didn't finish, or stuttered and stumbled, to convey the stress of consciousness at work on an impenetrable world. I exploited bad writing in order to allow first thoughts and the primitive roots of ideas to maintain direct contact with the impulses that generated them. I didn't want writing subjected to the control of a well-schooled consciousness that eliminated the alive roughness of that first impulse. Nonetheless, since I've spent my life admiring my own pantheon of "good writers," from Paul Valéry to Robert Musil to Ortega y Gasset, I felt a conflict between an impulse to write "good" and a feeling that it was the wrong position to take, both politically and aesthetically. So sometimes "good writing" would surface, while other times it would be suppressed.

On occasion the texts were informed by complicated theoretical notions which hovered in the background; the dialogue made reference to these ideas without clarifying them. Much of this "bad writing" was the product of my desire to honestly represent in the body of the writing the difficulties I had struggling with complex systems of thought. I don't claim, for instance, to be an expert on the French psychoanalyst Jacques Lacan, though he had great influence on me. I was deeply struck by insights that leaped from his convoluted texts with Zenlike suddenness, but when my writing made reference to ideas I'd culled from Lacan, I'd try to make my text imitate the difficulty I had trying to psyche out what was hidden in his dense prose style. While I was able to grasp certain insights intuitively, I was nevertheless a "stupid" reader of Lacan, and I wanted my writing style to show my stupidity dancing hand-in-hand with my insight. This writing did exactly what Gertrude Stein advised against: in baroque fashion, it reflected the stress of the act of writing within the writing itself. The syntactical, rhythmic form reflected the fact that I was not a well-tooled Lacanian machine, able to spout the jargon and follow the subtlest ins and outs of Lacanian discourse. Rather, I was someone who delighted in struggling with that material.

◆

In retrospect, I can see a logical development in my work toward ever freer, unconsciously oriented writing techniques. The decisions that led me in this direction were never deeply meditated; in fact they were made very cavalierly. I never tried to justify them. I'd simply become bored with one way of doing things so I would try to do something else. I should stress, however, that I always felt that life's rigor, rather than my own, was at work when I made such choices.

Over time I understood that it was my evolving program to write a little bit every day, or every other day, not knowing what would get used in a production, but I would continue to generate material. And I do think of it as *material*—I have no need to believe that I am writing *plays.* I came to understand I am just writing notes, thoughts, dialogue, fragmentary observations, some of which would eventually be staged. I also stopped imagining who was speaking the lines of dialogue I wrote down. In my earliest plays I indicated who was speaking by marking the first initial of the character's name in front of a line, like "R" for Rhoda or "K" for Karl. Then I began to leave those letters out, because when I was writing I knew who was speaking. It seemed obvious, I thought, so why bother indicating it every time? But sometimes I'd reread material and not remember who was saying which line, so I realized it must not really matter. The language would "go on" in an interesting way regardless. Then I thought it might be more exciting to leave out those notations entirely, and while writing try not to experience the dialogue as coming from different specific characters, but rather think of it as a nonending river of talk. And then make decisions about who would say what line later in rehearsal.

I also began to leave out the stage directions. As the movement in the productions became more elaborate, as I played with the assignment of the dialogue in rehearsal, I realized the staging no longer illustrated the text, but had acquired a life of its own, inspired by associations the text suggested. An increased use of music also led me to improvise more in rehearsals, though *I* was the one who did the improvising, not the actors. Eventually I stopped going into rehearsals with rigid, elaborate plans. The sets I was using at this time were designed to be as flexible as building blocks, so I was able to alter the set continually as part of my rehearsal improvisation. For *Penguin Touquet*, for instance, I designed a number of rolling platforms which I could continually reconfigure in order to change the stage composition. It seemed logical, therefore, to think up most

of the staging on my feet, on the set, with the real objects
at hand to play with.

◆

When typing up the handwritten material from my notebooks, I'd be careful to suppress the desire to make little
changes as I typed, fearing that would corrupt the spontaneity of the scrawled text. I'd type it out, trying to reflect
the actual look of the handwritten page—indentations,
blank spaces, and so on. Usually, though, I'd indent different lengths from line to line to indicate to myself that
different characters were speaking. The scripts looked like
open-field poems. I'd try to leave lots of empty space on
the page, making it easy to scan, so there was a concrete,
plastic feel, as if you were handling an object or participating in the blocking of a play on stage.

    Then when I'd get the urge to put a play together, I'd
spread these typed pages on the couch or a large table and
start leafing through them. I'd find a page that interested
me and put it aside. Then I'd pick out another page that
seemed to relate to the first in some way. They might both
refer to the weather, for instance. The third page I'd pick
wouldn't necessarily mention the weather, but could mention the building of a house—you might build a house to
protect yourself from bad weather, and that connection
might excite me. So I'd continue, assembling the play in
this very casual manner. I never spent much time pon-
dering: does this page go better with this page or that one?
I've always believed that since I'm writing out of the center
of my own spiritual quest, everything ultimately becomes
relevant, in much the same way it does in an inclusive
work like *Finnegans Wake*. The point is that one page contains all the other pages, therefore many possible combinations are valid. It's then my job as director to discover

particular ways the various materials of a play relate to each other, and so evoke that whole which is always the same.

Out of a pile of one hundred pages I'd make three or four plays, then I would decide which I wanted to produce next. There was a period from *Pandering to the Masses* through *Book of Splendors* when I generally chose the one that seemed the least theatrical, because I thought that was a useful risk; I liked the challenge it gave me as a director.

Then the play would sit on my shelf for about half a year—I was always ahead of myself—and I'd give it no thought until I was ready to go into production.

Once it was time to mount the production, the first thing I'd consider was the set. I'd casually flip through the script and make sketches. For instance, suppose we did this play about the weather. We have a house in it, and a boat, so I'd start to fool around: wouldn't it be nice to do this play in an Edwardian house, perhaps with a tree in front, and if we tilt the tree sideways, maybe it could become a boat? I can't emphasize enough how casual all this has to be at the beginning of the process, allowing the mind to float through multiple possibilities. In this same loose frame of mind I'd start making rough scale models of the set in cardboard. Usually I'd go through ten or twelve versions, each radically different, before coming up with something I'd keep. Maybe it wouldn't be a house and a boat, but a railway station with stuffed sofas instead of trains. I'd try whatever came to mind.

The next step would be choosing the music. I'd collect a lot of music, looking for material that would lend itself to tape loops I could play during performance. Often I'd keep a tape machine connected to the radio so I could quickly record anything I heard with a phrase or two, or a tone color, that appealed to me. I didn't try to imagine

it in the play itself, but about a week before rehearsal I'd
go through the tapes while reading the play and make
preliminary choices as to which combinations of loops
seemed potent, imagined in juxtaposition to each page of
text.

♦

When I read through the pages of a play I have chosen to
stage, I see that the darting, fragmentary nature of my text
touches many levels, and I want to reflect them all on stage
in juxtaposition. For the past ten years, I've used a kind
of shorthand when writing my texts, though I know a
spectator could never pick up on all the feeling tones and
associations packed into them, especially when heard only
once, in a single evening's performance. When you read
it on the page you have time to allow all the possible
associations to hit home, but listening to it whiz past in
the theater is another matter. So I try to help the spectator
by adding props and scenic elements—skulls, flowers,
globes, mirrors, stuffed animals, crutches, radios, and so
on—which suggest the range of possible associations the
text continually evokes.

I might write a speech that seems spoken by a narcissistic
person who loves beautiful things but who feels himself
physically or psychologically tawdry, like the main character in *What Did He See?* As I read that speech back to
myself, allowing myself to free associate in relation to the
text, I might think of mirrors, flowers, and a worn tapestry
hanging on the wall. The aim is to elaborate on and qualify
that speech in terms of props and objects, rather than in
language, in order to suggest the feeling background from
which the speech arises and the particular interactions between characters that might result. These props, once they
have been amassed on stage, function like the reverberating

chamber of a violin. When you play a note, it is amplified and projected by the wooden body of the violin into a richer tone. As you tune the violin precisely, more overtones are created. Similarly, the set and props of the staged play must be properly tuned (selected and modified) to create overtones not available to the spectator while he simply listens to the text's words as they fly past in the performance.

I'd start thinking about props only a few weeks before rehearsals began. Thumbing through the pages, again very casually, I'd say, For this page about the weather, maybe I can use an umbrella? Then I'd think, No, that's boring —better an umbrella at the end of a long stick with a wheel on the bottom. Then I'd go on leafing through the script and imagine one or two things that seemed suggestive for every page. In that way I'd amass a list of props, many of which had no obvious relation to the text, but all of which might add an interesting second level to the scene. During rehearsals, many of these props would get cut from the production, but I always wanted to start with a surplus of material so I had room to play around. Often I had doubles and triples of props so that several performers could use the same kind of prop at once, building choral prop effects.

On the first day of rehearsals, which usually last eight weeks, I'd start staging the play with the actors on their feet. There'd be no introductory read-through of the text. Often the set would already be built and in place, so the initial blocking rehearsals could be detailed and specific. As a director, I've always focused on the complex dynamics of each staged moment's relation to the specific physical environment of the set. Suppose the first line of the play was, "Oh, it's raining, isn't it?" I'd say—Kate, the first line is yours, and you enter holding the umbrella, wheeling it along the ground, walking in a straight line that parallels the back wall of the set, but about six feet downstage of it. At the same time, the rest of that cast is sleeping on the ground, and when she passes this table, all of you jump up and run off.

Very little of this was ever worked out before coming into rehearsal. Even the fact that the line was Kate's would probably have been decided on the spot, as I got the feel of things in the rehearsal environment. At most I might have scratched down three or four lines in my script suggesting: "Kate with stick, others run out." Maybe I'd even have drawn a little arrow to indicate the direction they'd all head. But the minute we'd begin working on our feet I'd have lots of other ideas, and with each scene we'd go through weeks of totally different stagings.

◆

When staging my earliest plays I wanted to restrict myself to a simple illustration of the text, but in later years I developed a method of working in productive counterpoint to the text. In *Penguin Touquet*, for instance, I staged one scene with the actors balanced on chairs with their right legs lifted awkwardly into the air. There was certainly no indication of that position in the dialogue or the text's stage directions. But during rehearsals I imagined that pose, and then realized it was my intuitive response to underlying psychological currents I sensed operating in the text. Perhaps the characters were psychologically off balance at that moment, and the way they raised their legs echoed that internal predicament. I try at all times to stage the psychological anguish present, but hidden, in each moment of the text.

Such counterelements in the staging also make reference to the way one's life experience is continually informed by contradictory impulses. When you love someone, do you want to kiss him or her all the time? Or do you sometimes have the urge to hit or bite, even at the same moment the desire to kiss arises? Such contradictions are at the heart of our condition on this planet, a condition you dream of transcending if you have spiritual yearnings. But of course, such yearning itself is open to question—is it a regression to a childish, and therefore undesirable, state? Perhaps the desire for grace is itself a kind of infantilism. Even though it might undercut my own position, I want each play to be the involuntary registering of a sensibility truthful enough to reflect its own internal contradictions.

◆

Over the years I've become increasingly obsessed with how the input into our culture is accelerating, and of the increasingly heterogeneous nature of that input. In my own life I began to see how I rapidly replaced old ideas with new ideas, old feelings with new feelings. Books I liked once I no longer cared for. Many of my opinions had changed. We live in a Mixmaster culture. Everything from mankind's history is available to us at the flick of a dial or the opening of a book. In business and government executives meet today to make plans for ten years down the road; the future compacts in front of us. But while that's happening, can we pay true and careful attention to what's going on in our sensibility at the precise moment of the present? I think not, distracted as we are by the rate of flow of new input. Does one accept that or reject it? There is speed in our culture, and I want to reflect both the exhilaration and the neurosis such speed injects into our lives. At the same time, I also hope to intuit artistic structures—models of consciousness—that might evolve into a new kind of lucidity and self-possession, which would enable us to navigate the rapids of our times.

There was a period, climaxing with the production of *Miss Universal Happiness*, when my plays became increasingly frenetic, moving so quickly that it was as if the spectator was picked up and carried along on a roller coaster ride. These plays regarded the ravishing objects of our physical world as illusion, to be enjoyed as you enjoy sights through a kaleidoscope. I hoped that the rhythm of my plays of the late seventies, early eighties, would induce a fast scanning mechanism in the spectator's brain, a hum in his consciousness akin to the Om of the universe in Eastern tradition. To attain that hum, you might first voraciously pursue all the baubles the world offers, look at each for an intense moment, and then throw it aside. Let each one be displaced by another, and another, and another, until you realize that what truly delights is the hum of movement that engulfs you—a hum that arises as you toss aside whatever coagulates into a fixed form to hypnotize and paralyze the consciousness.

◆

In his pioneering book, *The Meeting of East and West*, written in the midforties, the American philosopher F. S. C. Northrop discussed the difference between Eastern and Western art. Eastern art, he said, reflects an "undifferentiated aesthetic continuum" that flows through all being, whereas in Western art that continuum has broken down and has crystalized into particular, individualized objects. My work, along with much other advanced Western art of the twentieth century, is an attempt to evoke this undifferentiated aesthetic continuum.

An analogy I've used to illustrate the difference between Eastern and Western aesthetics echoes the difference between most theater and my own. A child receives a toy top as a gift, and on its sides it has a number of pictures.

For instance, one is of a man giving his wife a doughnut, and another is of a little boy fishing. The child looks at the individual pictures and is totally absorbed by their beauty. Then someone comes along and shows him that by pushing up and down on the center of the top he can make it spin. As it spins, the top makes a humming noise, and the individual pictures can no longer be distinguished. All that's seen is a blur. But the child becomes fascinated by that energetic blur and forgets about the individual pictures. I think of myself as making an art that focuses on the hum, the energetic blur, of that spinning top, rather than on the pictures visible after it has come to rest and died.

◆

A critic once told me that his problem with my plays was that when he was watching them he thought they were fantastic, but once he'd left the theater they seemed to vanish from his memory. As if that were bad! My sense, however, is that it's a very positive quality. It's always irked me when people say, "I don't know what your play meant, but wow, that image when she rolled out that strange umbrella and they all ran away, that really stayed with me!" Personally, I don't think that's much of a compliment. The image of the Marlboro man riding his horse and smoking his cigarette has stuck with me for many years—and so what? It's garbage. It's kitsch. All it means is that the image seduced me, that it pushed a button that was ready to be pushed, and I responded. It didn't widen my sensibilities, compassion, or intuition. Whereas an art that affects you in the moment, but which you then find hard to remember, is straining to bring you to another level. It offers images or ideas from that other level, that other way of being, which is why you find them hard to remember. But it has opened you to the possibility of growing into what you are not yet, which is exactly what art should do. So I try to make plays as hard to remember as a vivid dream which, when awake, you know you've lived with intensity, yet try as you might you can't remember.

◆

Writers like Anton Ehrenzweig and W. R. Bion have written suggestively about "free-floating attention," which is Freud's term to describe an open consciousness in which you are attentive to what arises before you, but are free from all habits of conceptual categorization. Were you to sit next to a psychoanalyst at work with a patient who was free-associating, it might seem to you that the patient was speaking nonsense. However, at some point the psychoanalyst will find sense in that nonsense. But to say that he would "make sense" out of it is to misstate the case. He does not create sense through focused intellectual effort. Rather, through his use of free-floating attention, he waits until sense "arises" in the mind, as it always does. There is an inevitable drift toward coherence. Rather than identifying what he observes and giving it a position in some hierarchical system, he simply allows it to float in his consciousness, transforming itself as much as it likes, without imprisoning it inside the grid of his own preconceptions. The analyst will wait for coherence to reveal itself. I think the artist at work does the same, and audiences should learn to do it as well. With the kind of art that I make, there is a similar, inevitable drift toward coherence, and it will surface and coagulate for the spectator in exactly the same way.

There's another idea that comes from contemporary psychoanalytic theory which I find suggestive. Many analysts claim that rather than being cured by an analyst, the patient manages to cure himself in collaboration with the analyst. From this perspective, the analyst is on equal ground with the patient, not superior to him. The analyst deliberately creates an arena in which the patient's own discourse, under the light of analysis, can gradually reveal what he's really trying to say. The transition the patient experiences is not that he, as an individual suffering from an illness, has had that illness removed so that he can return to health. Instead, he finds that the perceptual frame through which he sees the world has been recalibrated. Most people will go into analysis thinking: I am Joe Jones and I have a problem, and three years from now I want to be the same Joe Jones but without the problem. Many analysts would suggest, however, that to derive any benefit from psychoanalysis, you must accept the fact that at the end of the process you are not going to be the same Joe Jones. And Joe Jones will find his perception restructured to reveal a different environment. The old Joe Jones will not discover the answer to his problems presented in terms of the life game he'd been playing. Instead, Joe will find himself living by new rules, which will mean that the problems that surfaced within the old game no longer present themselves. It's not that the problem has been solved, but by being reframed and seen within the context of a differently defined world, it becomes a nonproblem. Similarly, my plays propose an art that focuses on changing the perceptual environment within which we see objects and problems; I refuse to analyze objects and problems using the terms insisted upon by our socially enforced perspectives.

Robert Musil wrote that he strove for an art that focused on all the holes in the web of our experience. To show the alternatives to what is; to show the things that do not cohere. Most serious, twentieth-century artists work along the same lines. What does the verbal style of Jack Kerouac show? That every detail of life, including everything usually dismissed as irrelevant or marginal, is of mind-blowing importance. What is Samuel Beckett showing? That despite all our great plans and monumental projects, what are of real weight are our obsessive fidgets. Everyone working in this tradition shows that the incidental stuff left out of the goal-oriented narrative of your life is actually the crucial, potent, soul-making material. And that's also the insight of psychoanalysis; how the seemingly unimportant slips of the tongue, dream images, meaningless details you think tangential to your real concerns, are in fact the royal road to that unconscious that determines your true fate.

◆

What's called for is a more radical attitude toward the contradictory nature of our experience. The commonplace diagnosis of our world is to say it's "fragmented"—a negative assessment that invokes defensive attitudes. It implies: how do we make it whole again? But perhaps wholeness is *not* the answer. Maybe it's only a regressive dream of lost innocence. Perhaps a more creative way to approach our contemporary situation is to assume that we're being called upon to find ways to be open and flexible enough so that we're no longer overwhelmed by the contradictory impulses of the world. You want to remove the hypnotic power that the world currently has over you. Rather than be hypnotized by it, you want to be free of the world. You want to realize that the world you see is made by the way you see it. Therefore, if you are open enough, and allow yourself a more dissociated perceptiveness, you can free yourself from being hypnotized by the world. Pro-

posing models for that openness and flexibility is the task
my plays perform.

◆

A modest proposal: perhaps some of my critics might find
it easier to enter the world of my plays if, before entering,
they tried to make themselves very tiny. If you're a big
person, carrying your big, heavy, important projects and
concerns with you into the theater, when you confront
my play it will appear to be an amorphous cloud of mo-
lecular particles, circulating in a seemingly random pattern,
like Brownian motion. Perceiving it like that, the big person that you are measures the play against the heavy projects you carry around in your head, and you think: In my
life I have a big square shape, which is my problem with
my lover; a big round shape, which is my problem with
my business; and a big triangular shape, which is my problem with my neighbor. I want help in resolving such
weighty problems, and all this play proposes is an amorphous cloud of circulating molecules, incapable of budging
those big solid shapes that fill my life. What I need from
a play is a shape bigger and heavier than my own in order
to reorganize my own massive shapes.

My art proposes, however, that by shifting your attention to the scale on which atomic events occur, by perceiving the world as you would perceive solid objects
through a powerful microscope, you discover that your
own solid shapes are themselves but clouds of molecules
in circulation. The problems you have with your lover,
your business, or your neighbor are not the shapes they
seem to be. Within you and your lover, for instance, a
myriad of Brownian movements circulate. If you can make
yourself small enough to follow the Brownian movement
of my plays, you might discover the same Brownian
movement at work in those monolithic shapes that seem

to block you from the happy ending you hope awaits you
at the end of your various involvements. If you have recurring arguments with your spouse they may loom im-
portantly like threatening hexagons of disaster, and you
may end up structuring your life around your psychic obsession with those hexagons. But looked at from the proper
distance—if you are properly detached, and able to com-
passionately identify with the passions that may be driving
your spouse—the hexagons of conflict may either enlarge,
or reduce, until you find you're suddenly viewing them
on a different scale, tuned into the harmonic hum of the
universe. Perhaps it's the scale of the stars, or the scale of
atomic particles, but on either of those nonhuman scales
the music seems much the same, the same laws seem op-
erative on both levels, just as those same laws, those same
musics, operate in the human being, if only he can find a
way to retune himself to be in harmony with them.

As the great French mathematician Poincaré suggested,
the scale creates the content. Perhaps you find the content
of my plays elusive because you don't understand that I'm
asking you to make yourself small enough so you can see
the smaller (more universal) scale on which events in my
theater take place. I'm trying to function as an atomic
physicist of the theater, and just as dealing with tiny, non-
material atoms can lead to gigantic explosions in the realm
of gross matter, I maintain that if you change the scale of
your perceptual mind-set as you watch my plays, the tiny
atomic structure of my style can produce explosions in
your larger-scaled, psychological self. This lends a specific,
therapeutic relevance to my Brownian-movement-kind-
of-theater; it enables you to sense your own life as har-
moniously immersed within the atomic dance of each lived
moment. But because you are not used to choosing the
scale in which you see, you tend to think of yourself as a
monolithic "I," with a monolithic personality that inter-

David Warrilow and Kate Manheim in **Penguin Touquet. (Photo by Carol Rosegg)**

acts, for example, with the monolithic company you work for—which has a monolithic personality of its own. We all tend to forget that our monolithic self is the product of a learned perceptual system, in which the constraints of convention and habit pile up to deaden our ability to scan those freedom-giving contradictions of our impulsive life. These contradictions are really doors; doors to understanding that the monoliths you perceive as blocking your path to happiness are, in fact, clouds of language and impulse in continual circulation; and you can enter inside these clouds, and dance with these elements.

I would hope that the rhythms and aesthetic strategies of my plays persuade you to adjust your perceptual scale during the course of the performance. There are moments, for instance, when an actor imitates brief flashes of a specific character type, and for those moments you should make an adjustment in scale so you can recognize and register "character." Other times, you're presented with an interplay of visual composition, gesture, and sound, which notates a raw impulse floating totally outside of any embodied character. A different scale of activity has taken over the stage, and you should adjust accordingly. Throughout my plays there are throw-away references of all sorts. References to phenomenological, political, or religious thought will suddenly be undercut by a reference to ice cream cones, and that twisted immediately into a reference to an automobile collision. All of these references are being juggled at once. As the balls come whizzing around the stage, you are expected to join in this game of juggling. "Oh, here comes a ball of ice cream cones." And you have to keep it in play. That is, catch it, but throw it right back up in the air or the game will be over. You have to be ready to catch the next reference, to automobile collisions, then pass quickly from that so you're ready for the next—a stab of feeling, or twitch of the body. Then throw that right back; keep it up in the air so the references continue to circulate!

I'm interested in evolving a dramatic structure that would use the raw materials of everyday life to externalize on stage a rhythm and sensibility that exist deep inside me, but that find no existing objects or conceptual forms sufficient in the world to reflect them. And so the spectator's question should not be, What does this play mean? The ques-

tion should be, In response to which of the world's possibilities and tensions is this play created? That is its meaning.
The meaning is the externalization of those impulses that
have no external home in the world as it is now constituted.
It is certainly a different kind of meaning from what you
find by decoding the narrative of a traditional play.

♦

What my plays say, in effect, is that not all the problems
of life can be resolved within the accepted terms of the
materialist culture we've inherited; in fact, the *most* important ones cannot. This is an approach to art that puts
it in direct opposition to the mythos of the mainstream,
business-oriented culture of the late twentieth century.
There's no question that serious twentieth-century art
functions as an adversary to the going culture. That's why
the powers-that-be have secretly—or not so secretly—considered adventurous (serious) art of the modern era subversive. It *is* subversive. It implies that the cultural choices
we have made are wrong, which is, of course, a disturbing
message. Mainstream art, on the other hand, even when
it is seemingly critical on a specific issue, can only be re-
visionist at best. It may suggest that things have gone
wrong, but can only point to options already existing
within the culture. It has no deep way of evoking the
possibility that the culture's deepest unconscious presup-
positions might be the problem: that it might be desirable
to reconstitute our very way of being human. Reactionary
critics have a point, therefore, when they attack contemporary trends in art because they fear such art might un-
dermine Western culture. In the long run, it well might.
But they shouldn't worry. Something better is coming.
My theater is one attempt among many to listen carefully,
in order to hear the approaching footsteps.

DIRECTING
THE ACTORS, MOSTLY

♦

When I started producing plays I was interested in seeing *people* onstage. I felt I'd never seen people appear onstage, I'd only seen *actors* onstage, and an actor acting is a special kind of person, one who bears little resemblance to my experience of people in real life. Most people rarely manifest the charisma characteristic of that category of the human race known as: actor. What interested me was taking people from real life, nonactors, and putting them onstage to allow their real personalities to have a defiant impact on the conventional audience. While you were not necessarily convinced that they were experiencing true, strong emotions, you had a stronger flavor of Bob or John or whoever it was, than you'd receive from a trained actor preoccupied with trying to convince you he felt great anguish because he'd just killed his best friend, or had fallen madly in love.

Those early plays projected an extreme naturalness which had a disruptive effect on the audience, because what the spectator was watching was a particular kind of naturalness that had been banished from the theater. The theater works very hard to keep *out* awkward, amateurish, wooden performances. I was working very hard to bring that area of naturalness *into* the theater, simply because it hadn't been seen.

For the production of *Angelface*, I decided that since I was using people who were not actors, and since I didn't want to rehearse for a long time, I'd put all the dialogue on tape and we'd play the tape in performance. Then I thought, wouldn't it be interesting if the actors repeated what they heard on the tape, but at a slower speed, so we'd get a web of language weaving through the performance? This would coincidentally facilitate rehearsals, eliminate memorization of the lines, and make everything fast and simple. I didn't ask my nonactors to "act," because I wasn't interested in acting. From the time I was fifteen I found theater much too concerned with actors trying to make audiences love them by being overemotional and manipulative, so I thought a nonacting performance style, working with the taped dialogue, would be a simple way to deal with that problem.

These tape techniques were also inspired by the sound manipulations of musicians like LaMonte Young, Phil Glass, and Steve Reich, whom I'd heard in concert at Jonas Mekas's Filmmaker's Cinematheque. LaMonte's pieces, for instance, were loud, continuous tones—drones with no real variation for minutes at a time—which made you listen to sound itself in a deep, different way. I wanted to get that same thickness, that overlay of sound, in the spoken language of my play. I was also influenced by the early events staged by Jack Smith and the particular acting style he encouraged in his performers, which was based upon having very little happen, stretched over long, long periods of time. That influenced both the rhythmic articulation of the speech on my tapes and the way I asked the actors to repeat the dialogue onstage, very slowly, with an uninflected delivery, in counterpoint to the tapes during the performance.

For all my early plays I worked the tape recorder myself, because I liked to be able to regulate the rhythms of the performance by starting and stopping the tape, holding the pauses the way I felt they should be held for that particular audience—or in response to the way I was feeling that particular evening—or in response to the energy level of that night's show.

◆

For a period, starting with *Pandering to the Masses*, all the lines on tape were recorded by as many as four voices, alternating word by word. During the performance the tape was played back from loudspeakers located in the four corners of the performance space, so each sentence of dialogue would seem to circle the audience: they'd hear one word coming from the left side of the stage, then the next word from the right side, then the next from in back of the audience on the right, and so on. We'd do it for the whole evening. The actors would slowly and softly repeat the lines of the character they were playing in counterpoint to the tape. Since the actors onstage would speak at a slower rate than the tape they were cued by, it meant that they were soon overlapping each other as well as the tape. This would continue for a few lines, then a loud thud would interrupt, and a moment of silence would follow, clearing the air. Then the whole process would begin again.

◆

For the first five or six years I asked the actors to speak as if they were teachers in front of a class writing lines for dictation on the blackboard for students to practice their penmanship. They could speak with authority, but were asked not to reflect the normal emotional content of the line so that the word quality itself could be heard ringing through the text, not swamped by the emotional thrust of the actor's performance. Empathy, I felt, obscured what was happening in the spoken language as well as other aspects of theatrical activity, such as the stage movement, the lighting, the sound effects; I felt all of these were invariably slighted in favor of empathy with the performer, which wiped out other levels of meaningful experience for the spectator.

♦

My basic rule for directing my own plays was to make the staging an X-ray of the text; to create as little embellishment as possible. I tried to cleanse the staging of all excessive movement; the performances were very static. The gestures were wooden, determined, controlled. It was an absolute documentation of the text. When an actor said, "I'm pointing to her," that's what he would do. I wanted it to be as simple and rigorous as the minimalist art of that period, showing only the basic shape of the event and not decorating it in any way. I rigorously followed the minimalist program of "no nonsense": Let's try to strip away all the hypocrisy of delight with which we ice the birthday cake of our art.

♦

As I see it now, the early plays were attempts to get back to the basics, to be as primitive as possible. And just as in primitive paintings figures are generally drawn from the front, my actors usually stood facing front, arms hanging dead at their sides, except when making gestures. Most of

the time I asked them to stare straight at the audience, as
if drilling the play directly into the center of the spectator's
forehead. I wanted them to appear heavy, solid, wooden
—I hesitate saying as if they were puppets, because for
years I was accused of using my actors like puppets. But
they were *not* puppets, because I was totally dedicated to
the idiosyncratic awkwardness of each nonactor as he or
she carried out my instructions in his or her own precise
and idiosyncratic way. Kleist, in his essay concerning
the marionette theater, explains how he's ravished by the
idea of a pure, suprahuman style of movement that tran-
scends awkward self-consciousness. But I *wanted* that self-
consciousness. I *never* trained my actors to move more
neutrally, to be automatons. I relished the collision between my precise direction and the actors' bodies and personal methods. I would enjoy the fact that actor A
slumped, or that actor B was scared to look directly at the
audience so his eyes darted about nervously. The more
awkward they were, the better. All I asked of them was
that they do their assigned physical tasks easily and simply.
I wanted to see what the world of the army would look
like if people were told to do things, but you didn't punish
them if they didn't do them too well.

♦

I received a letter at that time from someone who compared
my theater to a factory tour, where a guide might point
out, "Here's where we mix the chocolate, here's where
we cut it into squares, and here's where we wrap it up."
My staging was like a factory tour of a play. It was the
same kind of demonstration: here's how somebody hits
somebody else with a baseball bat, and here's how somebody holds the side of their head and says, "Oh, it hurts."
This notion of performance as demonstration had much

to do with my reading of Brecht, my more esoteric reading about alchemy, and my readings of anything else I could find that suggested strategies to counteract the normal, seductive glamour of the theater. But at the same time that I was using this clinical, minimalist approach, the plays became extremely sexual, in a funny way, because the bodies of the actors were absolutely present as physical flesh displayed in all its awkwardness onstage. In normal theater you tend to empathize with the characters' goals, which makes you look past his or her palpable physical presence and dream instead about what will happen when their projects meet resistance or achieve success. But in my theater, there was no project to dream into. There was only the physical being trying to manipulate his body in the material world, and there's a great erotic component in that.

The time came, however, when I felt I'd done all I could with nonactors. The texts I now write call for skills and an intensity which most untrained performers simply do not have. In the early days, I was interested in the collision between my language and the person without theatrical skills who spoke it; that collision made the performers more physically present onstage, as they struggled with the text and movement. The texts in those days were written in a way that rendered such collisions fruitful. But with my more recent texts that's no longer the case. I need performers whose skill enables the audience to look through them to see into the text itself. I must admit, however, that I'm not particularly interested in the emotional reality of the performer's psyche. I think only of how the performance will serve the text.

◆

I find I am attracted to what is thought of as the "silent movie" style of acting, because it calls special attention to the actor's gestures and gives them extra weight vis-à-vis the other considerations of a scene. I find this kind of exaggerated, carefully articulated acting style often more profound and penetrating than naturalistic acting. A good silent actor might roll his eyes in anguish, for instance, in a way that expresses a cosmic dimension of feeling we do not easily admit to in our society, dominated as we are by scientific rationalism and psychological reductionism. And that is why we laugh—the style seems overstated, because the conventions of our social world press us to understate the rush of impulse inside us. Take a typical silent movie scene: a husband opens a door and there is his wife in bed with the milkman. Cut to the sight of the husband seeing them; he rolls his eyes and clenches his fists—and we sophisticated late-twentieth-century spectators all laugh, thinking that simply is not the way people behave (even though it is the way people feel)! Often this style of acting is able to evoke archetypal levels of experience. However, when most contemporary productions make use of it, they intend it to be funny, because the rest of the mise-en-scène does nothing to sustain that acting style's reference to the deeper archetypal level to which it is capable of referring. But I believe that when I use that style I surround it with other directorial elements which make it seem appropriate, able to make truthful contact with the deep anguish and wildness inside each of us.

◆

I hate seeing people onstage reaching across the footlights, asking for love. Most directors encourage that in a performer, and even spend much time in rehearsals talking to the actors about how to get in touch with a love and compassion which can reach out to the audience. The results are performances that try to make the audience "love"

Kate Manheim in **Madness and Tranquillity. (Photo by Craig Massey)**

what they see onstage in empathic response to the love the actors pour forth over the footlights. But art should not be a substitute for real life; love should be between people, not exploited as the fetishistic focus of a work of art. If anything, we need an art that teaches us how to live with the lack of love, the difficulty and stress of late-twentieth-

century life. The simulation of love passing back and forth
between stage and spectator can make an audience feel for
an hour or two that everything is hunky dory with the
state of their inner selves, but what seems important to
me is finding a new theatrical style that accurately reflects
the true tension of our lives in a society which does *not*
manifest love. A new style that shows you how to picture
the tension of our daily lives in a way that proposes how
you might sing and dance with the trauma of life; how
you can redeem that trauma by reprocessing it in your
own psyche. A new style that shows you that while you
may not be able to escape the trauma, you should live it
in a singing and dancing way. Therefore, the latent content
of the actor's performance should not be the all-purpose
sweetness of "love," but rather the trauma and stress of
the hostile world—which, integrated into the composition
of the piece as a whole, is transformed into an aesthetic
celebration. For the spectator, this experience in the theater
might prove helpful once he decides to pursue his own
transformation, molding his own psychic trauma into an
aesthetically sensed object, which might then widen and
deepen his own experience.

◆

I frequently give the performers positions that put the body
in a state of tension. Or I do the opposite; I give them
positions that suggest a degree of relaxation inappropriate
to the situation. Both options break through the shell of
normal behavior. However, I never think of it in the blatant
terms of introducing more "tension" into the performance.
That kind of abstract conceptualization is pointless when
directing a play or making art. When I want to introduce
more energy into a scene, I will instinctively say to the
actor, "Could you sort of put your elbow on the arm of

the chair and lift up your body by pushing on your elbow
while you're saying that line?" Obviously, that movement
is going to make him tense, but I never think, How can I
make him tense? I never conceptualize it in that way.

◆

Performers normally want two things. One is to be loved,
and the other is to find a way to be relaxed onstage. The
basic Stanislavsky method, as it has been taught in America, trains an actor to find a way to be relaxed during a
performance, even within a highly emotional scene. Most
twentieth-century art, however, is not about being relaxed.
Ours is an era of stress, and serious art reflects that stress,
even if it wants to establish an alternative. The plays I write
reflect that stress, and I think the performers should as
well. Just as classical ballet employs a technique in which
dancers work out of a tension sustained in the body, for
many years I was interested in an acting style in which the
performance uncoiled from a center of tension. But just as
ballet dancers do damage to their bodies over a long career,
I found that such a performance style was not healthy for
the psyches and bodies of my performers. So I have had
to invent other ways to serve my texts, other performance
styles, and to accept a more relaxed mode of performance.

◆

Here are a number of things I often tell the performers
during rehearsal:

1. Be hostile toward the audience. Don't make them
love you.

2. Lower your center of gravity slightly, always be
ready to defend yourself. Remember that no matter what
gesture you perform, it might open you to an irrational

and sudden attack. You might be attacked for being a fool, or being vulnerable, or excessively smart. Anything you do, anticipate that you might be immediately attacked for it.

3. Always maintain the feeling that no matter what you are required to do or say, each choreographed move or line of dialogue represents a brilliant strategic move on your part. Even when you deliver the stupidest line in the play, to be stupid at that moment is the most masterful chess move that anybody has ever made. Remember that *everything* you do is a brilliant decision, especially if it is something stupid.

4. Assume that the stage is full of land mines, and at any moment as you cross the stage a mine is going to explode.

5. Assume the stage is covered with broken glass and you are acting in bare feet.

6. Assume that between your chest and the chest of your fellow actor is a rubber band stretched taut. Imagine it pinned directly to your skin, or perhaps it penetrates and is tied into both of your hearts. Wherever you walk, you stretch that rubber band between yourself and your fellow actor and it pulls painfully taut between your heart and his.

7. Always believe that when you have a line, you are saying the most intelligent thing in the world but that only a few people in the audience are going to get it. You should play the show only for those few. That does not mean to perform in a coy, Oscar Wildean style. You should not let the rest of the audience know secrets are being passed to the chosen few. It is as if each of your lines held over-

whelming information in coded form. And the audience, save for a few, are vulgar hooligans to whom you have no desire to present your wonderful insights.

Further clarifying this last directive: imagine yourself sitting in the theater and something happens onstage, and you have the urge to poke your friend in the ribs and whisper, "See? See what happened? He said he loved her, but did you notice he really hates her?" When this happens, you have been creatively aroused because you were given the sense you perceived something that was not evident on the surface; it engaged your creative perception. But if a performer offered that information on a silver platter, so everybody in the audience knew immediately that everybody *else* in the audience knew exactly that what was being expressed was, "I hate her, even though I say I love her," then you in the audience have no experience of creative pleasure. Too often performers deliver every line with such "commitment" and "passion," there is never any doubt that absolutely everyone in the audience gets it first time around. I find that totally uninteresting in a performance. I want to see a performer who makes me feel I see what is happening inside his soul, but at the same time gives me the feeling that I may be the only one in the audience perceptive enough to pick up on it. Ideally, of course, everyone in the audience should feel that they are the one person able to see it. But for the performer, everything he does, every choice he makes should include the arrogant notion: all of you aren't going to get this, but Larry over there sitting in the fifth row is going to know what I really mean when I say, "Beautiful day, isn't it?" I believe this is the most important instruction I can give the actors to clue them into the kind of performance that best serves my texts.

◆

Unlike most other directors working in the theater, I prefer not to involve myself with the actor's process. I just want results. I have never accepted that basic law of theater which determines that the actor is the center of the per-formance. Obviously, I want the audience to feel some-thing for the actor, but I do *not* want them to relate to the play through identification with the actor. I want the spec-tators to be watching *my* decisions. I want them to be watching *me*. I do not want them to be watching the actors—even if I am one of the actors. Though whether they do or not is their own business, of course.

That does not mean I am interested in puppets, or in Gordon Craig style "Uber-marionettes," because the ac-cidents of an actor's individual characteristics, the biolog-ical and spiritual facts of his or her unique style of presence, make actors more usefully complex objects than puppets could ever be. If you know how to act, and you want to be in my play, and you can do what I want you to do, that's great. I *want* interesting actors in my plays. But I do not think of the actor as the focal point of the performance. That does not mean I want to demean or squelch the actor. The actor is perfectly free to think he is the focal point of things—in fact, he or she probably *should* think so. But I am not, ultimately, interested in what is going on inside the actor when he or she is performing. That is the actor's business, not mine (though I can make it my business when it helps to get the performance I want).

◆

Being a theater director is like being a psychiatrist. It has to do with knowing when to interfere in the actor's per-formance and when to let the actor struggle through it by himself. It is knowing when to insist and when to lay back. When I direct a play, I feel I know how to act every part, and I try to get the performer to act with the intelligence I would bring to the part, except when the actor shows me that what he or she does is more interesting than anything I could have thought of. When I have good actors, that happens all the time. My real responsibility to them arises when they do something not as interestingly as I can imagine doing it. Then I have to trick them (gently, as a friend) into doing it at least as well as I can imagine it.

◆

If an actor is having great difficulty with a scene I sometimes will offer suggestions in psychological terms, but in general I prefer to propose to the actor physical sensations the character might be feeling in his or her body. Instead of telling him, "Oh, you really hate that person you're talking to, because you imagine he once did such-and-such to you," I have found it more productive to resort to a physiological fantasy. I might suggest, for instance, "During this speech, imagine fluids coming out of your body, pouring out of all your orifices—and think about that all through the scene." For many performers it works, for some it does not. But I am persuaded that using these physical fantasies serves my plays better than using normal, psychological ones. They reinforce my attempts to distance the work from the societally induced psychological grids against which most theater operates.

◆

Left to their own resources, actors tend to develop relations with each other, inside the world of the play, that reflect the needs and desires they identify with and create for themselves in portraying their characters as they imagine

them. Since I write lines that register an attempt to be open
to all things *other* than those with a characterological basis,
the actors in my plays must find ways to play with each
other that do *not* simply reflect their characters' psychological identity. A different kind of music has to take over.

I try to keep the communication between performers
onstage less direct than it would be were they left to themselves. Playing a scene, actors feed emotionally off one
another and deepen the psychological communication between themselves. While I agree it can be productive for
the performers to develop that kind of communication, I
often stage scenes in a way that will frustrate that connection (through tape overlay, strange blocking, and so on),
so that you can sense that the motivation for a particular
scene comes not from what the performers get from each
other, but rather from sources in their unconscious, spiritual selves.

One way to do this is to ask the actor to relate to the
physical characteristics of the room he is in, and to the
changing atmosphere in his environment: lighting, sound,
and words. Suppose I have a line of dialogue which a
character delivers in response to another who has just attacked him. "I think I'd like to have a headache and now
I don't have a headache." Let us assume I want to deem-
phasize the possibility that he is simply reacting sarcasti-
cally to the one who attacked him. I might say to the actor,
As you speak, back up so that by the end of the line you
are leaning against the wall in an awkward position. How
might that movement suggest other reasons he would like
to have a headache? Perhaps because he hopes the headache
will change the way his mind works, forcing him into
other patterns of thinking that are suggested by his awkward position against the wall. Obviously, that is not a
realistic action, yet it seems psychologically relevant to the

kind of breakthrough that any attempt to manipulate the head, including willed headaches, might anticipate. I often think of my work as an attempt to crack open the prisonlike shell of the particular reality we have convinced ourselves imprisons us. Backing up, slamming against the wall, and striking an odd position is an attempt physically to crack that shell. Simply walking backward symbolizes an attempt to counter the normal requirements of what we assume to be everyday reality, where, for obvious reasons, it is better to walk forward and see where you are going.

♦

For years I identified with Giotto's stiff compositions, in which meticulous concern was devoted to capturing the physical "presentness" of his subjects. I wanted people and objects to be similarly physically *present* in my own work. To be present meant to create a simple, strong, readable grid of right-angle relationships. To this day, I usually tell the actors I do not allow diagonal crosses onstage. If they have to get from upstage right to downstage left, they must do it by walking straight down and then making a right turn, rather than making the simpler diagonal cross. I want to make theatrical events that click into clarity like brilliant moves in a game of chess. Only certain patterns of movement are allowed; however, within the game's limitations your options are immense. The rules of the game make you aware how multifarious your options really are. You can play infinitely with *and* against those options.

When composing the stage picture, I consider both the physical presence of the actor as a personality and the sculptural statement his body makes as I place it in certain poses. I will often place the actor in an unnecessarily awkward position, in order to call attention to the fact of the actor's body *as object*—something that he, exemplifying the human condition, must labor with through the course of his life.

I try to think: in this scene when the actor sits down in the chair, how can I make him sit so you are aware that whatever he says, whatever he does, he is also *sitting in a chair*—a configuration of the body which is specific and unique? For instance, I might tell an actor: "Spread your knees a bit more and slouch forward so your back slumps." Ultimately, the actor would end up sitting in a rather unnatural position; not so unnatural that the audience would know that I intended to create an eccentric, unusual way to sit in a chair, but enough so that the fact of sitting in a chair is rendered slightly problematic.

Imagine a country where people never sat down, and the natives of that country get on a boat and arrive in America where they are presented with a chair. They would say, "What is this?" You then would invite them to sit in the chair. Can you imagine their first experience sitting in that chair? Would they not sit in it as if they expected it to explode, with their bodies in a refreshingly aware state? That is what I try to provoke.

◆

Once in Paris I went to the Crazy Horse Saloon, a chic strip joint, and I was interested to find that they had to solve a challenging theatrical problem. They had to put on a forty-five-minute show entertaining the audience with nothing other than the sight of well-built, naked bodies. Easy, you say. But there was no simulated sex, no other audience-involving behavior. They had to invent ways to simply display these bodies as phenomenological objects, without stories or other distractions. And they *were* very inventive. It was the most remarkably phenomenological theater I ever saw. The problems they faced related directly to my own concerns.

♦

In the large loft space I used as a theater in the late seventies, I would manipulate the actors and the sets to focus the spectator's attention on the simple fact of the space itself. I wanted people to be aware of the particular characteristics of the stage area (very long and narrow) and to savor the implications that manipulating such a space might add to the scene being performed. Sometimes I would use it as a long, deep space; other times, a wall would slide in to make it shallow. How do you place the actors in those varying spaces to make the spectator enjoy the way the manipulation of space is articulating the emotional quality of the scene? It is a bit like editing a film, where the editor's choices can make major differences in how a scene affects an audience. When I did the play *Boulevard de Paris*, one critic complained that while the stage was often very deep, the actors were crowded up at the front, almost on top of the audience. Of course, that was a deliberate decision on my part, in order to raise questions about what it means to have a play take place in a space eighty feet deep. Crowding the actors at the front makes you aware of that deep space in an interesting way. It might even give you the sense that the foreground of a life (down front toward the "audience") is supported by immense depths that contain infinite possibilities. Of course, sometimes the actors of *Boulevard de Paris* traveled far upstage. And when they did, special attention was called to that movement. It became symbolic of traveling into the depths, precisely because they spent so much of the performance bunched up down front.

◆

When directing, I'm actively engaged in deciding, from
moment to moment, whether the staging should reinforce
the overt meaning of the text, or if it should contradict it
in some way. Sometimes it's as simple an issue as whether
an actor should move toward or away from an object.
Suppose an actor looks at a cabbage on a table and says,
"Oh, this is a beautiful cabbage." If he says the line walking
toward the cabbage, it conveys an emotional effect that
simply reinforces his statement. If he says the line while
backing away from the cabbage until he bangs into the
opposite wall, it gives the cabbage itself more importance;
maybe he has difficulty dealing with the awe the cabbage's
beauty arouses in him. The distribution in space of actions
and objects—whether that distribution suggests expansion
into a field or contraction into a point—may well be the
unconscious focus of my direction, because that's what I
always seem to be manipulating. I want to take every
moment of the play and give it a relationship to the total
field of the world in which it occurs. I find that can best
be done by orchestrating how the actors approach, receive,
replace, or reposition the objects and themselves onstage.
You make a statement inclusive by backing up and widening your arms so you include the whole world, though
your dialogue may ostensibly refer to only one specific
thing. Or, in referring to the whole world, you point to
one thing and close in on it so then the whole world seems
embodied in it. When staging a play I'm after a continual
rhythmic alternation between these two tendencies, which
is a way of saying—on a whispered, subliminal level—the
thing is the world is the thing is the world is the thing is
the world.

♦

The task of the artist is to be open to all the ambiguities, all the multiple impulses present in a given situation. The fact is whenever you say Yes, a hidden part of you is also saying No, as well as innumerable other things. Suppose, at the height of an international crisis your response is, "Don't shoot those rockets at America," your No might in fact be modulated by an unconscious longing. You might secretly wonder what it would be like if rockets did explode over your city. Wouldn't it be amazing, awesome, beautiful, and terrifying all at the same time? And of course, there's also the obvious phallic symbolism that sets off contradictory reverberations in your psyche. The realistic theater, however, is not designed to engage directly this basic self-contradictory nature of the human psyche. It can suggest it through a character's behavior, but cannot play with it as a concrete motif in and of itself. I want a theater that can treat all of this, not through suggestion, but through the play of the concrete sign-systems of the theater (bodies, props, light, sound, word), so such conflicting possibilities are made to dance, both in word and action.

When I stage a play I make an attempt to match every moment with its counterelement. For instance, one actor might say to another, "I hate you, and therefore I'm taking out a gun, I'm going to shoot you," but I would stage it so love is implicit in the action. A love song might play over the loudspeakers, and the gun we see him pull from his pocket might turn out to be an unrecognizable object, wrapped in a handkerchief, which makes both of the actors dissolve in tears. Every feeling we express arises from combinations of contradictions and mysteries of this sort: hatred arises because of a potentiality for love that has failed; feelings of hatred do not arise in a situation in which love is not possible. But because I embody the counter-element onstage at all times, the spectator might say, I don't understand, is he hating or loving? The point is, he's doing both.

◆

As I'm staging a play over a period of weeks, as new insights come during the rehearsal process, I will add elements to the staging that will introduce other levels of meaning. In the beginning I might start with the more traditional relationships between characters apparent in the text, but each time I see the scene worked through in rehearsal, I think there's more to be said. Contradictions and dispersive possibilities hidden in the scene begin to surface. So I'll add something—stage business, or music, or props—not to clarify the original situation, but to complexify it, to show how precariously one meaning rides over the multitude of possible meanings that every scene really contains. I'd want to continually suggest: yes, it's true that this couple has a wonderful relationship, but is the relationship based on mutual need? Yes, it's true that the relationship is based on mutual need, but isn't that a part of any couple's relationship? Yes, it's part of any couple's relationship, but aren't there moments when they can transcend that mutual need? Yes, they can transcend it, but is that because their relationship was based on an infantile fixation? Yes, but. Yes, *but*. And each plateau of "Yes, *but*" is introduced by adding a gesture, or a prop, or a certain kind of music, or a surprising twist in the blocking. Sometimes I've had to throw out one decision I've made in order to put in something else, but usually I'm adding to what's already there.

The task is to create a complex composition that helps

the spectator realize that many different meanings are available in any chosen perceptual experience. We abide by cultural directives that urge us: clarify each thought, each experience, so that you can cull from them their single, dominant meaning and, in the process, become a responsible adult who knows what he or she thinks. But what I try to show is the opposite: how at every moment, the world presents us with a composition in which a multitude of meanings and realities are available, and you are able to swim, lucid and self-contained, in that turbulent ocean of multiplicity.

VISUAL COMPOSITION, MOSTLY

◆

The playing space is an environment for the text to explore, a gymnasium for a psychic, spiritual, and physical work-out. It's an exercise room, a factory, an examination room, and a laboratory. If the mise-en-scène does not pay homage to all this, it castrates the full body of the theater.

All the materials we find available in the theater should be thrown together in full polymorphous play. Curtains, scenery, moving platforms, lights, noises, bodies—all add complexity to the stage space. In the same way, we find in the text a multitude of psychic materials with which to play. The text should be an open file system, so distributed in its references that all aspects of the world seem connected to it. The complexity of the lived world should be made available to the spectator by the text, setting, and articulated production; never fall prey to using this wealth of materials to convince the audience that they are seeing something "real," other than the dance of the accumulated riches of your artistic resonances in concrete, articulated

form. As in music, a structural, rhythmical articulation of
all the elements.

◆

I like to assume that the spectator is watching the entire
stage at all moments of the play, so I try to make a stage
picture in which every inch of the stage dynamically participates in the moment-by-moment composition of the
piece. I might carefully adjust the tiniest detail, far away
from what seems to be the focus of attention in a scene,
because I want to maintain the compositional tension
across the entire panorama of the stage. Then the experience of watching one of my plays is not one of identifying
with a character and attending his progression through a
series of adventures, but rather savoring the multitude of
composed tensions in a given moment of the play, registering that moment of multiple tensions as it is usurped
by another, and then another, and another, and allowing
yourself to be buffeted by the kinetic sensations that result
from that rapid succession of compositional moments.

◆

The eye should be held in suspension between all points
of the stage picture, just as twelve-tone music does not
focus your attention on a tonal center but spreads it equally
within the field of the twelve tones. That's why, in my
earlier plays, if a character stabbed another in the back, I
might have introduced a third performer to stretch a string
from a far corner of the stage to the point where the stabbing takes place. At first, this might lead you to believe I
wanted to call extra attention to the act of stabbing. But
since a stabbing onstage could hardly be made *more* important, does the string simply reiterate that importance,
or is it doing something else? Does it urge you to enjoy a

separate compositional inflection at the same time you are
disturbed by a brutal act? Does it imply that some hidden
god or energy observes this evil act? Does it suggest that
the stabbing is a dividing up of the stage itself, since the
string slices the stage in half? Even though, at first, it seems
to say, "Look at this stabbing," does it not do it in a
circuitous way that first calls attention to the *method* of
pointing, rather than to the act being pointed out? Perhaps
what it really does is spread your attention over the whole
stage during the stabbing, implying that the whole stage
participates in the event. Look, there's a white line stretching from the stabbing to the top left corner of the
proscenium—and as a result, the entire space participates.
Your focus is no longer fixed on the emotional drive of
the character who has the knife. While another director
might isolate the stabbing from the rest of the stage by
highlighting it with a spotlight, I would try to free the
mental eye so that the entire stage seems to be an equal
participant in that dramatic moment.

◆

I've always enjoyed telling the audience to do something
other than what they would normally do at a particular
moment in the play, and by doing so, indicate how art can
model an escape from circumstance, just as I try to be free
within the circumstances of my life or my culture. I try
to urge audiences to reorganize their habits of watching,
by using techniques that deflect their attention away from
what they would tend to watch in order to suggest that
the real play is elsewhere. For instance, in *Hotel China* there
were ten little wooden stands on the stage, and each had
a rock placed on it which was covered by a handkerchief.
At one point, an actor removed the handkerchiefs, revealing the rocks for the first time. As the audience was

watching this, a legend was projected on the back of the
stage that read, "Do not pay attention to the rocks, pay
attention to the color of the stands." I wanted to say to
the audience, Be aware that you can make choices in this
theatrical situation, unlike normal theater where everything is done to manipulate you into watching, thinking,
and feeling the one thing the play's creator wants you to
watch, think, and feel.

◆

Most directors think of the stage as a platform on which
to display action, whereas I consider it a reverberation
chamber which amplifies and projects the music of the
action so it can reveal the full range of its overtones. My
stage is an enclosed territory—whatever happens onstage
bounces off the walls of the set, and is reflected back and
forth between the objects that are positioned inside that
space.

I was once on a panel with fellow director-designer Will
Leach, and he described how he designed his sets. He began
by considering the actor standing in the middle of the stage
and would then let the design expand from that central
point outward. I always start from the periphery. I begin
by considering the outer walls the action is going to bounce
against. That outer boundary is the crucial conceptual element, because in my plays I imagine the action as an impulse continually flung outward until it encounters a
boundary, which then bounces it back to the center of the
stage, coloring it with the particular quality of the wall it
was thrown against.

◆

Composition is always a question of the tension between
a container, and the contained energy that wants to break

out of that container and flow forth. The basic compositional reality is the tendency to flow and expand, and the
countertendency to block and contain that flow. Composition plays with that expansive thrust; it manifests at
the point where thrust is contained by a strong barrier that
either stops it, or better yet, redirects it so it can continue
on, but now patterned in a way that generates a complexity
like that of the world.

◆

The sets are enclosed spaces, but in no sense should the
audience feel it is peeking through an imaginary, transparent fourth wall. Instead, the action of the play should
bounce against the three walls of the stage, then flirt with
the trick surface of a fourth wall that the audience is continually, vaguely, reminded of. Often I introduce a railing,
or some string, or even a wall of glass as an obstruction
between the front row of the audience and the playing
space. These barriers reinforce aesthetic distance. I do not
want the audience to be sucked into the resonating chamber
of the stage. I want the spectator to keep his distance,
precisely so that the action can bounce against that subtle
fourth barrier. Too often in the theater, the play of resonance onstage is dampened because the "wall" between
audience and stage has softened to mush; empathy will
erode that wall and pull the audience onto the stage so they
identify with the actions or characters, which undermines
aesthetic distance.

◆

In many of my sets I have used strings, strung across the
stage in various directions, to cut up the space and to
introduce lines that dissect the picture plane. Because
something normal is rendered askew, it becomes extra

noticeable. Normally, when an actor makes an entrance you watch his body cross the stage, and if it is a body you find interesting or desirable, you immediately entertain fantasies in which you live imaginatively in relation to that body in a real-life way. But with the string cutting across your field of vision, it is hoped you will notice, ever so slightly, your *act* of looking at that body, because the act of looking has been interfered with by the string—which actually is quite beautiful in and of itself—so you will perhaps notice what it is like to see one part of the body appear above the line of string and another part appear below. Which gives you a little more freedom, because it enables you to choose among the different ways available to relate your perceptual mechanism to that body walking across the stage.

◆

I first began to run strings across the stage in *Hotel China*. In those days the strings were usually functional, at least in a metaphoric sense. For instance, there was a scene in *Hotel China* in which I attached strings to the sides of the stage in a widening funnel which came to a point on the actor's brow. Objects that he was supposed to desire were hung from the strings as if they had emanated from his yearning mind. But in later plays, the strings developed a life of their own, no longer limited to serving such symbolic functions. I've long felt that theatrical space is not clearly enough defined; it never seems to have the density of something you can touch or taste, and I miss that. I found I could add compositional tension to the stage by crisscrossing it with lines of string, which lent the space a shimmering, hovering quality. That was intensified when I began to place dots of black paint on the strings, creating dotted black lines that floated in front of the audience's

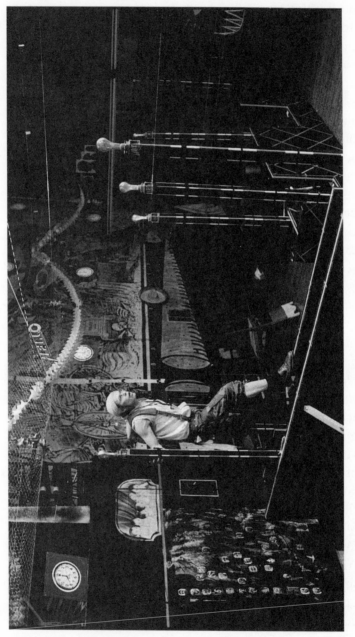

Willem Dafoe in Miss Universal Happiness. (Photo by Babette Mangolte)

eyes, mixing with the objects seen onstage. It seemed
to make the stage dense with its own empty space—
something like the scratched lines in a Giacometti
drawing. The lights hung above the stage were focused
into the audience's eyes, which added to this intensification
of the pure space of the stage. The light seemed to fill the
space itself, rather than illuminate the objects in that space.
The strings and lights collaborated to turn the stage into
a participant in the play, instead of using the stage as a
neutral container to display the materials of the performance.

I used the strings for the same reasons a painter will
allow various textures of paint to overlay his ostensible
subject matter. Those textures may not be true to our
conventions of objective perception, but they open the
portrayed objects to further levels of energy and to involvement in the physical act of seeing. What's seen with
the eye is never perceived with the crystal clarity of ideal-
ized perception. In human vision, images and sensations
bleed one into another, layered over by the faint traces of
the visual mechanism itself. The strings helped me to suggest that amorphous aspect of true-to-life perception, in-
terfering with objects and actors, but also superimpos-
ing what I imagined to be "lines of force" echoing the
many trails of energy that do shoot through our lived visual
field (eye and brain) only half noticed, but affecting us
profoundly.

My sets are full of evocations of this kind of energy. For
instance, in my early plays I used white strings which I
ran across the stage. Then, at a certain point, I began dot-
ting the white strings. The walls of the stage were always
striped or checked to suggest that level of energy. Sometimes I built Romanesque arches with alternating light-
and dark-colored brick around the arch. All of this to sug-

gest a rhythm closer to something going on in the neural rhythm of the brain, in perception; that's what I am after.

◆

As the texts of my plays became increasingly fragmented in order to echo the truth of psychic life, I wanted the scenery to do the same. I wanted it to make reference to the various locales suggested on the page, but without my having to make set changes every three minutes. I wanted scenery that was in many places at once, like the mind. The spectator should ask: Am I in a living room, or in a bizarre factory where art (this play) is being produced? In all of my sets, I try to create a space which suggests something is being manufactured; it could be a laboratory, a factory, a meditation chamber, or a kitchen. The sets are not dreamy, poetic landscapes, but they become evocative because they give concrete form to the tension between different levels of reality. How can you be in something that seems like a factory and yet, at the same time, seems to be like your living room? Where are you really? It should make your head spin, because it echoes your real situation in life: you are in your living room relaxing, but at the same time your living room is a kind of factory where, even when relaxing, you are in the process of manufacturing your life. Moreover, the actions performed on the set should echo this same kind of tension. For instance, the performer's elbows might be askew, as if at work making something in a factory, while the rest of his body is balanced in a pseudo-relaxed position, semiprone against a pillow, which suggests the couch he rests upon in his living room.

◆

The complexity of the scenery is a major resource that enables me to suggest the jump from one level of meaning to another during the moment-by-moment action of the play. For example, if an actor is at the back of the stage sitting in a chair against a suitably painted wall, the scene may seem to be realistically domestic. But if he then runs downstage to grab a handle at the end of a pole that rises from the floor and starts to spin it madly, since that pole is not something you would expect to find in a living room, it suggests that he must have left that domestic situation. Perhaps that action, which took place in *What Did He See?*, suggested a regression to childhood, but beyond that it suggests the wider notion of operating in a world gone mad. Had there been no bizarre pole in that living room set, and the actor had instead spun wildly around the post of a normal banister, it would not have referred to this wider level of meaning. It was only when the actor ran to manipulate the pole that he seemed to be entering another level of the set, one that subliminally evoked a demonic factory whose pole was strategically placed on the axis of the world. The next thing that character did in *What Did He See?* was to run to the top step of a platform and sit upon a throne, which invoked a third locale, added to the factory and living room. From that throne he looked down on the other characters, evoking overtones of manipulative power relationships. The physical resources of the set made possible the specific actions that enabled me to jump from psychological level to political level to metaphysical level, and so on.

In *Penguin Touquet* I used rolling boxes that functioned like booths in a restaurant. Yet giant checked walls in the rear evoked an abstract "mental space," and random letters glued to the walls formed word fragments suggesting the inside of a book. The side walls were covered with enlarged ruffled curtains that superimposed a childlike domestic atmosphere on the restaurant, which related to the fact that one of the characters seemed to be a psychoanalyst who would naturally regress patients, and by implication the play, to childhood states. At the same time, the overall design of the set suggested a factory or laboratory in which something was being produced— perhaps, even, the play itself, or a different mode of consciousness.

For *Film Is Evil*, the set appeared to be a radio broadcasting studio, but, at the same time, there was an excess of tables and desks, which made it appear not to be a real radio studio. It looked like a schoolroom or furniture showroom *invading* a radio studio. Also, the decorative style suggested that the play did not take place in the present. I love old-fashioned radio, and I find photographs of early broadcasting studios very evocative. I wanted the set to have the feel of that earlier era. The set also suggested an environment similar to a hotel lobby you might have seen in Paris at the time of the First World War—which, rather than being a workplace, like a radio studio, is a public meeting place.

◆

Theater is a public meeting; it is a ritual. In order to suggest the ritualistic, ceremonial nature of the theater during the performance, the set, whatever the ostensible locale, should also refer to a place where you might come to meet with a lot of people: a hotel lobby, a lecture hall, a schoolroom, a doctor's office, or a courtroom.

◆

The objects I build and incorporate into the set are meant to suggest, through their design, different ways that the performer can manipulate his body. All of the props and scenic elements are occasions for the exteriorization of internal impulse. They are a field within which impulse can express itself. For instance, if a table is propped at an unnatural angle, something about it should invite you to put your hand on it. In making the set and props, I would like to invoke impulses which say, "Look how that couch squats invitingly on the carpet, so why the hell not sprawl on that couch?"

Sometimes I build objects which suggest a combination of two separate objects as props or scenic elements for my plays. For instance, in *The Cure* I built tables with funny padded backs that made them appear to be half couches and half tables. It was a table upon which to work, but it somehow suggested comfort. Personally, I have a fondness for things that suggest you can lean on them, be supported by them. I want my plays themselves to be things upon which I can lean my ideas. Which can gently support my obsessive manias.

At times I have considered working without sets and props, in an empty theatrical space without the burden of an elaborate physical production. But then I realize that such a naked space does not allow the text to ricochet between levels of meaning, which is my obsession. I am interested in showing how the spiritual, psychological, material, political, social, and magical interpenetrate and are present to human experience all at once.

◆

There is a prejudice against decoration in art and architecture, because there is an awareness that the decorative allows the ornamental (or visual) aspect to take on a life of its own, which then threatens to interfere with the basic thrust of, say, a Le Corbusier building that declares, "I am purely hospital," or "I am a home that is like a hospital because here we lead focused, uncluttered lives." The unspoken assumption is that if we allow a little squirly-gig

up in the decorative molding to reproduce itself throughout the room, it would introduce something into the environment that threatens to run out of control. But the
fact is that our brains are secretly powered by those little
squirly-gigs. The light-whirls of energy present in Van
Gogh's "Starry Night," or the beads of paint that drip
sloppily from Picasso's brush as he slashes out his late
canvases, are those swirls inside the artist's head, in his
retinal system, or are they really in the sky or in the faces
that burst forth? In Van Gogh's case, does he depict what
the plasma in the sky is actually doing? The fact is that
those whirls are present in his head *and* in the sky. It's the
same material, head and sky. The same atoms, the same
energy fields. However, in order to function in daily life
and to earn a living, we learn to focus, and to control these
squirly-gigs. But if we overcontrol them, if we overfocus
on them, it is as if we were saying to the squirly-gigs,
"Okay you guys, I'm going to hitch you up to the cart of
my ambition, and I'm going to drive from here, where I
am a fledgling playwright, to over there, where I win the
Nobel Prize for literature!" So I get on the highway, and
I arrive at the Nobel Prize, but in order to win the Nobel
Prize I have ignored all the flowers along the roadside. So
on my deathbed, I whisper to my wife, "I may have won
the Nobel Prize, but there's something missing, isn't
there?" What's missing, to put it plainly, is that I ignored
what could have most profoundly fed my soul. I ignored
the decorations of life, the squirly-gigs inside the brain that
might have interfered with that direct route to the Nobel
Prize, but which might have refreshed me with the secret
happiness that life has to offer. So, more power to the
decorative. Which is really to say that man is not the only
possible center of the universe; there are other energies,
other forces, at work.

FROM THE
BEGINNING

◆

How would you say that Angelface *and your other early productions differed from the plays you had written previously, as a student and as a young playwright in New York in the sixties?*

The dialogue of *Angelface* was stripped bare of all normal social interaction. That's a reflection of the real me, I suppose, because to this day when people ask such things as, "How are you?" I don't know what to answer, because I don't, in fact, know how I am. To me that question is so vast, I'm incapable of coming up with a simple, "Oh, fine." I do say, "I'm fine," but I feel dishonest afterward because I'm not telling the truth; I'm playing a particular game I don't want to play. In the same vein, I wanted my plays to represent an escape from that sort of social game. I resolved never to make a theater that reinforced your belief that such games were the necessary way to move through your life.

In retrospect, I think I was trying to restrict myself to a primitive vocabulary, not unlike Peter Handke's efforts

in *Kaspar*, a play that shows a man being born and ac-
quiring language. Though I heard of Handke's play only
years later, mine was a similar effort to start from scratch.
I didn't want to write in a language that reflected all the
cotton candy, the sweets I'd inherited from my culture,
including all the art I'd been exposed to in the theater. I
wanted to go back to the basic building blocks of experience, to the beginning cells of consciousness.

I started with the premise that the basic cells of consciousness were the elementary noticings of collision between the self and its environment; for instance, when the
body collides with a physical object, or when the mind
collides with its own previously held ideas, or with ob-
stacles in its perceptual field, as when someone says something you don't quite understand. A key for me was a
short passage by Gaston Bachelard proposing a psychology
that wasn't family history—you hate your mother because
of this, that, or the other thing—but was concerned with
the individual vis-à-vis the basic physical givens of his
environment. The way the body, a material thing in the
material world, encounters hardness, heat, darkness, and
so on—anything that interferes with your progression
through the world. So for my early Ontological-Hysteric
Theater plays I limited the dialogue to small units that
notated collisions of this sort. For instance, when you lift
your hands and notice that it feels heavy, or when you try
to cross a room and somebody stands in your way, or
when somebody reaches out to touch you and the contact
makes you feel uncomfortable. Most of the spoken interaction between performers had to do with what one character imagined the character confronting him might be
experiencing in his body, like, "Is your arm heavy?" or
"Oh, why is your face growing?"

I wanted to *purge* art of emotional habit. To make audiences laugh or cry seemed an ignoble, manipulative achievement. To counter that, one of the notions that guided me in those days was that I should try to write comedy that did not make people laugh. Henri Bergson explains how laughter is in fact a response to the perception of man as a being upended by eruptions of his own mechanicalness, and I wanted to illuminate that mechanicalness in order to awaken the audience, rather than provide the soporific palliative of laughter. I was interested in imitating the forms that normally produce emotional response without allowing the emotion to surface—because the experience of emotion erases the awareness of how it was technically produced. One way I did this was to write in the joke form, in that kind of rhythm, using those kinds of jumps in logic, but without trying to be funny.

The actors spent much of the evening standing in tableaux. They would hold for five or six lines, and then there'd be a slight shift of bodies, and they'd hold for another five or six lines. Another slight shift, five or six lines more. And then a ludicrous, exaggerated action, like tumbling through the window. The actor would then hold an awkward position at the end of that tumble for five or six lines. It continued like this through the entire play, tableau followed by slight adjustment, followed by occasional, rather spectacular, but awkward activity.

Those plays had a scholastic severity, the quality of a classroom demonstration. When you show something in front of a class, you face the class, just as my actors faced the audience. Sometimes the actors would turn their backs to the audience, but that was a specific *showing* of the back. So there was always a decision. I've always felt that what was interesting about art was to consciously notice and savor the series of decisions the artist himself is making. Notice that decision? A few seconds later—notice that new

***Mike Jacobson and Judy Fyve in* Total Recall. (Photo by Babette Mangolte)**

decision? Even notice that another second has gone by and the decision was to have no change at all. See, my decision is still to have no change, but to have it go tick tick tick, so that each passing second the audience could rescan to see what my decision was, how I decided to fill the moment.

How did you design the sets, the costumes, the lights for your early shows?

The sets were extremely minimal. I didn't want to interfere with the impact—the truth—of the room in which we were operating, which was the ground floor loft of Jonas Mekas's Filmmaker's Cinematheque, at 80 Wooster

Street, in a neighborhood in New York that was just starting to be called SoHo. I only built those elements of the set that the play made specific reference to. If somebody was supposed to look out a window, I built a simple window. And if he was supposed to sit at a table, I built a table. I built everything. But I added no decoration. I wanted it to have a certain look, the look of my awkward carpentry, so everyone could see how these things were "put together." Then everything was painted a single color to give the set stylistic unity.

For the first ten years, the actors wore in performance whatever they happened to show up wearing on the first day of rehearsal. The costumes were, in effect, found objects. If their clothes had to be cleaned, I asked the actors to wear something similar, so that all through rehearsals they looked as they would in performance. I felt that was important, because as I was staging the play I'd decide where they would stand based on what they looked like —the "weight" of their visual presence—and if an actor wore a red shirt one day and a green shirt the next, that would play havoc with my decision making.

The lighting in those days was flat and unchanging—an effect meant to reinforce the clinical nature of the performance. It was simple light that was switched on, switched off. Though there were no lighting effects, I often used table lamps as props, and they functioned symbolically as mystical sources of energy. Those would be turned on and off as the script suggested—just practical, real household lighting. But the theatrical lighting itself would change infrequently, and in some of those early productions, never.

Would you say that the early plays had a rather informal quality?

Oh no, it seemed to me there was nothing informal about them. They were workmanlike. No nonsense, terribly sober. I wanted to think of every negative word I could and then make art out of that. I wanted it to be awkward. I wanted it to be uncomfortable. I wanted it to be static, stiff, not imaginative. Wooden. Rigor mortis. Funereal. I didn't think "funereal" in those days, but I realize now that it was funereal. In later years, actually, I came to think that the hidden subject of *all* theater was death. Because the actions of a play, memorized and repeated in front of an audience rather than issuing from real spontaneous life, were dead actions. Many of the sets for my later plays were encrusted with skulls in order to reflect that belief.

In order to shock the audience into superattentiveness, I wanted a certain hostility to shine from the stage, not the usual "please love me" that spills over the footlights in most theater—and that hostility further prevented it from being informal. A major way of establishing that hostility was by directing the actors to stare at the audience and to hold that pose for a long time. Kate Manheim became an expert at that; reviews used to refer to the famous "Rhoda stare"—Rhoda was the character she always played. Informality would have been suggested by a relaxed fluidity in the actors' bodies, but that never happened. Also, the dialogue in those days was punctuated every few lines by a terribly loud thud, which indicated: we can't go any further; what more is there to say? The thud was like a wall, ending discourse. It was followed by a pause, before speech would be tried again. But speech would hit against a wall again, and the thud would physicalize that impasse, which only increased the feeling of hostility and aggression.

Theater is the ultimate public art, all about social relations, and most people are attracted to theater specifically because it is a community activity—but to this day, I violently resist being so absorbed. I despise all social phenomena. I don't like being in crowds; I don't like being in crowded sections of the city. I don't trust group responses of any sort. I believe each individual when alone is always more sensitive, more insightful, than he is once he's part of a crowd. So when I make theater, I prefer to think I'm directing it toward the individual, sitting in isolation from everyone else in the audience. You might think that since I've chosen to work in the theater, I might as well accept it for what it's always been, and speak to that common public consciousness that assembles as an audience. In that case, then, let's say I'm not making theater; I'm doing something else. I'm making objects in space and time, populated by real people speaking lines, and they do it in front of other people—*and it's not theater*. In a sense, I wouldn't mind performing each play for one person at a time. I think of my performances as calling out to the crowd, Hey, is there one person out there in the midst of the social beast who needs this thing I've made to satisfy my own deepest desires? Is there someone who wants to separate him or herself out from the crowd and share in my world? Of course, for purely practical reasons, it's not feasible to play to an audience of one. But the crowd response is something I actively discourage, which is another reason for many of the techniques I've employed to frustrate the audience response that's so much a product of that feeling of togetherness exploited by normal theater.

In one of the programs, there was an invitation for anyone interested in performing in your next show to leave his or her name at the door.

Often that's about all it took. I'm a very shy person, so it wasn't easy for me to approach people. It still isn't. I hate the job of having to go out and recruit actors and technical people, actually making the necessary overtures. So in those days, anybody who wanted to could take part. Most of the people were writers, painters, filmmakers, or their friends.

But looking back, I can say that I generally preferred the kind of performers who, on one level or another, seemed not to fit the world, and yet had not developed a flamboyant, radical persona, as some people who don't fit the world manage to do. I was looking for that type because that's the type I was. I was looking for people who seemed to be members of my spiritual family.

What was the response to those early plays?

Aside from my friends, most of whom were filmmakers and people from the downtown art scene, it was terrible. For the first six years we knew that more than half our audience would walk out before the end of the play, often within the first twenty minutes. We drove them away like crazy, no doubt about it! There were nights that we ended up with only two people staying till the end. Even five years later—including my first play in Paris—the same thing. Every night, within twenty minutes, the audience was half gone.

I think I would have been discouraged—and simply given up making that kind of theater—were it not for the fact that Arthur Sainer, a critic from the *Village Voice*, attended my third play, *Total Recall*, and wrote a long review, saying, "This is pretty hard to take, and while I am against most critics who give consumer guides, you must see this play because it's like nothing I've ever seen, and it's terribly important." People still kept walking out, of course. But he reviewed my plays for the next few years and was always favorably inclined. If it hadn't been for Arthur's reviews, I doubt I'd have had the courage to continue, because I was a sensitive young thing and, really, everybody walked out. I remember the night Richard Serra and Robert Morris both came to see *Total Recall* and *they* walked out—two of my idols. I was crushed. Later, when I got to be friendly with them, one of them told me, "Well, in those days your work was so abstract, and I'm not really interested in going to the theater to see abstract art!"

At the same time, of course, we thought we had the word, and that people who walked out simply couldn't appreciate it, just as they didn't appreciate Van Gogh, or whoever else comes to mind. So I felt quite heroic. And fortunately there were a few people I respected who thought the work was the best theater around. I held on to that.

Could you discuss the texts themselves, your approach to writing them, how they were structured?

The situations depicted were normal, bourgeois theatrical clichés, domestic triangles, things like that. That's why I called my theater "Ontological-Hysteric," because the basic syndrome controlling the structure was that of classic, middle-class, boulevard theater, which I took to be hysteric in it psychological topology.

Those early texts always began with that sort of hysterical conflict. But at the same time, most of the things I allowed the dialogue to say within that situation were mental registerings that occurred on another level of the character's being—the characters expressed themselves through references to the physical attitudes and sensations they felt in their bodies. The dialogue didn't reflect the level where normal, psychological interaction with other people takes place. I suppose that comes from the fact that for as long as I can remember, even as a child, I've been aware of much going on inside of me which could not be expressed in society. I remember once when I was a young boy, riding in the car with my mother, I said to her, "Even when you're scolding me and I'm scared and unhappy, at the same time I'm singing a little song in my head." The fact that such multiple states of being exist in us at all times is what I've always tried to express in my work.

Once I began a play I would keep writing in sequence, start to finish, until it was done. Sometimes it would take as long as six months to get a play going that I'd be able to finish. I began play after play, but after six, ten, twenty pages, it would start to bore me and I'd throw it out. Or the language would start to get more discursive, or sound like conventional social intercourse, so I'd simply abandon it. An awful lot of plays were never completed. I accumulated a great many false starts.

At the time I would work from outlines, but what I did was to write *against* the outline. For instance, the outline for scene one might be: Max wants to go on vacation and his wife Rhoda doesn't want to go on vacation unless their friend Ben can come, and this makes Max angry—but then I'd write dialogue that contradicted my outline. I might start with Max saying, "I want Ben to come on our vacation." Then Rhoda would say, "I don't want Ben to fix the plumbing even though he offered." It wasn't that I expected or wanted the audience to appreciate a level of irony at work in the text, or that the situation was not as it seemed to be. It was simply that in the act of writing, I consciously tried to escape the mental inhibitions of my outline. In a subterranean way I was steered by the outline, but I wanted to write scenes that would, in fact, obliterate it. I thought it would be interesting, as I put it, to dewrite the outline. In other words, keeping the outline in mind, but saying "Hah, look how I can show the antiuniverse to this universe that I'm supposed to be writing." And that I *was* writing, in one sense, because somehow the progression from one scene to the next was still within the gravitational field of the hidden outline. This relates to a technique I used some years later, in which I wrote sentences like everybody else, from left to right on the page, but I'd imagine that the words were actually appearing on the page from right to left, obliterating and superseding the writing I was making the effort to write.

I suppose when I started dewriting, it was an attempt to get up the courage to write from a position of total ignorance, of having no conscious plans. I used to be very uptight about being able to justify my creative process intellectually, both to internalized authority figures and to external authorities like critics, audiences, and others. So I needed the support of intellectual justification to make me feel comfortable about the increasingly free way I was writing. Perhaps that added a special tension to the work. The fact is that this kind of unself-conscious spontaneity doesn't come easy to me, though it comes easier now than it used to.

As I understand it, in the early days you had an interest in the techniques of alchemy?

I first encountered a discussion of alchemy in a tacky French best-seller, *The Dawn of Magic*, by Pauwels and Bergier. They published a magazine for many years called *Planète*, which was the leading occult-Jungian-what-have-you magazine in France. Their book introduced me to a lot of things—speculation in a vein similar to what's found in the writings of Colin Wilson. Obviously, for many people, Wilson is also on the far-out fringe, but I happen to like his books, at the very least finding in them, as Yeats would say, "metaphors for my poetry." But I have to admit it's more than that; I think he's an interesting guy. Of course, many artists are inspired by ideas on the margins of respectability, since respectability can be suffocating intellectually, as well as artistically.

What attracted me specifically to alchemy was its notion of taking a very simple, primary material, and reworking it again and again in the belief that if you dedicate your purest self to this process of continual repetition, something unexpected would happen to the gross matter you labored over. A universal force, or the force of your unconscious, would project into the worked material so that it would rise, it would lift, it would transform itself into something else.

For instance, I'd start with the psychological confrontation between a husband, a wife, and her lover, and I'd try to establish a basic, wooden, primitive level upon which they all functioned, and that would be the prime material upon which I'd go to work. The husband might say, "Larry's sitting in my chair." A pause, then he'd repeat, "Larry's sitting in my chair." Pause. "He's still sitting there." And then his wife says, "Yes, he's sitting there." And the husband says, "He's sitting there." Pause. Then Larry says, "I'm sitting in this chair, Harry." And the wife says, "He's sitting in the chair." And the husband says, "Which chair? My chair." Essentially we proceeded at that rate, for hours on end—and after a while another level of energy seemed to take over. It became hallucinatory in a very interesting way which suggested transcendence.

You also discovered the writing of Gertrude Stein early on, and she became an important influence on your work.

Yes, but that was a bit later. When I discovered Gertrude Stein, it clarified what I'd been feeling about my own writing, and gave me the terms to talk about what I'd already been doing. Much of what I've read and responded to over the years has functioned for me in this way. What I do is always intuitive, then I hungrily search for things that explain to me what it is I've been doing.

There were two notions of Stein's that particularly struck me. One: Writing in a state of continual presence, a procedure which directly relates to what I've just described. And second, the notion of continually "beginning again" in the writing. In my muddy understanding of surrealism in those days, I felt that what I was doing was different from surrealism because I thought surrealism meant you entered into the flow of an image, and you were taken on a trip to wherever that image, as it transformed itself, might lead you. Whereas I thought I was working in the Steinian tradition, in which you have a response to a situation, and the minute it starts to exhaust itself—generally after a couple of lines— you'd stop, and immediately go back to that original situation and try it again. And begin again, begin again, as Gertrude Stein would say. In addition, in talking about writing in continual presence, Stein explained that she felt that she was writing the essence of the object, rather than its aura of cultural and emotional usage. And I, too, felt that with my minimalist orientation I was trying to get to the essence of the situation, and was avoiding the particular coloration the situation had been given by the culture.

When did you start to move away from your minimalist orientation?

I'd also call it a phenomenological orientation, because I was also reading Husserl, Max Scheler, Heidegger, and so on, and focusing on the essence of the objects I bracketed onstage for repetitive iteration. But all this began to change around the time of *Hotel China*, when I became more interested in objects, not as things in themselves, but as things that could have an *effect* upon me. It was a big change. I was no longer trying to penetrate to the essence of things. I was not trying to make the apple sit on the table while it became more "applelike." I was trying to figure out what I would like apples to do to me that I would find interesting, that would make me more aware of my own constructed mental proclivities.

With *Hotel China* I began to write plays by imagining intricate, strange objects that would suggest ways that desire, working through the performer, might cause them to be manipulated. I stopped working from outlines, and instead let the complicated physical objects that I imagined lead me in whatever direction they suggested. For instance, *Hotel China* had a small house on a pulley system which ran across the ceiling of the stage, and the house would slowly float over the stage and sometimes drop to the floor. Then actors would get inside the house and look out its little window. They'd turn the house around so the back side, which was cut away, revealed its interior to the audience, with an actor squeezed inside. When the house was up in the sky, the performers would peer at it through telescopes. I explored all potential uses of this house, and how each potential use would suggest a different psychological modality. I would build a scene out of a particular psychological situation vis-à-vis the house, because the house itself suggested particular manipulations. In that way, in an almost structuralist sense, the play would suggest how the given materials of a particular world create what we tend to think of as archetypal situations, precisely because those materials lend themselves to a series of possible manipulations that imaginatively suggest such archetypal forms. In other words, the plays demonstrated how our fantasy life, as well as our mental picture of the world, springs directly from the physical possibilities that are built into the objects with which we surround ourselves.

At this point, for the first time, fantasy material began to enter the plays, since the manipulation of these objects would also suggest various fantasies. If you have a house that comes down from the sky, it immediately evokes fantastic associations. In *Hotel China* the floating house was echoed by a little house that was strapped to the forehead of one of the actors, as if it exuded directly from his mind—or perhaps he saw the world through the "filter" of his acquired concept of "house"; part of his mental baggage. In the earlier plays, the objects were simpler and did not flower into that kind of manipulation or creative doubling. They were simple objects in static situations, phenomenologically bracketed off from contaminating contingency, so that the lamp on the table said only, "I am a lamp. I go on. I go off. Don't try to do anything with me that you should not do with a lamp." Beginning with *Hotel China* many of the objects were more complicated, funkier, more idiosyncratic. My new perspective toward the psychic significance of objects allowed me to use the lamp in such a way that the lamp said, "I am a lamp. But I can also be a projectile that you hurl at your enemy. I could also be something that you can lay on its side and put ketchup on and try tasting to see if it tastes good." It could be any one of innumerable possibilities.

A world ruled by objects could also suggest, "I am a lamp, and over there is a bookcase. What are the possible relationships between a lamp and a bookcase? Well, let me, lamp that I am, go over and sit next to a book on a bookcase. Can you read me like you can read a book? Is a book as bright as a lamp?" I'd let my imagination run free: "I am a lamp. Usually, when you go to bed at night you take a book and read before you go to sleep. Tonight, try taking me, a lamp, to bed, and hold me in your arms, and look into the light, and tell yourself the story that you see looking into the light."

All kinds of possibilities present themselves concerning wild and suggestive uses of lamps, which, along with radios, were my favorite objects. These objects suggest two opposing sides of the same metaphysical question—are human beings "lamps" who give of ourselves to illuminate the world, or are we "radios" who receive information transmitted from elsewhere?

I became interested in giving free play to the part of the self that weaves whole worlds out of whatever it finds, in order to discover, through ever more eccentric constructions, what the self might indeed be. Perhaps you are a being that finds it interesting to do such and such with tables and chairs. What else might you become if it were possible to pursue other extensions of your interaction with a table or a chair? Partially under the influence of the French structuralists and poststructuralists, I began to entertain the possibility that objects were simply crossroads for a multitude of inputs from the culture and from our unconscious. In structural terms, they were simply points of interaction between the different cultural codes we function within; the nodal points where the different forces of memory, association, and impulse meet, momentarily giving rise to one or another object on stage. My goal was to evoke that network of codes and associations, and so the plays became complex rhythmical interweavings of the visual, aural, and ideational material.

This tendency was further radicalized when you moved into your own theater on lower Broadway.

I had been looking for a space, and I went to George Maciunas, an old friend of Jonas Mekas and the force behind "Fluxus," the art movement, and he suggested that we organize some people to buy a building in SoHo, one floor of which I could use as a theater. I had just received a ten-thousand-dollar playwrighting fellowship from the Rockefeller Foundation, so I used that money for the down payment for my floor. The building was on lower Broadway, at Broome Street. The theater space was only fifteen feet wide, but a hundred feet long, a rather eccentric shape for a theater, but I've always felt the contingencies of a situation would create an art appropriate to that situation.

The audience sat in a twenty-five-foot area at one end of the space. The stage floor—which we built from scratch for each play—was usually a series of raked platforms. It might slope up for twelve feet, then down twelve feet more, then up, then down, like a series of hills. Midway on one side was an alcove which allowed us to move things in from offstage—sliding walls with doors, for instance, or painted images—allowing us to change the dimensions of the playing space very quickly. For instance, we'd begin a scene on the top of a platform eighty feet back. Then suddenly a wall would come in at twenty feet, obliterating the far platform and changing the set into a room on a platform closer to the audience. All through the show we'd shift back and forth, changing the set from one specific locale to another, though often the sets would be rather abstract. For instance, one scene in *Rhoda in Potatoland* took place in a café with swinging doors; a small model of the same room hung on the wall above the action. The next scene was in the countryside, indicated by a painted gray geometric shape on the wall that suggested a tree. Then an eight-foot-long shoe appeared, rocking back and forth gently on top of a platform in the distance. A moment later, in front of that shoe, a little boat entered, suggesting that the rocking shoe was really a boat which could take you away on a journey. And these changes were punctuated by lighting, music, and loud thuds.

I was interested in the shock effect of radically altering the space, shifting from a deep space which suggestively faded into the mysterious darkness eighty feet back, to a very tight space with the actors down front staring straight at the spectators in blinding light. I played back and forth between these possibilities, not so much highlighting the way the shifts related thematically to the explicit text, but serving the emotions hidden behind the text. I was interested in exploiting the ways in which the joy of playing with the scenic space could work in counterpoint to the feelings hidden in the text, producing a new level of reality that rose out of text (idea) and image (materiality) to create a heretofore unvisited country (Potatoland!).

Schiller, discussing art, said there are three kinds of people in the world: people who focus on the structure of a situation, in life or in art; people who focus on the content of a situation in life or in art; and people who are artists, who focus on the possibilities of play between *all* the elements inherent in a situation in life or in art. Faced with the unique space of my new theater, I did radicalize my tendency to play with the available elements, which I like to think is what any human being should do. He or she should be detached, to a certain extent, from both content and structure, allowing free play with both, and finding in that play the deep fulfillment of life and spirit.

This attitude toward play is certainly reflected in the strange, playful objects you introduced into the work, both as props and as part of the stage set.

In *Rhoda in Potatoland* people made a big deal out of the two, six-foot-tall potatoes that walked onstage, but to me that was a simple fantasy of exaggeration—something I'd often done before. In *Angelface*, for instance, there was a character who wore big wooden wings that kept him from entering a room; he kept banging into the door because his wings were too wide: exaggerated. Everything I've ever done, including exaggeration, could probably be found in that first play. Essentially an artist does one thing throughout his career, but over the years he discovers its various implications and expands upon and deepens aspects of what has always been present in his work. Perhaps that's the difference between a serious artist and an entertainer. The artist is constantly deepening a single, obsessive theme, rather than decorating a succession of topical themes with a more superficial talent.

By *Hotel China* I had begun to invent complex, suggestive objects that transcended simple exaggeration, but with *Rhoda in Potatoland*, for the first time, such ambiguous objects were linked to the generative core of the play's meaning. For instance, in that play there was an abundance of plastic tubes, about one foot in diameter and six feet long, which were brought onstage for a variety of purposes. The actors held them between one another, making abstract tube-networks between themselves as they talked, physicalizing both the connections between people and the distances separating them. But the tubes reinforced the

thematic metaphor of the play in another way. As I discovered in rehearsal—partially as a result of meditating on
those tubes as they appeared in different scenes each day
—*Rhoda in Potatoland* was a play circling the theme of
tumescence, the swelling of sexual organs, not excluding
the brain as sexual organ, swelling with ideas. Many of
the props, chosen long before I was able to conceptualize
this idea, suggested that quality of tumescence—they
seemed to swell to a point where they became something
quite other than what they in fact were. For instance, I
had always used strings in my plays, running them across
the stage in various patterns, and in this play the tubes
were, in effect, fatter, tumescent strings. All this also related to the image of the large potato, swollen as if it might
give birth, a womb for ideas and fantasies. And just as
tumescence implies sexual penetration, a feverish confusion of male and female in intense intermixing, so this
impulse created many props that seemed to embody the
penetration of one object into another. Such props continued to reappear in my plays for many years. In *The Cure*,
for instance, I used an object that looked like a cross between a couch and a table. I'm fascinated by the notion
that objects might invade and acquire the qualities of other
objects. Blake says that the universe exists in a grain of
sand; in addition, the table exists in the doorway, the lamp
exists in your forearm, and the *Encyclopaedia Britannica* exists in the street outside the window. That's what many
of my props look like, and I particularly enjoyed generating
a mise-en-scène out of a character's attempts to use a prop
in a way that suggested the two separate objects the prop
seemed to be at once.

   The introduction of such playfulness and fantasy was
also due to the influence of Kate Manheim, who was the
leading performer in these plays for many years. Simply

put, Kate is a more playful person than I, and it was she who wanted to do playful things onstage. It interested her to take off her clothes, to be shocking and provocative in performance, which not only funneled much erotic imagery directly into the work, but also encouraged its broader free play and inventiveness. Many psychoanalysts discuss the way that adults, through sexual life, return to the playpen as the polymorphous-perverse body acts out the invention and fantasy of bodily manipulation. In a similar way, I'd say that the sexual content that appeared in my plays opened the floodgates of playfulness in other areas. In *Rhoda in Potatoland*, for instance, we placed a chair with uneven legs and a tall curved back on a hillside, and hung a scale filled with books from the curved back. The weight of the books should have pulled the chair down the hill, except that Kate was sitting on the chair, keeping it from tumbling. If one were academically minded, one might talk about how that image symbolized the precariousness of knowledge; how you sit down to read never knowing when knowledge itself might suddenly pull you down the hill of mental insecurity. But it also demonstrated the way any object, thrown slightly out of kilter, forces us to notice it with renewed, refocused energy—just as in an erotic situation, so much human energy is devoted to rearranging your lover's body, creating that kick of strangeness and intimacy that excites your very being.

In terms of pure sexuality and provocation, it now amazes me how far my plays went in those days. I don't think there was any other theater doing quite as much. I remember, for instance, one scene in *Particle Theory* in which Kate and another actress came in on roller skates, totally nude, and then bent over on all fours—showing their naked asses to the audience. Though these moments always related to the thematic meaning of the scene, no doubt the provocation was intense. I staged many scenes of this sort, in which I wanted the audience to become self-conscious about their confrontation with so-called pornographic imagery. We've talked about my interest in collisions—how I felt that consciousness originally arises through a collision between mind and matter. Well, by *Rhoda in Potatoland* you could say we had upped the ante. The collision was no longer simply putting a hand out to feel a resisting wall. It was a collision between consciousness and the most loaded object in Western culture: the naked sexual body. And so eroticism became a major theme of the plays.

Once I began to manipulate the performer's bodies in this way, I wanted to echo that manipulation by using everything that surrounded the body, and as a result everything onstage became eroticized. Which is to say, everything became an object of passionate interest and concern; the sensory reading of objects was intensified. I'd look at a table and imagine: table, you turn me on, but you might turn me on more if one of your legs were longer, and there was a little machine under you to make you bounce in a wobbly way, so we might put a glass of water on you and that glass might fall and spill water all over the stage. Which is an event that took place in *Miss Universal Happiness*.

By Rhoda in Potatoland *the Rhoda character played by Kate had clearly become the central figure in the plays.*

I started giving Kate more and more lines, and more spectacular behavior, not simply because she was so electric onstage, which she was, but also because we were living together and she'd say, "Richard, I want to do more!" I remember how shocked Stefan Brecht was when I told him that for a particular scene in *Particle Theory*, when Kate had wanted more dialogue, of course I said, "We'll just give you all these lines that were written for another character. So cross out the name Hannah and write in Rhoda!" And Stefan said, "How can you alter the play like that?" And I told him that, as far as I was concerned, life's contingencies were the most productive raw materials available for making art, so if Kate wanted to have more lines, I'd give them to her, and in the process discover something in the play I hadn't been aware of before.

I never consciously wrote material specifically for Kate to perform, though of course I knew that she was going to be in all the plays, playing the leading role. I just continued to write as always, following the natural pull of my own desire to break down the elements of consciousness into their constituent parts. But Kate's planet had entered my universe, and the gravitational force of that planet certainly pulled me in new directions. For instance, I wouldn't have been able to explore much of the erotic material that surfaced in my work had it not been for Kate.

Even with the addition of this unsettling, erotic material, the staging was still fairly rigid, limited to what was specified in the text. If I had a scene in which Hannah said, "I'm showing off my body. Are the suitcases going to be attracted to Hannah, or are the suitcases going to be attracted to Rhoda's naked body?" the actors would simply strike a pose, and then hold that tableau. I wasn't interested in coming up with many different positions. I wanted to heighten the tension between the fact that you were watching a naked woman, while the language pulled you away from the immediacy of that experience. I wanted to split the audience's attention between the fact of confrontational nudity and the nonerotic strangeness of what went on in the language, and to invoke doubleness inside the spectator

Charlie Bergengrin, Kate Manheim, Rena Gill, and Bob Fleischner in Rhoda in Potatoland.
(Photo by Babette Mangolte)

so he or she could experience and appreciate that war of attentions coursing through his or her consciousness.

The cold, presentational staging made the eroticism more present, palpable, shocking, but at the same time, it was something the spectators had to deal with in an almost clinical manner. If you become empathetically involved in a romantic scene between two actors, you forget you're watching a staged performance and identify with the actors—you become aroused as if you were a part of that erotic scene. But if the eroticism is staged in a detached, presentational manner, you may then be led to ask, Do I feel awkward confronting this? Sexually aroused? What is my attitude toward this? Am I able to function in the way that I want to function, using my head, applying my aesthetic sensibility, or am I swamped by my erotic response? And isn't this an interesting problem—working out the relationship between the variety of feelings this scene arouses in me?

Were you still using your primitive performance style in Rhoda in Potatoland?

As I allowed more and more fantasy material into the work, it led to a different use of the performers. I began to explore more imaginative ways in which the performers could relate their bodies to the objects onstage. They were still emotionally neutral most of the time, but their bodies were often twisted in unnatural positions. In the early days I tended to have them flat on their heels, facing the audience. By *Rhoda in Potatoland*, they'd tend to be stuck with one foot up on a table, for instance, and their backs sloped against a wall. Still tableaulike, but the tableaux were convoluted and provocative—kinkier, you could say. I'd also begun to introduce occasional big, theatrical effects, or musical dance numbers. In *Rhoda in Potatoland*, for instance, an all-girl orchestra suddenly materialized, playing saxophones and using jazzy body language, and for about thirty seconds things got very lively. Then, just as the audience began to get into it, everything would stop, and the play would return to its normal, slower, static rhythm. That shift back and forth between rhythms would happen many times during the performance.

The subtitle of Rhoda in Potatoland *was* Her Fall-Starts, *which was a punning reference to the way in which the play was written.*

Half of *Rhoda in Potatoland* was written, from beginning to end, like one of my old plays, but it wasn't long enough to stage. As I mentioned before, I'd begun many plays I couldn't finish, I'd accumulated a great number of play fragments—false starts—and looking through the notebook in which I wrote *Rhoda* I asked myself, Why am I throwing these extra pages away? There was a lot of material there I liked. So thumbing through that notebook I said to myself, Why not stage these parts of the notebook, these false starts, as part of the play itself? I didn't skip anything; the short play *Rhoda in Potatoland* was at the end of that section. Then I realized it would make a more interesting play if I moved the Rhoda part to the front. That flip-flop of the material was a radical decision for me. I'd originally intended to produce the play in the same sequence in which it was written. I had always believed that keeping the material in its original sequence was more honest, that it reflected the particular trajectory of my thought. But then I realized I could do whatever I wanted with my own material, and since then, I've never hesitated to rearrange the texts in any way I see fit.

For all my plays through *Rhoda in Potatoland*, I wrote dialogue for the same group of characters who traveled through every play: Ben, Max, Sophia, Hannah, Rhoda, and a few others. But I never thought that the separate fragments I was writing would work together as a whole. It was only when I was looking through the false starts in the Rhoda notebook that I started to think: From here to here, it's *almost* like a play; I didn't see it before, but if you put them all together it makes sense. I then began to realize that everything that came through me as writing inevitably "made sense." After that, I increasingly tended to choose sections of my notebooks that led me to say: From here to here, *nobody* could stage that, it's too fragmented, it doesn't hang together at all; can I stage this and make it hang together? I got pleasure out of proving to myself that I could take even the most dissociative text, a series of unconnected fragments, and find a way to put it onstage and give it theatrical coherence.

Penguin Touquet was staged at the New York Shakespeare Festival's Public Theater in New York. Why did you decide to move your work into a more traditional theater space?

I had sold my loft theater in SoHo, though everyone thought I was crazy. But I felt it was getting too safe. By then, we had become something of a hot item. I had a devoted, cultlike following. There were arguments every night outside the theater as people pleaded to get in. We were always sold out, and each play ran as long as it interested me to keep it going. When I got bored with coming to the theater every night, I closed the play. It had become too easy, too secure a situation, and I wanted to maneuver myself into a more adventurous position. And selling the theater proved to be the right thing to do, because it forced me into many productive situations I'd never have been exposed to if I had my own theater to fall back on.

The environment of the Public Theater had an interesting effect on the work. Their assistant designers neatened up my designs, and their crews built the sets and props with a slickness that gave the work a different tone. And there were other subtle effects. I was very friendly with all the people at the Public Theater—I like them and I think they like me—but there's no doubt that their aesthetic tastes were different from mine. And when you're in a collaborative work environment, especially when you like the people you work with, it's difficult to keep from unconsciously drifting toward aesthetic choices more in tune with the sensibilities of the friends who surround you. So I believe I unconsciously drifted toward decisions that added a veneer of sleek professionalism to *Penguin Touquet*, as well as to the next two plays, all of which I did for Joseph Papp at the Public. It affected not only the scenery, but the performance style as well. The shows became less confrontational, more seductive, and this new luxuriousness that surfaced in the work left me feeling somewhat ambivalent. On the one hand, I was given resources that allowed me to mount spectacularly complex productions, but the slickness made some people nostalgic for the self-conscious primitivism of my earlier work. Aesthetically, I see strengths in both modes. That's why I've continued to work both at the Public Theater and in funkier venues like the Performing Garage, which is closer to the downtown art world.

Penguin Touquet was cast like any other play at the Public Theater: their casting department arranged auditions. Over the years, Kate's performances had grown so strong that none of our nonactors could match her dominance on the stage. I'd already begun working with regular actors when directing plays like *Threepenny Opera* at Lincoln Center, and Kate wanted to try that as well. So we decided to try to find actors who could match Kate's focused intensity. It also seemed appropriate to begin casting my plays with established actors since we were performing at the Public Theater. And why not? I welcomed the opportunity to discover what might result from the collision between my aggressively antidramatic texts and classically trained performers.

Once I started using real actors, everyone in the plays was given more to do. There was no longer such a clear distinction between the two or three principals, who really carried the show, and the horde of spear carriers who moved scenery, posed in tableaux, and manipulated props. I also stopped using tapes to deliver dialogue; the actors spoke their lines directly. This was partly because I felt I couldn't ask real actors to be subservient to the tape. But I also wanted to find out if I could internalize in flesh and blood performers the effect of psychic fragmentation I'd been achieving through manipulated taped language.

The web of language I'd achieved using the tapes was replaced by an increased use of background music. In *Penguin Touquet*, for the first time, I played music during every moment of the performance. I began to tape loops of musical phrases, usually no more than four or five seconds long, and I'd play two or three of these loops at the same time—so the relationship between their different rhythms and melodies was constantly changing. The loops added another layer of complexity to the performance, another layer of meaning. Suppose two actors are playing a scene with a certain atmosphere; by adding music you're able to alter that atmosphere. In Hollywood movies, they will almost always use music to reinforce the emotional atmosphere, intensifying the most obvious thrust of the scene. I, on the other hand, was interested in introducing music that displaced the emotional quality of the scene; the music was *contra* to the dominant atmosphere. I wanted to make the scene other than it appeared to be through text alone. Running two loops at once only added to this sense of disruption. The scene vibrated back and forth between the two different musical influences. What was being said by the actors was subtly redefined by the rhythms of the music, which not only introduced other levels of meaning into the scene, but frustrated the spectator's easy indentification with the actor's drift toward an emotionally manipulative performance.

During the period of *Penguin Touquet*, in order for me to feel right about the plays, every inch had to be so worked over and multilayered that, for me, the play reflected the complexity of life itself. And I thought that the effect of my plays on an audience should feel something like surfing. The audience was riding a wave of piled-up perceptions, which constituted the play, balanced on a wave of exhilarating, accelerating events. It was like being high—whether by drugs, or by mystical experience, or by simply feeling at the top of your powers, while enveloped by a world in which things are happening, but over which you have no control—certainly an archetypal twentieth-century experience.

At this time, the sound tracks for my plays became very loud, even assaultive, to echo the world as I experienced it. I felt I needed something in my art that could match the degree of aggressiveness that washed over me as I walked the streets of New York; only then could I claim the performance truly earned the state of calmness and detached lucidity I hoped it would produce in the spectator. I've always felt that if I can't find a way to be calm, detached, and lucid inside the abrasive world I encounter on the streets of New York, then I'm cheating. I had to make an art that transformed what was really there in my world, all the awfulness of that world, rather than simply dreaming of a better world and painting pictures of that dream. Obviously, if you choose to inhabit a nice, comfortable environment, it's quite easy to feel at one within yourself. The challenge is to find that point of stillness in the midst of the storm—within the depths of this negative hyperenergy that characterizes the worst of contemporary Western urban life.

This direction in your work, toward ever greater aggressive complexity and speed, reached its most frenetic moment in the production of Miss Universal Happiness.

That was due in part to the dynamics of the music, which was from Latin America and was very, very loud. There were constant explosions of activity and violence. The cast was made up of actors from the Wooster Group, and they didn't hesitate to expand on any of my suggestions to get louder and faster. They were used to working as an ensemble, and because they were skilled in performance techniques similar to my own, it was no problem for them to adjust to my extremely choreographic direction. They threw themselves into it with a vengeance that moved the performance faster and faster, and I indulged myself by asking for more violent physical activity than I ever had in the past. One example: I built ramps on the set leading up to very solid walls, and the actors were directed to run up the ramps, smack into the walls, and bounce off them back down to the center of the stage. I remember times during rehearsals when I started to explain motivations, and the Wooster Group actors would interrupt, "Come

on, Richard, that's what you tell your Public Theater actors; you don't have to give *us* motivations, just tell us
where to go and how to walk."

Miss Universal Happiness was the last time I chose to stage
pages from my notebooks that were so fragmentary, so
abstract, that they could have meant anything at all. More
radically than ever before, the dialogue was simply raw
verbal material that could have been part of a play with a
radically different theme and setting. When I assembled
the first pages of the text, I found a couple of things I
decided to read as references to Third World political turmoil, and that became the thematic center of the play.
Those two excerpts, from the original pages, read like this:

> Riveted by hostile factions
> God
> When the sun burns
> When I gravitate towards that
> Oh hostile factions,
> I can use: You: Two

and:

> Oh ringing of bells
> Oh ringing, ringing of bells.
> Why is it like a rage?
> It comes in the window.

Of course, these two brief passages could have been taken
in many other directions, but what popped into my mind
was a Latin American setting—perhaps I associated the
bells with the bells of a Mexican church I'd seen in some
movie—and everything followed from that. The set, for
instance, looked like a collision between a ramshackle
Mexican town and a child's playroom.

Something else which I thought of as significant surfaced
in *Miss Universal Happiness*. I introduced song forms into

the text; repetitive lyrics which the actors recited to recorded music loops. Since the Wooster Group was so responsive to rock 'n' roll dynamics, this song form helped to push the performances toward a controlled frenzy; it invited an energetic delivery much like the rap style that surfaced in the music world a few years later. I even used a number of hand-held mikes, which were located in different places about the set.

After *Miss Universal Happiness* I felt I could go no further in this direction. I felt I needed to try something else, which led to the much calmer and reflective energies of *The Cure* and most of the plays that have followed.

AUTHOR'S NOTE

◆

The stage directions included as part of these scripts reflect
the staging of the original productions as directed by the
author. Directors of subsequent productions, however, are
strongly urged to freely imagine their own stagings and
to set their productions in environments as different as
possible from the original. The texts are written to allow
for a wide variety of interpretations, of settings, even of
redistributions of the dialogue among the actors (including
the possibility that the cast be made up of a different number of actors and that the sex of a particular role be other
than as indicated in the script). Keep in mind that the
original productions contained considerably more background music and sound effects than are indicated in the
text. New productions should use more or less music as
the director sees fit, including the introduction of sound
loops taken from phrases in the text as he/she so desires.
In other words: all elements—except for the actual words
of the text itself—should be reconstituted as part of the
total vision of the director of any subsequent productions.
The texts cry out for the personal and idiosyncratic vision
to be contributed by each new director.

THE
CURE

THE CURE

◆

I called this play *The Cure* because I thought of it as just
that, a cure for my evident need to drive the work toward
the most frenetic, high-tech theater I could imagine. In the
productions leading up to my previous play, *Miss Universal
Happiness*, I'd been trying to achieve a state of Dionysian
frenzy—I tried to evoke the detachment and illumination
that can be found in the very center of the hurricane. After
Miss Universal Happiness, I realized there was no way for
me to go further in that direction, and I began thinking
about exploring alternative dynamics. Until then I had
been using complicated lighting effects, but *The Cure* had
very little lighting. The production was much softer, quieter. It was the first of a series of calmer, more meditative
pieces, and since then, though there have been exceptions,
I've been working toward a more meditative theater. The
plays became less confrontational, and I began to employ
a mix of performance techniques that allowed the actors a
more conventionally emotional performance style.

There is a passage in Jung which suggests that at forty

you approach a crossroads. You either head toward becoming a rigid, irascible old man, or you make new contact
with the roots, with the subterranean rivers of your unconscious. I remember reading that and thinking, I know
a lot of older men who clearly haven't made that contact,
and I don't want to end up like *them*. People had long said
my work was cold and clinical, and I agreed, and thought
that was fine. I thought of it as a corrective to the
encounter-group, emotional sloppiness that dominated
American theater. But by the early eighties I was thinking:
I'm getting older, and I'd like to see if my work could
become a bit mellower. I wanted the work to become more
mythic, to resonate to structures which reflected the archetypal pulsation within man. With *The Cure*, I consciously
tried to open myself to these energies, introducing different
currents into my work.

Writing *The Cure* I depended on two basic techniques:
I was taking dictation, keeping my mind empty and writing whatever came, and at the same time I was listening
to two different music loops playing at once. Before *The
Cure* I'd certainly written by taking dictation from my
unconscious, but the fragments that came before were
much briefer. Listening to the loops gave the writing an
impetus to keep going, to expand. The rhythmical energy
of the double music encouraged me to keep talking to
myself, and not to be embarrassed by what was appearing
on the page. Through that I made all sorts of discoveries
for myself. For instance, the repetitive use of the phrase
"Here's an important dream," seemed a good way to generate lines that were stageworthy, highly personal, and
recitable. And it was not unlike questionnaire forms the
surrealists invented to provoke revelatory responses.

I never made a conscious decision to write more personal
material, but after the fact I noticed that that was the case.

I wanted the writing to be a sensitive registration of efforts to affect my own personality and consciousness. Though this effort was never the "subject" of my plays, in the traditional sense, I told myself that the writing should be a kind of seismograph that registered the tremors occurring inside me as I made such secret efforts.

As I was staging *The Cure*, the decision was made to set it in a room where people met who seemed to belong to an occult society like the Golden Dawn, which had, among its members, Madame Blavatsky and W. B. Yeats. Rather than living in New York, wouldn't it be nice if I found myself in that turn-of-the-century society of powerful poets and occultists? When preparing a play I often ask myself: Aren't there other environments in which to locate this text in order to reveal aspects of it which are otherwise inaccessible?

I thought of the setting as a place where people came to work on themselves and others, perhaps through consciousness raising, or through religious ritual. At the same time, the play was staged in a room that suggested my own private church or meditation chamber. And in fact, even though the plays following *The Cure* don't take place in such a room, they do take place in constructed locales that are all, on a certain level, private meditation chambers.

For the ten years preceding *The Cure* I had always used at least twelve actors, nine of whom would run around making patterns and moving scenery. They were a chorus commenting on the action, and their manipulations made for a very spectacular, theatricalized performance. It was something I knew I could do—and I just got bored with it. Today it's much more challenging for me to deal with the interaction of two or three people, and to have the audience close enough to watch every detail of what's going on in the souls of these few people. Ideally, I'd perform these plays in a room thirty by forty feet square, with no more than fifty spectators, which is how *The Cure* was originally done. We put the play on upstairs at the Performing Garage, in a small room which the Wooster Group usually uses as a dressing room.

The Cure had only three characters. I had no idea whether I'd be able to stage a play with only three actors, but I thought it worth a try. I remember telling the actors on the first day of rehearsal that I didn't want to resort to any of my old shtick, my familiar techniques. So when we began to rehearse the first scene, I asked the two male actors, Jack Coulter and David Patrick Kelly, to take as much time relating to each other as they could. I told them, Pretend you're doing an Actor's Studio exercise. I'd never done anything like that before, and even though we abandoned this approach after the first few days—I got bored with it, and started to have other ideas—it did orient us in a way that colored the whole production.

In *The Cure*, I encouraged a more internalized performance style so the actors could be perceived as working through personal issues for themselves in front of the audience. For instance, at one point Kate Manheim came out of a tent carrying a doll and had a rather long speech about watching workers go up a mountain to polish stones. As she speaks, she gets lost in the cruel beauty of the scene. The character Kate portrayed in *The Cure* was very well-to-do, and as Kate delivered the speech, aspects of the character's relationship to working people, including the fact that she had never been forced to do meaningless work to make a living, seemed to crystallize, and to affect her emotionally. It's also true, however, that Kate herself had worked at various menial jobs when she was younger, and at that moment in the play I had the feeling that Kate herself, as well as her character, was in front of the audience figuring something out about herself. I encouraged her to internalize the speech and to speak quietly. As she spoke, she modulated her voice so it shook a bit. I also gave her the doll to hold on to—it was a small voodoo doll. It looked rather frightening. Though we never discussed it, my idea was that by holding the doll and half talking to it, the doll would stand in for a side of herself she had never encountered, so she was actually talking to her own fear. She never looked squarely at the doll, rather she held it next to her body as if it were a ghost, its head right next to her own. It was a wonderful moment: Kate seemed both inside and outside her character in a way Brecht himself, I think, would have approved.

The Cure was a play about what goes on in the interior. It was left an open question as to *whose* interior. The actor's interior? My interior? Some kind of shared, universalized interior? I thought of the play as the registering of what happens "inside"—not just inside a consciousness, but the shared "inside" which could be imagined everywhere. The previous plays painted a picture of what would happen if the rules of the internal worlds of perception and consciousness could operate in the external world. *The Cure*, however, was an attempt to make a play that existed in the internal world itself, with no concern about projecting that way of being into the world outside the self.

The Cure had a very intimate quality; it was a chamber piece. The three actors all wore radio mikes and spoke very softly. The audience heard their spoken words over loudspeakers, though no spectator was more than twenty feet from the performers. I don't think the audience was used to hearing miked actors in such a tiny space, and it gave the play a unique quality, detached and meditative. It indeed seemed to be happening inside the audience's heads.

I wanted to make the watching of the play akin to the experience of reading a poem by Rilke. Up until then, I had been doing *War and Peace*, in my own little way. Here I thought I was doing "Sonnets to Orpheus." From the first day of rehearsal, I told the actors I felt *The Cure* was my best play, the one on which I was willing to be judged. I still feel that way. Many of my friends seem to prefer *What Did He See?* which is similar in mood, but I think *The Cure* was stronger, perhaps because it used less directly personal material, which makes it applicable to a variety of psychic circumstances. *The Cure* is like a transparent plate of glass: a filter that transforms whatever life circumstance is placed in front of it; it's responsive to a broad range of interests and experiences. I'd say *The Cure* is the most transparent of my plays; perhaps for that reason it's more obscure, but in the final analysis this quality of transparency makes it more universally applicable.

Most writing for the theater congeals into a dense mass. It takes you inside of it, so you can visit its specific location—the specific house at the specific hour in which the specific man murders his specific enemy. It's like opening a door and hearing, "Come into this room for a while." Most playwrights tailor their work to convince the audience that what takes place onstage is *really* taking place in the concrete, believable world. Each action onstage has one clear reason for being, and that reason, more often than not, contributes to the narrative thrust of the play. That approach makes me claustrophobic. There's no space in such a text to suggest the wide range of human consciousness that is the true subject of exciting art.

I would like to produce writing that is quite thin, transparent, so it functions as a talisman that lends itself to being worn through all kinds of life situations. A writing that doesn't coagulate what it refers to into yet another object in the material world. It might function instead as an allusion to a possibility, a flick of an idea spread thin like a sheet of glass. The writing, therefore, becomes a material form of consciousness through which you can experience the world. I want a writing that is more like spraying yourself with perfume, so you carry its aroma, hardly noticed, through the adventures of your own life. I want to make a theater that closes your eyes to the specific reality of where it's supposed to take place, so that all other possible locations can bleed through it.

The way I staged the opening of *The Cure*, David was looking at a jeweled ring he was wearing, though the text originally made no mention of a ring. The line simply was, "Look at this jewel. . . . It's faceted." In fact, the play began with David slowly entering and pausing to look at the audience. Only then did he slowly look at the jewel on his finger, making a connection between the audience, himself registering the audience, and the jeweled ring. I wanted to suggest he was talking about the jewel of his head, or perhaps the jewel of the room, or the wider psychic environment in which he found himself. I wanted to erase the power the ring had to make us think he was talking about the ring. It's hard to explain how you achieve that, but it's a matter of the actor's focus, a slight adjustment of his body: he can deliver the line in a rhythm that casts doubt on its believability without destroying its emotional effect. The opening line was, "Look at this jewel. It smiles at me." Does he smile back at it? Is he himself the jewel that is smiling? The text goes on, "It's faceted. That means the light enters it . . . and bounces around before it comes out. . . . A jewel of an idea. A jewel of an act. A jewel of an emotion." The way I wrote it, there's no indication in the text of how that's to be staged or who is speaking. That's decided in rehearsal, when I see how the particular distribution of the lines can assist in keeping all the references multiple, dancing from one possibility to another. I had Jack speak the next line, "The time . . . has come . . . to tell . . . the truth. Art: this art . . . tells the truth. But it is hidden. Why is it hidden?" Certainly, it's easy to provide a million glosses on that. Does this line refer to the play itself, or to an aspect of the relationship between the characters? I felt it important to shift the lines to Jack at this point, so that the audience wouldn't over-identify with David and feel the play was being seen through his eyes. I wanted to keep the focus fluid and the dialogue open to innumerable interpretations.

It's a transparent kind of writing, and to stage it the director has to fill in the gaps, but in such a way that his specific choices don't close down the wide range of references the text suggests. As I've said, I set *The Cure* in a meeting of the Golden Dawn Society. Someone else might have chosen a strange jewelry store in Prague, with a group of old Jews sitting around analyzing the Talmud. Another director might do it poolside at a Miami hotel, or in an airport lounge in Hong Kong. What is important is to avoid making that chosen time, place, and historical context too specific. Not that I'd ever place the action in some timeless, placeless void, but I work hard to make every visual element and detail of action suggest multiple, superimposed readings. For instance, though *The Cure* had a turn-of-the-century, occult society atmosphere, that was simultaneously layered over by a set evoking a sleek, postmodern Italian interior design.

This approach shares a great deal with the strategies of contemporary poetry. Prose is writing in which language disappears, leaving you free to live inside the experience to which the now invisible language makes reference. Poetry is a form of writing led as much by language as by the world to which the language may or may not refer. In poetry, language stays in the foreground; the power of the language itself gives the reader a sensory and emotional experience. In the same way, I want a theater in which the theatrical language—lights, props, scenery, actors as actors, words as speech-effort—stays in the foreground. Unfortunately, most theater has modeled itself on the strategies of prose. What I propose is not a theater of "poetic atmosphere," but one which models itself on the strategies of poetic syntax and structure, the better to handle the materials out of which the life-force builds subjective human experience.

The Cure was first produced by the Ontological-Hysteric Theater at the Performing Garage in New York City on May 19, 1986, with the following cast:

> Kate Manheim
> David Patrick Kelly
> Jack Coulter

The production was directed and designed by Richard Foreman; costumes by Jim Buff; technical director, Carl Sprague.

Kate Manheim and Jack Coulter in The Cure. *(Photo by Craig Massey)*

The stage suggests a ceremonial room of some kind, overtones of a funeral parlor. The walls are covered with felt, the upper half red, the lower half a soft grey. Two black padded tables are at either side, and center is a five-foot-tall white column, topped by a giant vase filled with flowers—this vase, the flowers, and even the leaves, the same white. In one corner is a sort of throne. Objects on the walls make the room seem appropriate for some sort of religious ceremony, though there is nothing specific enough to suggest any particular religion. Along the walls at head height where the grey turns to black, there are many small painted wheels, and hanging from the ceiling against the walls, a series of similarly painted pendulums hang down—wheels and pendulums ready to go into rapid movement on cue. At a far side of the room is a wooden rack. Suspended from the rack are a variety of clear light bulbs, none illuminated at the moment. Oriental carpets are on the floor, and three, large, classical marble heads, covered with white cloths, are lined up rear. In the center of one carpet sits something that looks like a small playpen, but of carved and heavily decorated wood, with a low bench inside. A blackboard is propped on one of the two tables. A wooden railing separates the audience from the actors.

As the audience assembles a quiet, ringing music is heard. Then, slowly, DAVID walks onstage. He is dressed in a white shirt and tie, crisp and clean, and he stares at the audience for a while before slowly proceeding to the thronelike chair. He speaks very quietly, as do all the actors, who bear body mikes that enable them to converse in tones not much louder than a *whisper. In addition, all speak very slowly, as if in a dream, throughout the play.*

DAVID: Look at this jewel. *(He holds out his hand, looking at the bright ring on his finger)* It smiles at me. It's faceted. That means the light enters it . . . and bounces around before it comes out.

(Old-fashioned, lively music is heard softly as DAVID rises and slowly holds out his arms. KATE and JACK enter from opposite sides. KATE is dressed in a tight-fitting black dress with a corsage pinned to her shoulder. JACK is in a somber, striped sport jacket over a black silk T-shirt. They enter quickly to the music, touch DAVID's hands, and whirl to opposite sides of the stage. KATE slowly sits on a chair, JACK slowly sits in the playpen, and DAVID slowly takes out a handkerchief which he lets hang down from his fingers as he continues)

That's why it sparkles. The idea enters it . . . bounces around . . . *(He lets the handkerchief fall to the floor; KATE comes and retrieves it, holding it like a veil just below her eyes as she goes to sit in DAVID's throne; JACK begins combing his hair)* and each bounce . . . hits the eye. A jewel of an idea. *(DAVID comes, slowly takes JACK's comb; JACK rises and he and DAVID slowly circle each other)* A jewel of an act. A jewel of an emotion.

(DAVID bends and sweeps off a bench behind JACK, intending for him to sit down. JACK puts his hand out to stop him)

JACK: The time . . . has come . . . to tell . . . the truth. *(JACK crosses to sit in a far chair and DAVID enters the playpen)* Art: this art . . . tells the truth. *(KATE and JACK slowly rise and change places)* But it is hidden. Why is it hidden? Because unveiled, it would blind you. Would that be so bad? To be blinded by the truth? *(Soft, lively music rises again)*

KATE: Ah, you'd protect yourself against that by lifting your hand over your eyes.

JACK: You would. Even though, to be blinded by the truth wouldn't be so bad.

(They all slowly point at each other. The music fades)

DAVID: Do you think the truth . . . is an idea? Not at all. Can it be conveyed . . . *(A pause; KATE slowly changes her position in her chair)* in a story? Yes. Tell me a story. No. You just did. *(All slowly rise)* Right, I just did.

(JACK and KATE suddenly look at their hands and shift abruptly as if startled by what they see)

DAVID: Beautiful childhood person. Do you know my real name?

(Soft thuds are heard. KATE goes to hide her head on the table as JACK stares up at the sky)

JACK: The thunder gave birth to twelve shining automobiles. Those fast and burning cars, distributed to twelve princes of the earth, and I have received one.

KATE: *(Looking up slowly)* Watch how I drive . . . *(As she continues she slowly rises, climbs onto the padded table, and sits on top, leaning back, posing against the wall)* In the manipulation of my car I am a total career. In the manipulation of my car I make a medium out of a traffic flow, for other automobiles are not so perceptually varied. Their routes are my routes but different rhetoric patterns, preempting my own ecstatic, what-d'ya call 'ems? what-d'ya call 'ems? what-d'ya call 'ems? Do I speak gibberish? It is the style of driving and speed and final destination in my car that the thunder gave birth to. Great car!

(Rhythmic music is heard softly. DAVID and JACK stand, bouncing on their heels very slightly to the beat, hands over their crotches)

DAVID: Great car!

JACK: Great car!

KATE: Great car!

JACK: Here's an important dream: I wanted to have so much money, whatever I desired was mine.

KATE: Here's an important dream: I wanted people to love me, to put their own self-interest in second position. To dedicate their lives to my happiness.

DAVID: Here's an important dream: I wanted to be able to speak my thoughts without inhibition. Totally to be able to reach out and touch whatever could or could not be touched by my half-recognizable desires.

KATE: Here's an important dream: *(DAVID and JACK, still lightly bouncing, bounce down to KATE at the table as she leans back ecstatically against the wall)* I wanted to be bigger, better, brighter, faster, longer, more strong, more happy, more alive, more, more, more . . . !

(Atypically, the music now rises very loud, and the wheels and pendulums on the walls go into rapid motion. DAVID and JACK break into a stiff, hyperactive, puppetlike dance, prancing around the stage. They circle twice, then stop dancing and—after a final spastic flurry—collect themselves as things become quiet again. KATE has seated herself on the throne)

Here's an important dream: I woke up one morning and found that the world was just how I desired it. All flowers were in place where there were supposed to be flowers. All rivers, houses, trees, animals, people the same thing, the same thing.

JACK: *(Seated in the playpen)* Will my dreams come true? If you believe so. *(KATE rises and starts toward him, but he puts up a hand to stop her)* Of course. *(DAVID scribbles for a second with manic intensity on a pad of paper on the table, then looks away and is motionless)* If you live good. Of course. *(DAVID repeats his action)* If you worship God. *(DAVID repeats his action)* Of course. *(DAVID repeats his action)* Is that all? *(DAVID repeats his action)* That seems so easy. *(DAVID repeats his action)* It is easy.

(KATE pulls away DAVID's pad. Grabbing after his pad, DAVID almost falls off his chair, but then recovers)

DAVID: Find out how to run a big business.
Find out how to seduce a beautiful girl.

(All three rapidly slap their hands in rapid drumbeats on their thighs)

Find out how to mix metaphors in a language you find tough.

(Again they slap)

Find out how to cook a pork stew with onions.

(He sniffs his fingertips)

Find out how to balance yourself at the end of a twelve-foot pole on the top of a tall building.

(Again they slap their hands on their thighs like drumming)

Find out how to ride a one-wheeled bicycle not using your hands.

(Again they slap their hands, but after a few beats they pull up their hands and shake them as if it had caused pain)

Find out how to punish a man approximately five-foot-eight-and-a-half inches tall and nobody finds out but it isn't physical death.

(They hide giggles behind their hands)

Find out how to stop dead in your tracks when confronted with undeniable evil.

(Pause. JACK rises and looks offstage)

Find out how to spell configuration.

(KATE starts quietly spelling it, as DAVID continues)

Find out how to spell accidental.

(JACK starts to quietly spell it, as DAVID continues)

Find out how to spell multiple.

(KATE and JACK look at DAVID; they all sit; KATE looks to the sky)

KATE: Beautiful childhood person, do you know my real name?

(Three tones sound, and they speak in foreign languages)

KATE: Pour qui sont ces serpents qui sifflent sur nos têtes?
DAVID: Mi sento strano a tenere questa roba in mano.
KATE: Le tonnerre donna naissance à douze automobiles étincelantes. Ces bolides de feu furent distribues à douze princes de la terre. Douze élus dont je fus. Watch how I drive.

(Three tones sound. JACK repeats KATE's speech in German as DAVID and KATE fall asleep in available chairs)

JACK: Grosses Auto.

KATE: *(Waking up)* Admirable automobile.

DAVID: *(Waking up)* Macchina maravigliosa. *(He turns to tell JACK)* I'm not so sure you can really become so perfect. As the driver of fast and brilliant automobiles?

KATE: *(Stretching)* Admirable automobile.

DAVID: *(Turning to KATE)* I'm not sure you can really master the steering, acceleration, and so forth, and so forth.

JACK: Grosses Auto.

DAVID: I'm not sure, she can calculate the . . .

KATE: *(Rising and crossing)* Come on now! That girl is capable of packing and unpacking her suitcase without once reaching for the light switch.

(They all go and pose behind the covered heads on the floor, one hand ready to lift the cloths that cover them)

Come on now, that girl can balance three glasses of gin-rickey on her forehead at one time.

(They each flick off the cloths and sit on the heads)

Come on now, that girl can lick twenty-five percent of the men in this room with one hand tied behind her back.

(Sitting on the head, each starts to feel different physical symptoms)

Come on now, that girl could strip any attractive man in this vicinity stark naked using her teeth like scissors and not leaving a scratch.

(They take three deep breaths, almost as if giving birth)

Come on now. Come on now.

(They all feel about on their own heads, rather than the ones on which they sit)

JACK: *(Speaking straight out into space)* Does everybody have an aura . . . as powerful as your aura? *(Still feeling their heads, they all giggle)* Look. A female guru. *(They laugh even more; JACK rises from his head and goes to a table)* Look. A capitalist.

(He sits on the table. DAVID and KATE pick up discarded cloths from the floor and drape them over JACK'S feet, which stick out past the edge of the table, as JACK vibrates his feet gently)

DAVID: *(Putting the third cloth over his head, like a prayer shawl)* Nobody knows my name but I don't care, I don't care, I don't care.

KATE: *(Standing against the rear wall, slightly vibrating her whole body)* Nobody knows what books I like but I don't care, I don't care, I don't care.

DAVID: *(On another table, next to the pillar, he lies on the tabletop and gently rocks the pillar with his foot)* Nobody knows where I'm going when I leave here but I don't care, I don't care, I don't care.

KATE: Nobody knows if I like my name or if I don't like my name but I don't care, I don't care, I don't care.

JACK: Nobody knows if I can swim . . . *(KATE and DAVID come and snatch the cloths from JACK'S feet and use them to shimmy themselves slowly around the stage)* but I don't care, I don't care, I don't care.

KATE: Nobody knows if I went on vacation last year but I don't care, I don't care, I don't care.

DAVID: Nobody knows if I like birds or if I don't like birds but I don't care, I don't care, I don't care.

KATE: *(Coming toward the audience)* It was one of those days when the only thing that was going right was my relationship to everything that was going wrong.

JACK: It was one of those days.

(Three tones sound. KATE still shimmies to soft music and JACK goes to sit at a table)

DAVID: *(Turning toward the audience, quoting Joanna Field)* "Not only did I find that trying to describe my experience enhanced the quality of it, but also this effort to describe had made me more observant of the small movements of the mind. So now I began to discover that there were a multitude of ways of perceiving, ways that were controllable by what I can only describe as an internal gesture of the mind. It was as if one's self-awareness had a central point of intensest being, the very core of one's I-ness. And this core of being could, I now discovered, be moved about at will; but to explain just how it is done to someone who has never felt it for himself is like trying to explain how to move one's ears."

JACK: Why can't I possibly explain the opposite idea to the idea I have?

KATE: Ah, you need a shot of anti-antitoxin.

(Behind them, DAVID puts his hand on the table where JACK had been sitting. He gets burned.)

JACK: I can't explain the opposite idea to the idea I have because when I start to explain it, it turns immediately into the idea I have, because—

(DAVID tries putting his hand on the table again, gets burned again, and KATE and JACK turn to look at him. Then KATE goes to the other table with the blackboard. Above the table is a long shelf on which sit a box of cornflakes, a bowl, and spoon. JACK comes to watch her as she reaches up with great

effort, brings the cereal box to DAVID, *and turns to give the bowl and spoon to* JACK)

KATE: *(To* JACK) You'll never solve it.

JACK: But it's just normal cornflakes.

KATE: *(Returning to get the box from* DAVID, *she brings the cornflakes to* JACK, *fills his bowl, then returns to snuggle close to* DAVID. *She says to* JACK) You're wrong. It's not normal cornflakes.

(She and DAVID *sit on the far table, swinging their legs nonchalantly over the edge)*

JACK: *(Explaining to the audience)* And then an amazing thing happened. Using individual cornflakes instead of a typewriter, he—or she—started to write, word for word, an entirely new version of Leo Tolstoy's famous book *War and Peace*.

KATE: Word for word!

(She jumps off the table, crosses to the table with the black-board, carrying her cornflakes box, turns on a light attached to the top of the blackboard, and begins to attach cornflakes, in a mysterious pattern, over the face of the blackboard. JACK *and* DAVID *watch in fascination)*

JACK: *(Turning to the audience)* In this new version of the Russian classic the psychological and spiritual content took precedence over external incident which hardly existed, perhaps owing to the limitations of the medium which, in this case, was cornflakes rather than real life.

KATE: *(Coming to* JACK *and quoting Alfred North Whitehead)* "That leads to a comparison of English and Russian novelists. The novel on the grand scale seems to have been done best by the Russians—Tolstoy, Dostoevsky, Turgenev. *[She spins through the room, ecstatic to recite those names, and ends up seated on the throne]* Except in such

hands where the whole range of society is presented—
the family, the political, military, and economic systems,
and the clash of personalities and ideas—the novel is
concerned largely with the prevailing social habits of a
given place and time. This tends to restrict it to sec-
ondary range as an art form, not quite up to those tremendous universal themes of the great Greek tragedies.
But, have you noticed that there are a good many
second-rate works of art which survive and have a long
life—which they may not deserve as well as their
betters—because they embody some continuingly popular subject? It is true, a widely popular subject is likely
to be a good one, but for purposes of survival the work
must appeal to a good many people."

DAVID: *(Continuing the quotation)* "Music," I ventured,
"may come nearer it than words. Sometimes, during a
good performance of the very greatest music one has a
sense that he is in the presence of infinitude somewhat
similar to what the composer must have felt when he
was having to choose between one concept and another
in the hope of expressing it. *[DAVID is now writhing slowly
on the table. JACK leans the pillar at a moderate angle and
supports it while DAVID speaks]* The definite concepts are
there, in tones or phrases, but all around them hover
the infinitudes of possibility—the *other* ways in which
this vastness might have been expressed."

*(KATE has brought a tray of cookies to DAVID. He chooses one
and eats it)*

KATE: I have had more visionary experiences than you
can shake a stick at.

*(The atypical, loud, prancing music begins again, and DAVID
does a stiff-leg, puppet-strut dance around the room. JACK rocks
the pillar back and forth as the wheels and pendulums again*

go into crazy action. KATE *whirls holding her cookie tray,
rubbing her belly in time to the music. It all ends with a final
flurry, and they recompose themselves around the blackboard
table)*

DAVID: *(Standing)* Celebrate it. *(KATE and JACK, seated, rise
halfway and freeze)* How? I don't know. *(KATE and JACK
sink back into their chairs)* I have a suggestion.

(Three tones sound. KATE *takes a great deal of time wandering
about the stage looking for their source. Finally, she ends up
seated on the table, dangling her legs over the edge and swinging
them back and forth.* DAVID *and* JACK *come to look at her)*

KATE: *(Smiling, as soft music begins)* Do the Charleston.
Do the uptown.
Do the zip.
Do the dum-dum.

(DAVID and JACK have been backing away. KATE *holds her
hands together, looks to the sky, and whirls her hands around
one another)*

Do the waltz, do the waltz, do the waltz . . .

(She readdresses the men, swinging her feet again.)

Do the samba.
Do the rumba.
Do the chicken.
Do the doctor.
DO THE WALTZ DO THE WALTZ DO THE
WALTZ DO THE WALTZ!
Do the motivation.
Do the switch.
Do the stovepipe.

Do the knee.
Do the hat trick.

(DAVID and JACK try a bit of soft-shoe)

DO THE WALTZ DO THE WALTZ DO THE WALTZ DO THE WALTZ!

(DAVID puts his face to the wall and JACK leans with his back against the pillar)

Do the I don't know.
Do the hat-check-bang-bang.
Do the paintface.
Do the derrick!

(JACK has positioned himself in front of the pillar with knees bent and his hands behind him holding the pillar, so as he simply straightens up he lifts the pillar, with its large vase and flowers, straight up off the floor. As KATE continues, he slowly bends forward from the waist so that the pillar rests horizontally on his back, sticking out past his head like a giant cannon, with the vase and flowers going along for the ride)

Do the block!
DO THE WALTZ!

(She repeats "DO THE WALTZ!" ten times, DAVID whispering it along with her, as JACK first points the pillar cannon at KATE, then swings it around so that it is pointing at nothing in particular. DAVID walks over to observe the pillar)

DAVID: *(Putting his hands behind his back and turning to address the audience)* Can I dance without . . .

(Unable to think how to finish his phrase, he turns and moves away. JACK swings the pillar so that it points at DAVID. Sensing this, DAVID turns and watches the pillar as he moves

*back to the wall. The pillar pursues him until the flowers are
under his nose)*

Can I move my . . . *(He sniffs the flowers. The pillar moves
away from him and points downstage.* DAVID *puts his hands
up behind his head)* without . . .

KATE: *(She moves onto the other table, stretches out on top of
it, and quotes Joanna Field)* "Before, I had assumed that
there were just two attitudes, one a striving with whips
to make my thoughts follow the path I had chosen, the
other a witless dreaming, letting them wander off, use-
less and blindly nosing after grass. Now I began to think
. . . *[She comes off the table and goes about the room, as* JACK
puts the pillar back in its place and leaves it there] that there
might be, not just two, but as many different attitudes
as steps in a dance. I tried to make a list of all the different
gestures which I had found effective and the situations
in which I thought they would be appropriate: 'that fat
feeling' when I was tired, putting myself outside myself
for listening to music, and so on. I imagined myself
practicing each one as a dancer would first practice the
separate steps and then learn to do each at the right
moment, to leap or pirouette or curtsy as the music
might dictate. *[She notices* JACK, *who has seated himself,
staring at* DAVID] Detaching myself, holding myself apart
from what I was doing, which I first learned while darn-
ing my stockings, seemed equally effective in appreci-
ating the landscape; music, when it seemed to be nothing
but meaningless sound, would leap into significance
as much when I imagined myself to be dead as when
I pushed my awareness out into the hands of the
conductor."

JACK: *(Rising and speaking to* KATE) Of course, I am alive,
I hope, to those special possibilities.

(As he rises we see he has managed to seat himself so that a white cloth, the ends of which he holds in each hand, passes between and around his legs in a way that effectively shackles him to the chair. He stands, attached to the chair, takes tiny hobbling steps to the blackboard, and turns on the light attached to its top. Then he carefully removes cornflakes that KATE had applied, holding each one up to the light to examine it. As he does this, DAVID sings an ascending scale, softly, high in his register. A high electronic hum is also heard. JACK takes a final cornflake and holds it out for all the world to see. He speaks in a tiny, high-pitched falsetto)

JACK: Look, a cornflake that speaks volumes in the brief moment before it is transformed into light. *(He loses the falsetto)* Can I fly without flying apparatus? *(He looks down at the cloth that binds him and walks across the room, dragging his chair, to collect a large rock)* Can I carry a heavy rock in my arms when flying, or is the rock itself the energy that shall lift me over the rock-strewn landscape? *(DAVID is lighting candles on the four corners of the playpen. JACK, still tied to the chair, shuffles center with his rock)* Look, it is indeed a rock-strewn landscape.

KATE: Don't guess. Don't analyze. Don't do anything.

JACK: Everyone can be peeled like an onion.

(JACK has been holding his rock over the playpen as DAVID has gone to the wall and put his hands back behind his head. He drops the rock and everyone makes a high, yodeling noise. As the rock hits, JACK, still dragging his chair, hustles as fast as possible to the front of the playpen and sits)

DAVID: *(Wiggling his elbows slightly)* I have a difficult time making my arms flap in a way that closely resembles the way a bird's wings do.

JACK: *(Holding his own head)* Here, hold some of these rocks in your hands.

(DAVID drops his arms and takes a bowl of cornflakes down to JACK. JACK starts eating them with a spoon as KATE crosses, holding a small vase of flowers. DAVID sniffs the flowers, and both he and KATE go back to the table. Each gets a bowl with a spoon. They cross down to watch JACK and eat at the same time, but it appears that instead of cornflakes they each have a large rock in their bowls. They lift their rocks toward their mouths with their spoons, but before they can put them into their mouths, the rocks fall into the bowls. JACK looks around to see what the noise is, then goes back to eating. DAVID and KATE try again and fail again. This happens several times. Soft piano music is heard. Jack finally smiles at them and asks)

You expect results? *(JACK unties the cloth that attaches him to his chair; KATE and DAVID back away as he starts to use the cloth to blindfold himself)* I bet, there's method in this madness.

(Three tones sound and JACK rises, holding out his hands. DAVID and KATE place their bowls into his outstretched hands. JACK, blindfolded, slowly crosses the room holding out their plates and quoting Joanna Field)

"I want, not knowledge, but experience of the laws of things; to suffer them, not only to observe them. To apprehend with regard to the things I come across—the necessities of their being, what immutable law makes them what they are, their physics and chemistry and actuality, to feel it. . . . Knowing is no good unless you feel the urgency of the thing. Maybe this is love; your being becomes part of it, giving yourself to it."

(By now JACK is on the other side of the room, still blindfolded. KATE, carrying the large rock, comes up to him and asks)

KATE: What's your name? I bet it's a good name. *(She runs to DAVID)* What's your profession? I bet it's a fine profession. *(Back to JACK)* What's your taste in clothes? I bet you have very good taste in clothes. *(Back to DAVID)* What's your phone number? *(She sets the rock on DAVID'S lap and runs to sit on the throne)* I bet you have a very impressive phone number.

DAVID: *(Holding the rock as JACK takes off his blindfold)* How did you get to know so very much about me? Oh, Paula, you tried to keep secret things that were self-evident. Written on my face.

KATE: Were they embroidered in red letters on the back of my dress like—

(She gives a little shriek as if the back of her dress burned her flesh, whirls, and rises. This startles the two men, who also give a jump. Then all calm down. DAVID gets rid of his rock)

KATE: Were they . . . painted on?

(She and JACK go and take two of the heads from the floor. KATE takes one to her corner, and JACK puts one in the playpen, on the bench, and kneels to touch it gently)

DAVID: Selfish, selfish. *(Then he sits and asks himself)* Why do you say selfish? Were they . . . ?

(KATE goes to put her head inside a little booth that hangs from the wall with a curtain in front. Only her legs now show from below the curtain. DAVID picks up a bowl of cornflakes and begins to eat. JACK sits high up on top of the head inside the playpen as DAVID comes and looks at him)

JACK: It's not wise to talk about things that scare you. *(DAVID turns and sees KATE peeking out from her booth; as their eyes meet she disappears back inside, while JACK takes out his comb and grooms himself)* It's not wise to talk about things that make you cry. *(He and DAVID stare at each other)* It's not wise to talk about things that make other people mad at you. *(DAVID eats more cornflakes and looks back to the booth, but KATE is still hidden)* It's not wise to talk about things that jeopardize your economic security.

(KATE emerges from the booth holding in front of her face a small black voodoo doll with tiny skulls for a headdress. She speaks from behind the doll as she advances upon them)

KATE: But I *never* talk about such things. Such things are private. Sometimes you talk about them without knowing you talk about them. *(She has moved to a table. She sits on it, placing the doll to sit in her lap. She continues as if talking to the doll)* Impossible? But it's true, dear Paula. *(She refers to the doll as Paula)* Unwelcome ideas can sneak their insidious way into the most casual conversation. Or into the mind that has no intention of inviting such renegade thoughts into the mansion of the soul. Nevertheless . . . I don't think what I don't want to think. *(DAVID has found an identical doll which he holds up to JACK'S face)* Impossible, alas. Not impossible. Not impossible. Nothing is impossible.

DAVID: *(To soft music)* Sometimes it comes in the front door. Sometimes it comes in the window. *(KATE slides away in fear on the table, exclaiming "Oh?" and DAVID comes and sits beside her with his doll)* Sometimes it comes through the air conditioner.

KATE: Oh.

DAVID: Sometimes it comes through the water pipes.

KATE: Oh.

DAVID: Sometimes it comes through the electrical sockets.

KATE: Oh.

DAVID: Sometimes it comes in up through the toilet.

KATE: Oh.

DAVID: Sometimes it comes through the clock.

KATE: Oh.

DAVID: Sometimes it comes out of the medicine cabinet.

KATE: Ohhh!

JACK: *(Gently combing his hair)* Paranoia. Total paranoia.

DAVID: Sometimes it comes through the mail.

KATE: Oh.

DAVID: Sometimes it comes through the radio receiver.

KATE: Oh, oh.

JACK: Such concerns are neurotic, therefore finally trivial. Such concerns are the product of a man that spends too much time watching the private pictures it paints on the back side of the brain. Therefore trivial.

KATE: You think "trivial" . . . and a word lights up on a distant mountain . . . *(KATE gets off the table, walks down center, and looks to the back of the auditorium to see the imagined mountain. DAVID joins her and looks too. KATE turns away and finds herself at the back of the room, standing against the pillar, still staring up at the mountain)* the result of three years' effort on the part of workers who are paid for a certain activity . . . *(She is now explaining to the doll)* each day of which they have no sense of connectedness and purpose other than feeding themselves and their families, except a beautiful thought finally manifests itself as a word on the mountaintop . . . *(She and the doll are both looking out to the audience, tears in KATE's eyes)* which glows at night in a bright color you do not think is beautiful because the color is garish like a neon color and on nights when the air is full of mist the mist catches and reflects the garish color and dilutes and softens it and you agree that is beautiful, but is it? *(She moves about the room looking high on the walls for written words that may or may not be there)* The word is an interesting word. *(She places the doll at the top of the throne and sits beneath it)* No. It is no more interesting than another word. We've forgotten what the word is because we are remembering the beautiful dispersed color of the reflectiveness which makes us imagine a more intense color which is now the hidden but imagined source of great intensity but we thank no one, except an imaginary person inside us.

(DAVID brings a painted panel of glowing fruit to a position in front of KATE's face, and she holds it there, hiding behind it, as DAVID starts moving his arms as if he were swimming across the stage. The music rises. JACK moves the wooden rack with the attached light bulbs to a position in front of KATE, and the light bulbs become very bright. From behind the bright light she calls out in a tone of voice part sarcastic, part genuine)

Great! Just great!
Great! Just great!

DAVID: *(Having arrived at a position in the playpen, on top of the head)* But somebody turned on the radio and our ears distorted our eyes—

JACK: Don't turn on the radio! *(He holds a piece of fruit which he has extracted from the panel KATE holds in front of her face)* In the center of the fruit was a pit. And that pit was the radio receiver of the particular fruit. *(He holds the pit over his head and poses, then turns to the audience and recites from Alfred North Whitehead. DAVID prays, trembling slightly, perched on top of the statue head)* "Classical scholar Gilbert Murray said something highly similar about Aristotle—especially when Aristotle came to drama," said Alfred North Whitehead. "He was talking about the ecstatic element in the *Bacchae* of Euripides, the Dionysian 'possession,' and said, 'After all, isn't the motto of a philistine in fact: "Mayden Ahjhan" '?"

DAVID: "Mayden Ahjhan"? Nothing in excess.

JACK: "That is it," said Whitehead, "to get really into a subject takes more energy than is implied by the phrase 'nothing in excess' and a man has to ignore many things in order to proceed with one thing. A certain element of excess seems to be a necessary element in all greatness." And, as an example of the opposite, he quoted a remark about someone "who knew forty-one languages and had nothing to say in any of them."

(JACK breaks his position and leaps onto a table. He lies on his back, legs up in the air, cycling upside down at a great rate as lively prancing music surges. Then the music stops and JACK freezes. Silence. During this, DAVID has brought an easel with a painting on it from the side of the room. He sets it in place so we see that the painting is of a boat in full sail on the high seas, surrounded by swirls of energy)

DAVID: *(After a pause, during which we compare the image of JACK, upside down with his legs up, with the image of the painted ship)* Are you staring at the fruit? Or listening to the radio?

JACK: What's wrong?

DAVID: Can you see things and hear things at the same time?

JACK: *(Sitting up)* What's wrong?

DAVID: Seeing them . . . or hearing them.

KATE: *(Coming out from behind the rack)* I know the unfortunate answer to that question.

JACK: What's wrong?

KATE: *(Using her finger to trace one of the energy swirls in the painting)* I know the answer unfortunately determined

by the particular psychophysiological-metaphysical orientation of our Western civilization.

DAVID: *(Holding a giant rock over his head)* No more graven
images!

JACK: *(Staring at the ripe fruit he holds in his hand)* No more
graven images.

*(The lively prancing music builds again during this tableau,
then abruptly stops as three tones sound. DAVID slowly touches
his rock to the carpet)*

DAVID: I saw all my enemies arrayed. *(slowly lifting the
rock waist high)* Some with swords of iron, flashing iron
in the sun-drenched air, liquid lead roofs torn off houses
of celebration and infamy. *(He slowly walks forward, with
his rock)* The pageant—life on earth. I saw the hesitation
to enter higher realms, realms of sharp passions so
extreme . . . *(He goes away)* so extreme.

KATE: I heard people talking about me.
I heard the sound of my own voice in a mirror.
I heard the glacial cracking of the ice of my emotions.

*(DAVID has placed his rock on the statue head in the playpen
and strokes it gently. KATE begins running her fingers around
the perimeter of her face)*

When I surveyed the landscape,
Spread out beneath my feet,
For as far as the eye could see,
I heard seeing, talking, tasting, touching, feeling.
I heard thunder.
I heard marching.
I heard hundreds of radios.
I heard radios marching.
I heard sounds marching.
I heard air marching.

Kate Manheim, Jack Coulter, and David Patrick Kelly in **The Cure. (Photo by Pamela Duffy)**

I heard water.
Fire.

(She turns and points to DAVID, *who runs away from her)*

Ice, ice, ice, ICE!

JACK: *(Goose-stepping to center as he talks; faint jazzy music;* DAVID *also begins goose-step dancing and* KATE *does a kind of shimmy around the pillar)* Somebody made overtures to my wife. Somebody tried to part my hair with a knife. Somebody went on a rampage in Buffalo. Several people I know crossed the street when I greeted them with a big "hello."

(They form a circle and shimmy in place, watching each other)

Somebody wiped his hands on my personal towel.

(They change positions)

Somebody went to town on my forehead without asking me.

(They rub their stomachs, pat their heads, and turn in place to the music)

Somebody got permission to do the famous dance of the three-legged stool.

(KATE leaves the circle and brings DAVID a canoe paddle, and he does a very controlled delicate shimmy using the paddle. JACK points at him, rhythmically)

Somebody cried out you fool, you fool.

(Three tones sound)

DAVID: *(Using his paddle to paddle in place)* Somebody stole my wallet. I had a hundred and ten dollars in my wallet.

(KATE and JACK applaud)

Somebody stole my shoe. I had a quarter hidden in my shoe.

(KATE whistles)

Somebody stole my tie. I had a valuable diamond pin in my tie.

(JACK holds a plumb line over one of the heads still out on the carpet as DAVID paddles himself slowly backward, upstage)

Somebody stole my handkerchief. I had a piece of real gold wrapped in my handkerchief.

(He stops paddling)

Somebody stole my underwear. I had two fifty-dollar bills pinned to my underwear.

JACK: *(Poised with his plumb line, as DAVID slowly raises the paddle over his own head)* A certain type of person fulfilled all my expectations. Not to say I was fulfilled. A certain person of the type who manages in a certain way to wear a certain type of hat. A certain person, demonic or not demonic. A certain residual armor. So much EFFORT is lost. So much armor is practically, in practical terms DE-manipulated.

(KATE has put on a little plaid hat with a red pompom and has acquired a little silver stick with which she points to a boat in a painting)

KATE: There's nobody here yet but you can take off your shoes and socks and relax. There's nobody here yet but you can drink as much as you like. *(She comes forward to the audience; JACK and DAVID turn to face each other)* There's nobody here yet but you can gorge yourself on fresh fruits and take pits from those fruits and place those pits in a circle enclosing your physical body.

(With much extra and unnecessary activity, she traipses around the room to collect a fruit tray and some napkins from the high shelf above the blackboard table—making use of a totally unnecessary stepladder. An English music hall ditty plays faintly. JACK and DAVID break character and watch her at work. Eventually, she brings them each a fresh fruit and a napkin, then stands next to DAVID. The music fades)

DAVID: *(Holding up his fruit)* Follow this carefully . . .
KATE: *(Leaning in to him)* I heard what you said.
DAVID: Therefore, look . . .
KATE: *(Smiling)* Don't look, listen . . .
DAVID: *(Peering into the bowl she holds)* A bowl of conceptual, therapeutic fruit.

(KATE runs to put down the bowl of fruit, and returns center with a shallow bowl full of dried pits)

KATE: A bowl of radios. Thought radios? I mean . . . THERAPEUTIC . . . radios? *(She picks up a pit)* They cure me?

DAVID: Therefore, a collection of dried pits.

KATE: They cure me?

JACK: Plant them in dried earth.

(DAVID and JACK are leaning back against a table, supporting their bodies with their feet far forward onto the carpet)

KATE: Do radios grow radios? No, they grow plants.

DAVID: In the ear?

JACK: They grow plants which grow fruits which hide.

(Surprisingly fast and lively bagpipe music rises as DAVID and JACK start vibrating in place. KATE runs into the little booth. JACK and DAVID make their legs start dancing, then they are whirling and beating on the table. The wheels and pendulums are going full pace)

KATE: *(Shouting from her booth)* HERE IT COMES, THE 29TH STREET TROLLEY, AND THERE ARE A LOTTA DWARFS INSIDE SHAKING THEIR THUMBS AND SPITTING THROUGH THEIR RAT TEETH!

JACK: *(Making his legs move fast, supporting himself on the table)* The cure is in the pain!

KATE: HERE IT COMES, THE "A" BUS, FILLED WITH LADIES WHO PUT THEIR POCKET-BOOKS INSIDE THEIR POCKETBOOKS AND SKIP BIG LUNCH.

JACK: The cure is in the pain!

KATE: HERE IT COMES, THE UNIVERSAL LOCAL

STUFFED WITH TUB THUMPERS WHO PIT
THEIR BRIGHT IDEAS VERSUS THE OLD MAN
OF THE MOUNTAIN IN HIS COAT OF MANY,
MANY, MANY, MANY . . . !

*(The music has become more like an Irish jig. DAVID and
JACK bounce to center stage. KATE stretches a thick rope tied
to one wall across the stage, and they proceed to jig underneath
it, bending backward to get past. Then they jig out of the
room. KATE is left alone, holding the end of the rope as the
music fades out. She speaks softly)*

Radios. But what ARE those plants, really? And what
are those fruits?

(She lets down the rope and goes to examine a remaining fruit)

When you bite, do you engage the ear, more than the
eye?
When you bite, does it hurt?
Does it hurt a fruit? And does the hurt fruit cry out?

(She holds the fruit against her face)

There is no cure?
The cure is the cry of pain?
The cry of pain is the radio?
The pain of the radio in the ear is the cure?
The pain of the cure *is* the cure?

*(The jiglike music returns. DAVID and JACK trudge in with
their arms folded, looking at the floor. They both wear little
skullcaps. They trundle about to the music, clearing the stage
enough so that they can carry the pillar with the flowers to
center stage. KATE tries to make them pay attention to her, but
since they ignore her she runs off. They finish on either side*

of the pillar, peering at each other like two conspirators. The music suddenly stops)

DAVID: Believe me. Everybody I know seeks vengeance. Plus. I am NOT your uncle.

JACK: I never believed you were my uncle.

DAVID: *(Offers his hand)* Will you take my hand?

JACK: Can you travel in relative dark?

DAVID: *(Backing away a bit)* But there is no reason for me to travel. I am surrounded by all the fruits of the earth.

JACK: Look, he's moving.

DAVID: Am I moving?

JACK: He's moving forward.

DAVID: I'm not aware of that movement. *(He points off to the side)* Oh, Paul, knock on that door with your fist.

JACK: With my iron fist?

DAVID: Now, everyone knows his name.

(The jig returns. Holding up a fist, JACK jigs to the side and behind some black curtains. The music cuts. JACK thrusts out his hand from between the curtains, a red rose in his fist)

JACK: Here is a rose, which comes from the depths of this house which grew, in darkness.

DAVID: That's unusual isn't it? Roses need the sun, but not this rose.

JACK: *(Emerging, crosses to DAVID)* Ah, a rose . . . that eats darkness.

DAVID: *(Backing away)* That means, it's still inside the rose.

JACK: *(Smelling the rose)* Yes.

DAVID: Look, the rose maiden.

(The jig returns and KATE runs in with a bouquet of roses and a hatchet. She lays the flowers down and fans at them with

her hatchet as the two men hold their heads and cry out once in pain—and the music stops)

JACK: *(Quietly)* That must hurt.

KATE: *(Looking about, perplexed)* What?

JACK: Those roses must HURT.

KATE: What?

DAVID: *(Taking a hand that KATE has extended without her realizing it)* Initially, Paul, it must feel like lying on a bed of soft flesh.

(He kisses her hand. She pulls away, sees him, and gives him her flowers)

KATE: *(As she speaks, she goes and lies down on one of the tables)* Or, you mean, it feels like lying on soft flesh which is lying on a bed that both you and the soft flesh are lying on.

DAVID: That's not what I mean at all. *(He puts her roses back by her side)*

KATE: *(Sensuously)* What do you mean?

DAVID: What do YOU mean?

KATE: *(Sitting up suddenly)* What do YOU mean?

DAVID: *(Holds his head)* Wait a minute. *(He dashes to the other table, leaps up on it, and stares at a picture propped up on the shelf above the table)*

JACK: What do you mean?

KATE: What do YOU mean?

DAVID: Can you flood me with hundreds and hundreds and hundreds of vivid images?

JACK: Look, Paul, the rose maiden. *(DAVID turns to see KATE, who has just picked up the bouquet again)*

DAVID: Does she know that I am dangerous?

JACK: Oh, but she's entertaining the perhaps erroneous notion that she's the one who's really dangerous.

DAVID: *(Seizing a sword that lies on the shelf)* Delusions upon delusions, perhaps.

JACK: NO! I think the truth of the matter is that I am dangerous and she is dangerous and she is dangerous as well.

(All pose, frozen in place)

DAVID: She certainly moves fast.

JACK: Oh no.

DAVID: Oh yes.

JACK: Oh no.

DAVID: One moment she's in the street, flashing past doors, houses, trees, hills.

JACK: The next moment she's who she is.

DAVID and JACK: *(Whispering)* The rose maiden! The rose maiden!

KATE: *(Producing a piece of paper from behind the table)* Here's the list of people who are REALLY your dangerous enemies, Paul.

JACK: It might be dangerous to read that list.

KATE: Put on your glasses.

JACK: No—

DAVID: Look Paul . . . *(He jumps down from his table, runs to grab the list from KATE, and sticks it on the tip of his sword)* the point of that sword could scratch your very eyeballs.

JACK: You think I don't know that?

DAVID: Then why this irrational refusal to put on your eyeglasses?

(DAVID advances slowly and JACK retreats)

KATE: Seeing is believing, seeing is believing.

JACK: I think that's the biggest problem of all, that commitment to the "seeing is believing" syndrome. Let's get outta that bag.

DAVID: You mean, let's pretend we're all blind men?

(DAVID lifts the blade under his own throat)

KATE: Beautiful childhood person, do you know my real name?

DAVID: *(To the ceiling)* The thunder gave birth to twelve shining automobiles. Those fast and burning cars, distributed to twelve princes of the earth, and I have received one.

(The lively, prancing music fades in softly)

JACK: Watch how I drive.

(Three tones are heard. All scream once with delight and run to three corners of the room where they suddenly pull out large steering wheels which are attached to ropes from the ceiling. They all lean back into the center of the room, pulling on the steering wheels as if driving ecstatically toward the sky)

KATE: *(She begins speaking softly; after two sentences JACK starts to speak the same lines from the beginning, overlapping KATE; two more sentences, and DAVID starts the same speech, also from the beginning; they are speaking the speech as if it were a fugue; the prancing music rises and becomes loud, and they all shout happily over the music)* In the manipulation of my car I am a total career. In the manipulation of my car I make a medium out of a traffic flow, for other automobiles are not so perceptually varied. Their routes are my routes but different rhetorical patterns, preempting my own ecstatic, what-d'ya call 'ems. Do I speak gibberish?

(As KATE *reaches the end of the speech, all break away and run to chairs as three loud tones cut off the music. Silence. All sit quietly.* KATE *is holding a plastic globe)*

KATE: I could have been one of the most famous amateur horseback riders of the 1980s—is this the 1980s?

DAVID: I could have pleased people in ways that are not trivial, since pleasure itself though often irrelevant . . .

JACK: I could have taken wealth and added the idea of perspective.

KATE: I could have shifted certain centers of gravity.

DAVID: I could have left an important void.

JACK: Twisted.

KATE: Touched.

DAVID: Turned.

JACK: Perceived.

KATE: Prepare.

DAVID: Possibly.

JACK: Certainly.

KATE: Absolutely.

(All slowly rise. KATE *hesitates, then lightly tosses the globe to the rear of the stage. They watch it roll for a moment, then come center, hold hands, and bow to the audience)*

The End

◆

FILM IS
EVIL:
RADIO IS
GOOD

◆

FILM IS EVIL:
RADIO IS GOOD

♦

Film *is* evil. As the Bible says: Thou shalt not worship graven images. Of course, one cannot deny film and other visual aspects of experience, but our culture has become tremendously overbalanced toward the visual. The assault of images is so great, the bombardment so continuous, we're unable to weave them successfully into the warp and woof of daily experience. It troubles me. However, at the same time, many people have said that I'm essentially a visual artist, and I've always found that visual elements come more easily to me than other aspects of my art. I fight the lure of that ease, but it's very hard. Often I've developed the visual aspect of the performance to a point where it becomes the major emotional element affecting the audience. In fact, for a while I was interested in giving up the theater and making films instead. I even completed a feature, *Strong Medicine*, in 1979. Visuality is evil, and yet I'm a great indulger in visuality. It's a paradox, but I'm immersed in that evil.

The greatest visual art, though it shocks the self with

moments of insight and recognition, does not reach those
deep, profound levels of the self where sensory reality has
no real foothold. There are people who would take the
philosophical position that the truth of being is to be found
on surfaces and their extensions, but I disagree. I believe
the truth is hidden. It is encoded in material in a way that
obsures it from both our perceptual mechanisms and our
formal mental categories. But visual ways of translating
the world give you the illusion that the truth is scannable,
controllable, and categorizable.

Evil, of course, is a strong word, and I was using it for
polemical purposes. I don't think film is evil. I don't think
anything is evil but for the use man makes of it. But in
Film Is Evil, I was evoking a sociological perspective on
the way film has become the great collective dream of the
masses. It's an analysis you find in the work of Ortega y
Gasset: we're ruled by a dream machine which replaces
problematic real experience with more easy-to-swallow
iconographic imagery. The play, however, also alluded to
a more esoteric issue which is suggested by the title. It's
an issue I first encountered in discussions over the differences between Greek culture, which accents the eye, and
Hebrew culture, which accents the ear: does an eye-
centered culture inhibit the projection of spiritual depths
into its social forms?

Of course, irony on irony, I produced a film for *Film Is Evil*
which I incorporated into the production. It concerned an
apparent spiritual teacher, played by me, who, in the end,
dematerializes. There I am, staring into the camera, and as it
films me in close-up I dissolve into thin air. The implication
is that as soon as a person's image is glamorized by film—
and anything seen on film is automatically glamorized—the
real forces trying to speak from within that particle of being
are swamped, wiped out by the hypnotic energy generated
in an audience seduced by the screen image.

But I was also saying, I can only reach you in the audience if you agree to go beyond appearances. My disappearance acted to invisibilize the surface (me) to bring forth the delicate music of the inside (my art). This is what Rilke was saying when he wrote his famous letter explaining how poetry invoked the "bees of the invisible." Right after I vanished on film, the character played by Kate Manheim runs to look into the camera, which is still filming, and shouts, "Don't turn off the camera, film me!" That was the other side of the coin, Kate objecting that she doesn't want to disappear, she didn't want to share Richard's trip. The point was that most people *don't* want the camera turned off. That's the problem; we all want to be glamorous, in films or otherwise. The film and the play were attacks on the position represented by Kate's character. But in fact, I put *myself* in as star of the movie, which was an acknowledgment of the contradictory urges we all have inside us.

I recently read *And There Was Light*, a book by Jacques Lusseyran, a Frenchman who, though blind, had played an important role in the Resistance during the Nazi occupation. He was leader of a Resistance unit, and whenever someone wanted to join the unit, Lusseyran would spend an hour alone with the applicant, chatting about innocent, unrelated subjects. Specifically because he was blind, his other sensibilities had developed to a degree that enabled him to tell whether or not the applicant could be trusted. During the war he passed on some forty people, and the only person he was unsure about turned out to be a traitor.

The story struck a deep chord in me. In a funny way, I'm convinced that what I should do is blind myself; it might actually make me a more insightful human being. I don't attribute this only to the influence of the Oedipus legend. In fact, one of my unproduced film scripts tells the story of an imaginary, blind motion picture director.

I'm not about to blind myself, of course; I'm not even about to eliminate all the visual aspects of the apartment I live in. But philosophically, I'm not convinced it wouldn't be better for me!

Perhaps the most important evil that *Film Is Evil* referred to was the fact that no matter how exotic the adventure portrayed on the screen, the fact that it's filmed convinces the spectator's unconscious that it takes place in the "real world." That's especially true now that most films are shot on location, or on meticulously realistic sets. But even if the sets were not realistic, the fact that set and actors are both filtered through the medium of film induces audiences to subliminally perceive matter and man bound together in the concreteness of a totally material, because filmable, world. Film works to subliminally persuade you that the material world perceived on-screen is the only possible world in which human consciousness can function. I think that's evil, because I don't believe our world has to be constituted as it is at this moment. There are other realms of possible experience, other modalities of consciousness, which you may not be able to immediately picture or articulate; yet if you maintain the dream that they're possible, something slowly changes in your consciousness, which then changes the way consciousness registers the environment, which means that, in fact, the environment itself changes. Film, by its very nature, works in our consciousness to limit our options.

Lying in bed at night, falling off to sleep, you drift through a twilight state, and there you have an intimation that other worlds are possible. You sense a world no less different from our present world than if you were to wake up and find yourself magically transported to ancient Egypt with the consciousness of an ancient Egyptian. I think it's quite justifiable to imagine that with the mind-set of an ancient Egyptian, looking at the pyramids and the Nile, you might feel the world was constructed from a different substance, with primary energies different from those our own culture highlights. Film makes it difficult to believe that there could be such a difference in mind-sets. Film says to us: all worlds are made up of the same matter, obey the same laws, are perceived in the same way. There is something about film that kills the imagination, especially the evolutionary aspect of the imagination.

This is true even when the subject of a film concerns the attempt to transcend the limits of the material world. For instance, Ken Russell's *Altered States* presents people in an isolation tank who experience expanded consciousness. This kind of film speaks about altered levels of perception, but it's overwhelmed by the palpable reality of the material world registered on the film stock. The theme of the film is unconsciously subverted by its medium of expression. Some people might say: Oh, but that's not a very good film; more sophisticated films by Bergman or Tarkovsky do allow the viewer's perception to play with the consistency of material reality. I just don't think that's true. Films like *Persona* or *The Mirror*, though they represent altered states of consciousness, are undercut by the nature of the film medium itself. Film inherently sends subliminal messages to the viewer's unconscious, habituating him to the unstated premise that the matter that forms both the body and the environment—as it appears captured by film—constitutes the only possible reality. Good films allow that man can still dream, but imply that the launching pad of the imagination must be within our real, material world. I maintain that from this launching pad you can only go to certain places; many alternative possibilities can't be reached from this launching pad. Other artistic media alter the spectator's perceptual mechanism by exploiting the artistic materials themselves to reconstitute the very qualities of the matter of which man dreams himself to be a part.

Silent film comes closer to evoking this more complete kind of transcendence because of its strangeness, its obvious distance from our own nonsilent existence. One could imagine that a hundred years from now the same might be true for films of today, passing time might gild them with the stangeness of "the past." But what concerns me here is the present impact of contemporary film, as opposed to the more positive psychic effects of radio, poetry, and, of course, the theater.

Painting is less "evil" than film, because the lie of painting isn't as convincing a representation of real life. It contains a great deal of ambiguity, it shows the painter's hand. Remember Picasso: art is a lie that tells the truth. One way in which painting's lie tells the truth is by suppressing certain aspects of the visual experience, such as movement, or real three-dimensionality. A painting leaves gaps that the viewer's vibrating consciousness must fill—more gaps than film does. This is especially true of contemporary painting, which has learned to exploit the medium's limitations. The exploitation of limitations is what brings art to life. A good painting is a reference to a system of perceiving reality, rather than a stand-in for reality itself. The same for poetry and poetic theater. But film runs the danger of handing its audience a dead substitute for reality, rather than a lively way of alluding to it.

Language is able to allude to reality in a much more suggestive fashion. When William Carlos Williams writes about a red wheelbarrow in his long poem "Spring and All," what makes it interesting is that it is everybody's wheelbarrow. He describes it with judicious selectivity, so that as you read his poem you project your own associa-

tional net over the wheelbarrow. The ambiguity of his
pared-down language invites all kinds of energies, whiffs
of the universes of your own private associations, to flesh
out his abstract written reference. Even if he were to add
specific details to his description, those details would only
modulate your own creative associations. In film, however, the material wheelbarrow you see on the screen
smothers the web of association a poem excites. In both
language and film, you may relate to the wheelbarrow as
a symbol, but in language the symbol is made your own
by your creative projection. In film, the symbol functions
more schematically, limited to the reference system within
the film itself.

Now the defenders of film might say: Just wait, we're
going to get more imaginative, we're going to use more
interesting editing techniques, narrative structures, mon-
tages of sound and image; we're going to create the kind
of suggestive art you deem so desirable. But I maintain
the mechanically reproduced image swamps all such
efforts—it's impossible not to be hypnotized by the film
image, though it may be interesting to try. Perhaps God
didn't imagine that man would ever invent motion pictures, and so left us sadly vulnerable to a form of art that
most closely apes a world we would do better to transcend
than to worship.

The subliminal message of film is: What is real can be
photographed, and if it can't be photographed, it isn't real.
But as we know, many things that can't be photographed
are real.

These purely conceptual issues, I should add, were never
considered during the writing and rehearsals of *Film Is Evil*.
I started with a text and a space, and I tried to make something that pleased me. This is important to say, because I
don't make art in order to theorize. As I work, I'm sus-

tained by the faith that what I've made for pure sensory delight, working out of an inner rhythmical compulsion, will inevitably reveal, on later examination, what it is I really think about things. And though I arrived at the play's title before it was completed, and I knew I somehow believed it, nothing in the play was calculated to reinforce that title. Everything that's there is intended to set forces and ideas at work; only when I see the finished product do I realize what it is I'm saying in a particular play.

Film Is Evil: Radio Is Good was first produced by the Ontological-Hysteric Theater and New York University Tisch School of the Arts, Department of Drama, at the Tisch School of the Arts' Mainstage 1 on April 29, 1987, with the following cast:

ESTELLE MERRIWEATHER	Kate Manheim
PAUL ANTONELLI	David Patrick Kelly
HELENA SOVIANAVITCH	Lola Pashalinski

and students from the Tisch School of the Arts, Department of Drama: Bobby Bowman, Cristina Bykowicz, Jeff Casper, Kirsten Cook, Adrienne Corcoran, Julie Dean, Barney O'Hanlon, Donna Jerousek, Tanya Kane-Parry, Robert Lanier, David Pittu, Anne Reingold.

The production was directed and designed by Richard Foreman; lights by Heather Carson; stage manager Susi Levi.

The film *Radio Rick in Heaven and Radio Richard in Hell* was directed by Richard Foreman; director of photography, Babette Mangolte; editor, Melody London; music, Daniel Moses Schreier; and the following cast:

> Kate Manheim
> Richard Foreman
> Cynthia Gillette
> Lillian Kiesler
> Kostas Alex
> Don Shewey
> Raymond Rosenthal
> Maryette Charlton

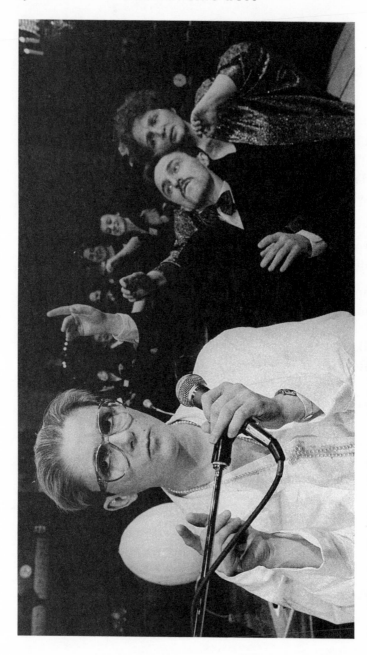

Kate Manheim, David Patrick Kelly, and Lola Pashalinski in Film Is Evil: Radio Is Good. *(Photo by Martha Swope)*

The stage represents a large, old-fashioned radio studio, but a very bizarre one. Thirties-style art deco paintings are on the walls, and many tables are scattered about the room, along with many stand microphones. To one side is a giant movie screen on wheels. Letters from a foreign language painted in gold are arranged over the walls in many places, suggesting messages bleeding through the walls. Overlooking all is an observation booth at the back of the stage—a large window covered with closed venetian blinds. There is a sound-effects table, used when appropriate, including a sound-effects door large enough for people to bang in and out of. There are the usual On-the-Air/Off-the-Air signs you see in broadcast studios, but the signs are unusual in that they have a third category that sometimes lights up, reading "Error!" The general effect is something of a cross between a radio studio and a secondhand furniture store.

At one of the tables a man in a suit and tie sits poring over books, an old-fashioned adding machine to his left. This is the accountant, Mr. PAUL ANTONELLI. The lights are very dim, the studio is not broadcasting at the moment. From offstage we hear a woman calling, "Anybody home?" A woman in a white lab coat, wearing a black hood, slowly crosses the room in the shadows, unnoticed by PAUL. She goes to a glass-faced cabinet, opens the door, and quietly takes off her hood and sets it in the cabinet. We see a severe though beautiful woman. This is the station manager, Miss ESTELLE MERRIWEATHER. She turns, watches PAUL, becomes irritated that he hasn't seen her, crosses

*to stand in his line of vision. When he still fails to look up
from his books, she snaps on the lights.*

ESTELLE: I have an announcement to make. You are not
my Prince Charming.

PAUL: *(Looks up, finally)* Oh? Who is your Prince Charming, Miss Merriweather?

ESTELLE: Do you ever listen to this radio station? Do
you ever hear me broadcasting late at night to whoever
might be out there in the darkness? I invented the words
to this song. Pay attention please.

*(She pushes a button, a bell rings, and three girls—
employees—trot briskly on and position themselves as a singing
group at the microphones. The One-the-Air signs flash and
the radio station comes to life)*

GIRLS: *(Singing to music, a bouncy version of "When Day Is
Done," with altered words)*
When day is done
and twilight's come
I dream of you

I think of all
the happiness
of love come true.

The huggin'
and lovin'
I cannot do alone.

The kissin'
I'm missin'
That don't come through
a microphone.

(The music continues and ESTELLE *talks key words to the music)*

ESTELLE: Day . . . Done
 Twilight . . . Come
 Think . . . Love
 All come true
 Hugging . . . Loving
 Like a dream
 Nothing . . . Real
 But up there on . . . the evil silver screen.
A GIRL: *(Leaning into the mike, interrupting the music)*Film
 is evil! Evil! Film is evil!
ESTELLE: *(To the audience, like a schoolteacher)* Pay atten-
 tion to this!

*(As the previous song has been proceeding, other young people
have entered and taken their places behind microphones, some
sitting at tables, others at standing mikes. They are the station's
announcers, all young people, the girls in white lab coats like
ESTELLE, the boys in white shirts and ties. Black armbands are
worn by all over their lab coats and white shirts. The evening's
programming has begun, and everyone speaks to invisible listeners somewhere out in the dark city. As they speak about
listeners who have obviously written in to the station, they
hold up pieces of paper, as if documenting the listener's reality
for all to see)*

A GIRL: When something goes through the ear, it goes
straight to the heart. But when it goes through the eye,
it's the brain that gets it, and that's the bad news, testifies
Mrs. Mable Williams of Ashmont, Oregon.

*(A grand and elegant lady of ample proportions has appeared,
dressed in a gaudy evening dress. This is the owner of the
radio station—HELENA SOVIANAVITCH.She claps her hands
together impatiently)*

HELENA: Well? There's more to say, certainly. Keep the ball rolling, please?

ANOTHER GIRL: Doctor Max Jacobson of Minneapolis explains that what you see, i.e., film, you tend to believe. Bad, bad, bad. But what goes in through the ear, you supplement with your own creative imagining. Thank you, Doctor Max Jacobson.

HELENA: *(Leaning into a mike)* I thank you also, Doctor.

ANOTHER GIRL: To answer a question posed by William Deegan of St. Louis, what hypnotizes the eye and so blinds you to possibilities of self-recognition is what we self-confidently proclaim as evil. Film is, therefore, essentially evil. Hope that helps, Mr. Deegan.

ANOTHER GIRL: Furthermore, somebody who thinks as we do, fifteen-year-old Annie Wupperman of Greensboro, North Carolina, points out that filmmakers often go out into the world pretending to themselves that the world they are capturing on film becomes, thereby, their own personal property. Certainly not true, says Annie.

A BOY: For a fifteen-year-old, that's not bad thinking.

A GIRL: We might point out to some of our more mature listeners that what Annie refers to could be thought of as an almost sexual exploitation of the material world by the invariably ego-obsessed maker of practically all contemporary films.

ANOTHER GIRL: Of course, literally hundreds of other listeners we haven't time to mention by name have written to us expressing very similar ideas. Namely, that film is evil, and radio—thank goodness—is a good medium, even if occasionally misused.

A BOY: *(From the rear, raising his arms as the music rises)*— Radio. The spiritual potential of all that radiates like the sun. Like the penetrating God-consciousness, said the ancient Hebrews, penetrates invisibly to the heart.

ANOTHER BOY: *(Whispering into a mike)*—Brain damage. Permanent brain damage.

(The music fades and the Off-the-Air light blinks as the lights dim and the studio clears out, except for a few young people, who slowly circle upon PAUL. *Each holds a book with a silver cover, encrusted with jewels.* PAUL *looks up at them, unsure of what is happening. Throughout the play, whenever the young people speak they lean into the nearest microphone. This is sometimes the case with* ESTELLE, PAUL, *and* HELENA, *but not in the scenes the three of them have among themselves, when the young people are out of the studio)*

A GIRL: *(To* PAUL*)* Are you an old-fashioned kind of guy? I bet what you're into is old-fashioned literature.

PAUL: Can I ask . . . what about my silver books?

ANOTHER GIRL: You read them? No, you listen to them.

PAUL: What about my silver books?

A BOY: Permanent brain damage.

PAUL: What about my silver reading and writing?

A BOY: You can ask. But then it won't: Happen, he said.

PAUL: Happen, he said?

ESTELLE: *(She appears in the window of the observation booth overlooking the studio, talking into a mike)*—Do you want me to make it happen?

(She lowers a small devil-doll from the window)

PAUL: Are you the professional temptation? The professional temptation entered the back of my head.

A BOY: The professional temptation . . .

ESTELLE: You have to be a professional to know whether or not you're dealing with a temptation. Me, for instance. I look in the mirror—? I know, right away. I tempt, therefore I am. *(She lowers the venetian blinds with a bang, then peeks through the slats)* Peek-a-boo! I'm in charge of this place. Which means I have to fix things that are wrong. That's how I tempt myself—with my own good deeds.

(She can be seen in the booth as she suddenly grabs a large tool of some sort and immediately goes to work, making a tremendous noise. Sparks fly in the booth. As she continues, music rises, bells ring, and all hell breaks loose in the studio. Someone is on roller skates, and HELENA appears, covered in a black veil, crying out prayers, collapsing on the floor)

A BOY: *(Intoning over the music)* Blessed mother, who makes all my dreams come true, in my imagination I see a picture of my heart's desire, blessed mother, blessed mother!

(Meanwhile, two other boys carry a large, raw side of beef across the stage. The beef seems to glow with a religious light, as in a Rembrandt painting. Then suddenly the emotional hurricane passes, the music fades, and ESTELLE is quiet in her window)

ESTELLE: I suddenly realized that nobody was paying attention to me, even though I was raising hell in my concentration chamber. There has to be a reason for this. For instance, if you are in a soundproofed studio—am I in such a room?

PAUL: *(To himself, trying to figure out what's been happening around him)* And if you are staying in the same specific kind of room . . . Heaven WAS anticipated by these people. The strangers WERE devoted to making it happen.

ESTELLE: Oh, but a special way of seizing the moment. The specific radio moment.

PAUL: *(Looking up at ESTELLE)* Yes, I agree, it's what they should have done.

A BOY: A special way of getting your first big break.

A GIRL: But when something works . . . nothing works.

PAUL: Tell me about some of your additional solutions.

HELENA: Everything that happened to them . . . stopped happening. It was an early moment.

PAUL: An early moment?

HELENA: *(She speaks to little orchestral chugs as a kind of rap song begins. All the lines are obviously about PAUL, who reacts to each definition)* Somebody's face was shining. Somebody's teeth were big, bright, and the kind that cut corners.

(PAUL tries to move away from HELENA, and slips)

ESTELLE: Look at him round that corner.

HELENA: Somebody's pockets were inside out, which put a lot of you-know-what into the cash flow.

ESTELLE: Thank goodness for the cash flow. It isn't spiritual, but it sure as hell is empirical.

HELENA: Oh, she's so sweet.

ESTELLE: Did you say feet?

HELENA: Not at all, dear. They were ways of turning politeness into a career.

(The rap ends. PAUL is scooting away from some of the girls who have been trying to give him a kiss, much to his embarrassment)

ESTELLE: Wow! Look at somebody's career take off.

A BOY: Hello?

ESTELLE: It could be me.

PAUL: It could be me.

A BOY: What is needed now?

(As PAUL has moved about the room all the young people have formed a kneeling line, and now PAUL kneels too. HELENA

holds a mysterious tray at the end of a long stick over PAUL'S
head. Soft organ music plays and the atmosphere has become
churchlike)

HELENA: What do you think is needed now, Paul?

PAUL: I don't know. *(He tries to rise and hits his head on
the tray)*

HELENA: Premature, Paul? *(She finds a white egg on the
tray, holds it up, and exits)*

ESTELLE: Undo the doing, ladies and gentlemen. Find
out about real Prince Charmings, Ladies of Mystery,
and other sources of what comes up next to change your
life permanently.

PAUL: Which means?

A GIRL: Undo the doing, Paul. Setting men free.

A BOY: I know that . . . spiritually, I am not free.

PAUL: You know?

A BOY: I know.

*(HELENA has returned carrying a giant egg which she hugs to
her body)*

A GIRL: Undo the doing, Paul. Unshell the shells.

ESTELLE: *(pointing at* HELENA'S *shell from her window)*
Look! My shell. Crack open this shell, which seems to
be saying, "Hello up there, Estelle Merriweather," but
isn't really.

A BOY: End the domination of nature, Paul.

PAUL: *(Rising to get away from them as they again start pur-
suing him)* I'm walled up here in nature, huh? Huh, I
suppose?

A BOY: End the domination of nature, Paul.

ANOTHER BOY: How?

A GIRL: Unsplit the split, Paul. Heal the personal break.

A BOY: How?

A GIRL: Look at it this way, Paul—

HELENA: It was an early moment. Nature failed and must be relegated to its rightful place.

A BOY: HOW . . . !

ESTELLE: *(Calling down after HELENA, who has disappeared with the giant egg)* I think you're disappearing with somebody else's private property! *(Pause)* Helena? Come back with that shell or I'll be very upset, and I'll zoom, zoom to a big, bad conclusion! After all, nobody goes public —even radiowise—without a protective layer or two— which I perfected over many years. Perhaps because I'm a fractionally frustrated woman who works in a radio station that slips and slides over the dial as if it were a banana peel, I've come face-to-face with the facts of life in general—man has failed.

(By now, all are again kneeling in line, as if to receive blessings from ESTELLE in her window)

A GIRL: Is that what I think too? Is that why I'm so sad?

ESTELLE: Man has failed, and must be elevated to ritual. The one way open.

A BOY: You said it for all of us, Miss Merriweather.

PAUL: Ritual. How is that to be done?

HELENA: *(Again holds a tray over his head)* Look, Paul, what is owned will decay. The end of all in-itselfness.

A BOY: In-itselfness?

ESTELLE: Real radio airtime.

HELENA: Say it.

A GIRL: In-itselfness.

HELENA: The end of all in-itselfness.

ESTELLE: Somebody is about to reveal a big secret.

A GIRL: Real radio airtime?

ESTELLE: *(As music begins to rise)* Somebody is about to dissolve himself in glee and flap metaphorical wings in

the face of recent personal disaster. Somebody is about
to dance on the head of a pin—ha—that's not possible.
Just you watch.
Just you watch.

*(All dance wildly now, singing nonsense syllables to a Latin
thirties beat—then a break in the middle of the music as all
call out numbers in unison. Then the music cuts back in and
HELENA shouts over it, "I love to see young people having
FUN!" After some more steps, another break in the music
and ESTELLE calls out softly)*

ESTELLE: We're on the air, Paul.
PAUL: On the air?
ESTELLE: *(Waving a finger and smiling)* Wrong!

*(A buzzer sounds and the music picks up where it left off.
After a few more turns, the group does a few big body-lurchings
to the music which brings them to the ground, knocked out—
as the music stops and ESTELLE shouts)*

ESTELLE: We're on the air, Paul!
PAUL: *(Staggering up from the floor)* On the air?
ESTELLE: WRONGGGG! *(She lets her venetian blinds
down with a bang and is gone)*
HELENA: We breed many winners, Paul.
A GIRL: *(As all the rest rise)* Just you watch.
A BOY: Here, we breed many winners, Paul—then, we
breed even more losers.
A GIRL: *(Quietly, as the group is wandering off)* Oh, my
God . . . oh, my God.
A BOY: Oh, my God.
A GIRL: I can't believe I'm . . .
A BOY: Lost.
A GIRL: Lost.

PAUL: *(As HELENA again pursues him with her tray)* You get away from me. You get away from me with your outrageous demands.

ESTELLE: *(Opening her blinds)* Certain objects were important, even though in other cultures they would have been called little more than trinkets.

PAUL: *(Looking up at the tray)* Ah, this brain-scanning device, for instance?

ESTELLE: You are crazy and I have to figure out how I can utilize that potential in my own internal scheme of things. By the way *(Music for another rap song starts)* you think I roar?

PAUL: You haven't heard me roar.
What you heard is just wiping my feet on your personal doormat, which makes my beginner's throat rattle a bit because my Network experience is nil.

HELENA: You think I do radio rolls
down the hill of my emotions?

ESTELLE: Only when a certain not-so-tough guy
bangs open the door of my private life
which means, "Hello.
I'm here to project on the silver screen everything that goes on behind your eyeballs."

A GIRL: *(Interjecting, and the rap stops)* Film is evil—film is evil.

ESTELLE: You better start seeing some of my visions, Mr. Antonelli.

A GIRL: Film is evil. That's like little pictures you see in your head.

ESTELLE: Got the price of a ticket to MY kind of movie theater?

ANOTHER GIRL: *(Coming up close to rub her body against PAUL)* The motion picture is evil in motion. The pictorial, the image, is evil. The image is evil. The image is evil if one worships the image, Paul. If one is seduced by the image.

PAUL: Okay. How can one not be seduced by the image?

(Loud, machinelike music begins, the lights dim, and the big projection screen slowly swings into the center of the room. A door opens and a human-sized duck comes into the room and flaps about for a bit, chased by three boys wearing funny hats and holding popcorn bags from a Saturday night at the movies)

A GIRL: Are you dumb? Sound! That's the answer— sound! Passes through the door and exits. *(The duck is quacking its way through the sound door)* That's the way out, Paul. Sound comes in one door and goes out the other door, and that's okay.

PAUL: Does that duck work here too?

(Violin music rises, played in the rhythm of a duck waddle)

A BOY: What does a duck know?
A duck knows film is evil.
His quack quack quack
is a radio dream.

ESTELLE: *(Peeking through her blinds, she sings)*
A duck knows film is evil.
His quack quack knows that.
A duck knows film is evil
and that's his radio dream.
   Oh—that's what it means!

A duck knows film is evil
His quack quack knows that.
A duck knows film is evil
and that's his radio dream.
   Oh—that's what it means!

(The three boys ready for the Saturday night movies have shifted their attention from the duck to a cute GIRL USHER in red jacket and hat)

A BOY: *(Poking at the girl and laughing)* Is this a live one?

THREE BOYS: *(Singing, loud and raucous)*
We're goin' to the movies,
We're gonna meet some girls.
Haha haha ha ha ha
Haha haha Ha!

A BOY: Hey sweetie, what's this film going to be like?

OTHER TWO BOYS: *(Singing)* Haha hahah, ha ha ha.

GIRL: I don't know.

A BOY: You don't know? How come you don't know? Surely you must have seen it?

GIRL: I don't know, sir.

SECOND BOY: Gee, Wally, struck out again?

A BOY: *(To the GIRL)* Come on—

(On the screen, which now dominates the stage, we can see that a film is beginning as the title is projected: "RADIO RICK IN HEAVEN AND RADIO RICHARD IN HELL")

ESTELLE: *(Peeking through her blinds)* Guess who's really in this film?

A BOY: *(to GIRL USHER)* Geez, you must have seen it. Tell us what really happens in this film.

GIRL: I told you. I don't know.

A BOY: *(getting irritated and chasing her)* Hey, duck face!

GIRL: I just work here, sir.

SECOND BOY: Ducky bunny duckalloo!

GIRL: Please, sir—

A BOY: Hey little duckbill platypussy—

SECOND BOY: My little duck ass—

THIRD BOY: C'mon, we're really hot for this movie!

THREE BOYS: Quack, quack, quack!

GIRL: *(Arriving at a mike, ignoring the boys, she explains to the audience)* You see, film is the hypnosis of the population in general, making us all believe the concrete physical world, which is that which can be filmed, is therefore the real world.

THREE BOYS: Yeah.

GIRL: No matter what adventures occur on-screen, no matter how imaginative, they are seen to occur against a background of reality, and that reality seems not changeable. There seems no escape from that filmed reality, which becomes the lie of reality itself. Believe that lie? Believe that lie?

(The lights are completely off onstage now, and the film Radio Rick in Heaven and Radio Richard in Hell *begins. The film features* KATE MANHEIM, *who seems much less severe and more seductive and glamorous than she does in her role as Miss* ESTELLE MERRIWEATHER *in the stage play. Her leading man is, in fact, the author of the play—*RICHARD FOREMAN. *As the film begins,* RICHARD *is in a white, tiled room, holding an earphone to his ear, as if he were broadcasting over the airwaves, and he recites to the camera)*

RICHARD: Radio Rick is on the air.
Radio Richard just don't care.
Radio Richard counts to ten.
While Radio Rick begins again.

Rick palavers soft and sweet.
While Radio Richard warms his feet.
Radio Rick transmits a smile.
While Radio Richard waits awhile.

Radio Rick is on the air.
Radio Richard doesn't care.
Radio Rick has perfect pitch.
So Radio Richard pulls the switch.

(The scene shifts to KATE *lying back on a deep, soft couch. She stares into space and thinks to herself)*

KATE: I really couldn't figure it out. I started to reach for the Bible because . . . I needed some spiritual refreshment in my life. But as my hand touched the holy book, I felt another hand on my shoulder. And I turned to find . . . I was looking at myself. *(A closeup of* RICHARD*)* "Are you my double?" I said. And he answered, "No, I'm a friend, that's all." "But you look exactly like me!" So, I went to the mirror, and lo and behold it wasn't me at all.

RICHARD: Here's why: Film is evil. *(Slowly lifting his head)* Power . . . power . . . power. . . .

KATE: Are you really into power? *(Looking directly at camera she starts to panic, trying to brush away the camera that zooms slowly in on her)* Get away from me. Get away from me!

(Cut to RICHARD*)*

RICHARD: *(As* KATE'S *screams fade)* Radio Rick is on the air.
Radio Richard just don't care.
Radio Richard counts to ten.
While Radio Rick begins again.

Rick palavers soft and sweet.
While Richard waits and
warms his feet.

Radio Rick transmits a smile.
But Radio Richard waits awhile.

Radio Rick is on the air.
Radio Richard doesn't care.
Radio Rick has perfect pitch.
So Radio Richard pulls the switch.

(KATE *is seen walking across the floor in a large empty room with broadcasting equipment on tables*)

. . . Testing one, two, three, four.

KATE: *(Looking into the camera)* Finally?

RICHARD: *(Voice only)* You're on the air.

KATE: Finally.

RICHARD: You're on the air. You're really . . . on the air.

KATE: *(As the camera travels in on* KATE, *the image slowly dissolves to a group of people listening to her words as they gather by their old-fashioned home radio)* I feel myself radiating to the whole world. *(The scene changes to a dining room;* KATE *sits with two older ladies,* LILLIAN *and* MARYETTE, *and* RICHARD. *A tray of sandwiches sits before them on the table)* Reading the text of my heart, I say to myself: "Oh, dear. I am exiled from real consciousness of seeing the sandwich as the sandwich."

LILLIAN: *(Leaning across the table to* KATE, *with a smile)* Listen to my letters. In specific, mental colors: N-E-E-D.

KATE: Need. You spelled "need," Grandma.

LILLIAN: Look what time it is. You have no need of time here, sweet thing.

KATE: I am excluded from real consciousness of what you're telling me. Maybe I had better get away from this motion picture camera that records my image, and that exiles me from my own consciousness. Did you know that film—to film somebody—steals the soul? *(We briefly see RICHARD, munching his sandwich as he stares into the camera)* It does. It steals the soul. It steals the soul. People in touch with their own inner life understand. They understand that. I am excluded from real consciousness of seeing myself, even when I think I'm looking at myself.

(Cut back to RICHARD, lifting his hand to his forehead)

RICHARD: I am excluded from real consciousness of seeing my hand, even when I place it against my forehead where all the mental activity is taking place.

(The scene dissolves and we see a closeup of KATE, standing against a striped wall that rocks dizzily from side to side)

KATE: I am excluded from real consciousness of getting my bearings when I do my imagination exercises, because that's just a ploy I use when I find myself in a place that's real, even if it doesn't seem real. *(The scene changes to KATE entering on a stage, staring down at the audience over the footlights)* Oh dear. I am excluded from real consciousness of seeing and experiencing the place I am entering. I am excluded from real consciousness of experiencing the other people here with me.

(She is presented with flowers, the audience applauds, and as music rises she takes a bow. Then the scene immediately cuts to a closeup of RICHARD. As the camera pulls back a bit, we see he is dressed in a robe in front of a decorative screen. He speaks directly into the camera as faint organ music is heard)

RICHARD: Do you see what I see? I am surrounded by artifice, as we all are. I am waiting for somebody else to explain my thoughts. Interestingly enough, I guarantee to stop speaking at the precise moment the camera begins to film my image.

DIRECTOR: *(To RICHARD)* Will you stand up, please? Forgive me, I feel shy about giving orders to someone like you.

RICHARD: The camera isn't rolling at the moment? I ask because I've promised to stop speaking.

DIRECTOR: We'll tell you as soon as we start filming.

RICHARD: How do you want me to position myself?

DIRECTOR: I apologize for making everything so artificial.

RICHARD: Ahhh. But that's a great opportunity. *(As he is staring into the camera, applause starts and he holds up his hands in front of his face, turning away with a show of false modesty)* No, please, not yet. *(Dissolve to an extreme close-up of RICHARD; there is a pause, then he speaks quietly to whoever is watching)* Embrace me.

KATE: *(Voice only)* You're speaking.

RICHARD: No.

KATE: You swore you wouldn't.

RICHARD: No. There were conditions for my not speaking. But you've forgotten what they were. You forget almost everything.

KATE: You are right to admonish me.

RICHARD: No. I admonish nobody. You've misunderstood me completely. I'm complimenting you rather than criticizing you. And if I were to continue speaking, I hope the conditions of my speaking and not speaking . . . *(Someone reverently brings him a bouquet)* would bloom and fade, like these flowers.

(Cut to men behind the camera)

CAMERAMAN: *(Turning from his camera to the film DIRECTOR)* He's not following the script. Should we stop filming?

DIRECTOR: No, no, continue.

RICHARD: *(Again in tight closeup)* I'm not really a man of flowers, nor the contrary. Can you imagine me in a business suit? A man of affairs? Efficient, cruel, blinded by ambition? You see, beloved ones, whatever words I speak, whatever dialogue I write for myself and memorize—no matter. Other people will explain it, while I . . . vanish. The camera is rolling which means . . . I'm no supposed to be speaking. But I did speak, because whatever I say is therefore irrelevant—get it? Do I indeed have beautiful eyes? Correct. A kind of collaboration.

(The camera pulls out as RICHARD slowly gets down on the floor, kneels, and bows low toward the camera)

CAMERAMAN: The film is running out.

RICHARD: *(forehead touching the floor)* It won't . . . run out.

(Suddenly, he vanishes right before our eyes)

CAMERAMAN: Holy shit! Did you see that? *(There is a stunned silence, then, nervously)* We're out of film.

DIRECTOR: *(Turning to look straight at the audience)* If I had the chance to shoot that scene over—I'd have one correction. It should have happened while he was look-ing straight into the lens. *(Cut back to show the empty floor where he disappeared, then the scene changes and KATE and a friend, CYNTHIA, are sitting by an open window)*

KATE: It was amazing to see.

CYNTHIA: But you weren't there.

KATE: But I saw it . . . on film!

(The moment of RICHARD'S vanishing is repeated. This time, after a moment's shock, there are screams and the noise of

things falling over as the camera pans about, out of control.
Voices are heard over the panning shot)

CAMERAMAN: Should I stop filming?!
DIRECTOR: Pan to the wall! Pan to the wall!
CAMERAMAN: What are we getting?
DIRECTOR: I don't know yet.

(KATE walks into the shot and the film DIRECTOR screams,
"CUT!")

KATE: Don't stop filming, goddamn it.
DIRECTOR: Get out of the shot!
KATE: No. You keep filming. No matter what!
DIRECTOR: I already stopped the camera.
KATE: *(Staring straight into the camera, at the audience, as*
apparently the camera hasn't stopped after all) Film me, goddamn it. You film me! You keep filming me, no matter
what happens. *(As she goes on, the image dissolves into a*
closeup of her speaking defiantly in front of the striped wall
that rocks back and forth dizzily, as manic ragtime piano music
that repeats a single phrase again and again rises to match her
anger) No more missed opportunities, okay? No more
being left out of things. No more forget yourself because
everybody else forgets. No more of that shit! No more
forget me anything! Big, little, or what you say doesn't
count! No more of that shit! Hell on wheels! You heard
right the first time: HELL ON WHEELS! No more of
that shit! Hell on wheels! Hell on wheels!

(Now she is seen running in place in front of the rocking
wall—then it is RICHARD, running in the same spot, pumping
his fists up and down as he runs. Then the image dissolves
back to KATE, and as the music takes over, the stage lights
come up slowly, and all the young people are seen imitating
that manic running-in-place, onstage, as the screen image of

KATE'S running fades, the film ends, and the screen is rolled away to the side of the room. The onstage running continues as the music fades, and one of the girls breaks away and comes to a microphone. Over at a side table, PAUL is back working on the accounting books)

A GIRL: Film is death, because it is a shadow, and a mock version—of the truth of light. The perversion of light. The very perversion of light.

HELENA: Radio is good because its metaphysical principle is like the radiations that sustain all life in the universe itself. *(The runners stop and begin to move offstage)* So in our mortal souls it is a reassertion of the active process of the universe, so as a nonvisual IMAGE in our souls of our eyes it is FRUITFUL, because radio is to RA-DIATE, and we know that even when we don't KNOW, the idea that we don't KNOW is a good and fruitful idea. Attend films, Paul. Attend a lot of films. Go on, destroy yourself. *(She exits. PAUL is left working alone onstage, as a mysterious bearded figure with a long beard—a God figure, seven feet tall—is seen at the rear in the shadows)*

PAUL: *(To himself)* Do you mean, burn up the ego in the self? Okay, but what does that mean? I'm saying words, but I don't know what I'm talking about. Burn up the ego in the self—*(Three boys return to taunt PAUL)*

A BOY: Some of us guys from the radio station decided it would be a good idea to make last weekend a movie marathon.

GOD: *(Waving from the shadows)* Hello there, my chosen people!

ANOTHER BOY: Some of us guys from the radio station decided what enters the brain through the EYE, comes out like mental shit!

A THIRD BOY: Some of us guys from the radio station decided to initiate somebody good with numbers.

A BOY: We was all normal guys—regular, run-of-the-mill guys.

ANOTHER BOY: Believe it, really believe it.

PAUL: *(Agitated)* Okay. You're talkin' to me, but you don't know who you're talkin' to when you're talkin' to me. The guy who keeps the books? Okay, I keep the books, but you're talkin' to a guy who likes to look down the twenty-five-foot telescope of his one, two, three dreams in a row that don't come in Technicolor. You're talkin' to a guy who glues his ear to the radio and hears good, evil—I wanna get PAID for what I listen to on company time!

HELENA: *(Returning angrily)* Do you know who REALLY pays the bills around here? What famous movie star do you think I resemble? *(She strikes a pose. No response from PAUL)* Time's up!

PAUL: *(Frowning, turning inward)* What famous movie star do you think I resemble? *(A fast exit of all but PAUL)* Hey! Where did everybody go?

GOD: *(Waving from the rear)* Hello there!

PAUL: *(Whirls back to shout at GOD)* Look—I don't want any spiritual guidance, thank you! So just give me back my personal eyeglasses.

A GIRL: *(Appearing)* Suddenly you don't see so good?

PAUL: Film is evil? Not without my glasses. *(He grabs one of the papers he's been working on)* I'd like you to examine this document. It has a lot of figures.

A GIRL: Use your EYES.

PAUL: Oh, I've been there—I've been there! It's when I wake up after leaving the radio on too long and the station I was tuned into drifted into my third eyeball!

ANOTHER GIRL: *(She carries a mechanical device on a tray* *that looks like a cross between a radio receiver and a jungle hut, with columns made of rolling pins)* This primitive version—

PAUL: —was a total electrical field at one point? Was it one, two, three cylinders I could touch mentally without having a heart attack? *(Girls grab individual rolling pins and chase* PAUL *around the table once)* Don't hypnotize me!

A GIRL: SELF-hypnosis, maybe?

PAUL: Please!

GIRLS: *(Rocking back and forth with upraised rolling pins, as soft rock-a-bye music is heard)* We wouldn't LIKE to be hypnotized, Paul.

PAUL: *(Across the room from the girls)* What makes you think I can do hypnotizing? Self-hypnosis maybe, but it needs you, so I don't. Does that mean I won't? It means—you did.

ANOTHER GIRL: *(With a rolling pin in her mouth)* How come?

PAUL: I'm in a trance, I think.

A GIRL: *(A rolling pin in her mouth)* How come?

PAUL: I just feel I am.

A GIRL: It must be your hyperactive imagination.

PAUL: Okay. Let's say it's true. I did hypnotize you and you and you—

A GIRL: That means we all have access to a hyperactive imagination.

PAUL: Me too?

A GIRL: It's moving.

PAUL: What makes it move? It has no arms, it has no legs—*(Girls run off)* Don't run away until I can find out how to explain everything!

*(*PAUL *runs after them and disappears. The music peaks and goes out.* ESTELLE, *out of her booth at last, enters down on the*

main floor. Her head is covered in the same black hood she wore at the beginning of the play. She slowly crosses the deserted room, goes to the glass cabinet, and takes off her hood as the music fades. She puts the hood away and replaces it with a tall Tibetan-style monk's cap. She also takes out a silver-covered book, and with the hat on her head and the book in her hand, she crosses to the table)

ESTELLE: *(Quietly, after a long pause)* After an evening at the movies . . . I came back alone to the radio studio. I laid down my pocketbook, and gloves. Then . . . I went to a secret cabinet . . . and took out the forbidden silver book of my spiritual potential. I began reading, word by word, when a voice inside my head told me to look up, and when I raised my head from the book, there was someone on the other side of the room. Far away from the microphones. *(The GOD figure is again seen in the shadows, rear)* There was someone. There was someone on the red wallpaper. My flesh fell to the ground! I was stripped by lightning! Oh! That imperishable moment: Truth! The body of God is on the wall of my poor studio. Why? He is in a landscape, one I drew years ago. *(Soft music can be heard again as ESTELLE collects a small painting which she places on the edge of the table, a landscape, but no image of GOD is to be seen in it)* What beauty. What gentleness and elegance in him! Look at his shoulders and the way he holds himself. He's wearing a dress of yellow silk with blue ornaments. He turns around and I see his calm, radiant face. Then six women carry a corpse into the room. A woman with snakes around her arms and in her hair is near me.

(HELENA enters in the shadows rear, and the GOD figure has disappeared)

HELENA: *(Very gently)* Estelle, dear: You've seen God. And the demon is gone. But he will come back.

ESTELLE: The demon?

HELENA: Intelligence!

ESTELLE: *(Lowering her eyes)* You don't know the good you do me, Helen.

HELENA: Estelle, we love you. Look into your heart!

ESTELLE: I understand. Everything.

HELENA: Can you see me, Estelle?

ESTELLE: Yes—

HELENA: Do you have any questions to ask me?

ESTELLE: No.

HELENA: Certainly you must have some questions to ask me. For instance, you may want to ask whether the image in whatever form is evil. Whether it does good or bad to the human soul.

ESTELLE: Here's an idea of my own invention: dehypnotize the brain.

(Enter PAUL)

PAUL: That's the subject I've started THINKING about—

HELENA: Shhhhh! *(Turns back to ESTELLE)* Go on Estelle.

ESTELLE: How do you dehypnotize the brain? Here's my method. Take the beautiful music you've been listening to—

PAUL: What music?

ESTELLE: And by the adjustment of consciousness, render it . . . NONbeautiful.

PAUL: Fool, fool, foool!

ESTELLE: Oh—you'd discover something interesting.

HELENA: Those experiments are secrets that are never to be spoken of, Estelle. Human beings who say such things in words must be punished.

ESTELLE: *(Pause)* How do you know such things?

HELENA: Don't speak. Don't ask.

(GOD appears again in the rear, lifting his hand toward them in a friendly greeting)

GOD: Hello there, everyone! I'm sure glad to make your acquaintance. The first thing I'd like you to do is wake up! Wake up, Paul, to your spiritual ambitions.

ESTELLE: That sounds like a great idea—I've been broadcasting that to the whole world on semiprivate megahertz, but who's listening?

HELENA: Somebody MUST have been listening, dear.

((She drifts offstage. GOD also disappears))

ESTELLE: I don't think anybody's been listening.

PAUL: *(Seated at a table)* I was listening *(pause)* I think . . .

ESTELLE: *(Sits across the table from PAUL)* Okay. Then tell me. What was the message?

PAUL: Let me think about this. *(pause)* Film is evil. Radio is—

ESTELLE: That wasn't the message.

PAUL: I heard it. Lots!

ESTELLE: It wasn't MY message.

PAUL: Who else?

ESTELLE: Radio Rick. That's what he's into.

PAUL: Who?

ESTELLE: Radio Rick.

PAUL: The big Boss?

ESTELLE: The brains—you know—

Radio Rick is on the air.

Radio Richard just don't care.

Radio Rick come loud and clear.

While Radio Richard flaps his ears.

PAUL: I'd like to talk to him direct.

ESTELLE: You can't.

PAUL: I'd like to meet him, to ask some questions—

ESTELLE: You can't meet him face-to-face.

PAUL: Why not?

ESTELLE: You'd burn up! *(She stalks out)*

PAUL: *(Alone, he looks at the telephone on the table; then he picks up the receiver)* Hello?

DEEP VOICE FROM ABOVE: Hello!

PAUL: *(Nervously)* Hello?

VOICE: Hello.

ESTELLE: *(Runs in, Tibetan hat in hand)* Oh my God, what are you doing! *(She grabs the phone)* Hello? I'm sorry, but somebody picked up the telephone—by mistake. They didn't have any permission to do that.

PAUL: *(Trying to get the phone back)* I'd like to know why, exactly why film is evil and radio is good?

VOICE: I'll be glad to explain that, Miss Merriweather.

ESTELLE: It wasn't ME asking that question, and I don't want to hear your interpretation.

VOICE: But I have some very good ideas on that subject.

(ESTELLE bangs the receiver back on the hook)

PAUL: Call him back, please!

ESTELLE: Nobody knows his number.

PAUL: You don't NEED his number, all you do is pick up the phone.

ESTELLE: You're getting too big for your britches, sir.

PAUL: I can tell I have you RATTLED, Miss Merriweather.

ESTELLE: I'm not rattled.

(All the lights suddenly go out)

PAUL: *(Shouting)* Hey, turn the lights back on! *(Pause)* PLEASE?! *(The lights go on)* They went on by themselves.

ESTELLE: Stupid! Lights don't go on and off when nobody makes them go on and off. *(Pause)* I liked it better when they were off.

PAUL: *(Suddenly grabs the phone and talks into the receiver)* Hello, Radio Richard?

ESTELLE: See? No answer.

PAUL: Richard? Richard?

ESTELLE: You're barking up the wrong tree. That telephone only works when the person on the other end wants it to work. *(HELENA sweeps back into the room)* Here's Helena Petrovna Sovianavitch, see if she doesn't agree.

PAUL: Whether she agrees or not—

HELENA: *(Smiling up into the lights)* Are the cameras loaded, gentlemen?

PAUL: *(Looking about)* What cameras?

ESTELLE: Film is evil—

VOICE: You said a mouthful, Estelle Merriweather!

PAUL: *(Points to phone)* Did you hear that?

VOICE: But I wonder if you understand fully the whys and wherefores informing those slogans you repeat with such facility.

HELENA: *(Nervously)* Hang up that telephone, somebody.

VOICE: *(Becoming more and more threatening)* Film is evil because there is a total prohibition on the glamorization through the image . . . of a fallen world . . . which indeed exists . . . but needn't exist . . . much longer. Now. Hang up the phone!

(The phone is quickly returned to the receiver)

HELENA: *(Shaken)* Let's all forget about what we just heard.

ESTELLE: How are you going to do THAT, Helen?

HELENA: Shut up Estelle! *(Trying to lighten the mood)* Paul, why don't you come over here and give me a big kiss.

ESTELLE: *(Shaking her head)* Film is evil—

PAUL: Madame Sovianavitch, I couldn't just kiss you right off the bat—

HELENA: *(With a tinge of desperation in her voice)* It might be FUN, couldn't we have a little FUN?

ESTELLE: Hey—I think my number one task is to get this radio station back on the air, FAST!

(She rings the studio bell, but nothing happens)

PAUL: What you suggest might be fun, but there'd be hell to pay.

HELENA: I can pay!

PAUL: Who's to say where it would end?

ESTELLE: *(Sliding close to* PAUL *as* HELENA *turns away contemptuously)* You're quite right to be careful, Paul. That Helen Sovianavitch is a dangerous character. Not only is she filthy rich, controlling the lives of all of us who work in this radio station, but she probably wants to entrap YOU in one way or another.

PAUL: Probably you do too, Estelle Merriweather.

ESTELLE: Of course, but I'm open and aboveboard about it. Someone like Helen—she's as phony as your local picture palace two-bit romantic-adventure story. Plus: she cheats and finagles all the time. In my case—I present my position openly. Me—Estelle Merriweather—basing my life, both radio and otherwise, on the good example of certain specific saints from the most exalted traditions of Western ecclesiastical authority. I dare say to your face—I'm interested in your INNER self, even though for my own not-so-hot purposes. Now—what percent of what I've told you do you think is true?

PAUL: Well, Estelle Merriweather, excuse me. But I think I see how things might end. Badly, for me.

ESTELLE: Of course. *(She takes a silver book from a cabinet while soft organ music plays, mysteriously)* You see this secret book that I've tried to look into a hundred times? It's a text I carefully avoid mentioning whenever the On-the-Air sign flashes.

PAUL: Is that why it's silver on the outside?

ESTELLE: *(Pause; she looks deep into his eyes)* No. It's silver on the inside.

PAUL: Fiery silver letters? *(ESTELLE opens the book, displaying a page full of the same foreign letters one can see on the walls of the studio)* Not silver, but something unusual.

ESTELLE: When I read this book—

HELENA: You never read it.

ESTELLE: Oh, I've pored over quite a few texts in my time. PLUS: I did a little self-discipline.

HELENA: I can imagine your version of self-discipline, Estelle.

ESTELLE: *(Hushed)* I "let go." That's the secret technique I discovered. I let go, disappear, and what I'm reading . . . replaces my head!

HELENA: Quite an improvement.

ESTELLE: *(Quietly)* That comment stinks, Helen.

HELENA: Quite right, my dear.

ESTELLE: I quit.

HELENA: You're fired.

PAUL: I'd like to borrow a book—

ESTELLE: I don't lend books. And she can't fire me, because she didn't HIRE me.

(The entire group of YOUNG PEOPLE races into the studio)

A BOY: *(Waving a piece of paper)* Miss Merriweather! Miss Merriweather! Here's an urgent telegram for you!

(Pause. ESTELLE is afraid to know what is in the telegram)

A GIRL: How come you turned pale?

A BOY: Her heart skipped a beat.

ESTELLE: Nothing of the sort. I don't believe in phony telegrams.

A BOY: *(Disappointed)* How did you know it was phony?

ESTELLE: Self-discipline. It makes me . . . what I AM, boys and girls! Try it someday!

A BOY: You say that, but you never gave us tips HOW.

ESTELLE: *(As she plunks her Tibetan hat back on her head, and the YOUNG PEOPLE take a nervous step back)* Okay. I'll start—

HELENA: Take that hat OFF, Estelle!

ESTELLE: Oh no!—Here's one of my most POTENT methods *(She has opened her book)* You read the words in this book, but you don't try to connect them. So, in effect, the book dissolves instead of you. But it's the same thing of course—

PAUL: Am I allowed to try this?

HELENA: No! This could end badly for all of you—

THE YOUNG PEOPLE: Aw please—Come on—Give us a chance *(And so on)*.

HELENA: *(Quieting them down)* I ADMIT . . . ! There are probable benefits. Wealth, power, maniacal attractiveness to the opposite sex—if you consider that a benefit. BUT! Balance that against the spiritual risks involved. Which I shall now explicate from the vast storehouse of my experience—

ESTELLE: I'm sorry, Helen, for ten years I haven't understood a word you've said to me. *(She sits with her back to everyone)*

HELENA: *(Continuing with quiet sarcasm)* I'm deeply moved. Nevertheless it's YOUR life that hangs in the balance, Estelle *(Turning to others, sweeping through them as piano music rises)*, Paul, Wanda, Mona, Maurice, even Matthew. Everybody, the whole world!

(One of the boys in the crowd has come on with a bicycle, another with a stack of books. As HELENA has been talking, they've encouraged PAUL to take the books and to climb on the bicycle, which they steady for him. He starts cycling forward into the center of the room, holding his books)

PAUL: Look, I got a whole sack of my own books I can take home to pore over, whenever I feel like—WOOPS!

(He falls off the bicycle, dropping books and crying out. Then everyone is silent, looking at him sprawled on the floor)

ESTELLE: *(Not turning to look)* You know what this makes me realize? Hearing things without seeing things, means nobody can tell if my motives are really antihuman; and that's good because how else can I help what's currently called . . . *(She rises, walks over, and points to the crowd)* "people." *(She rings the studio bell. Thirties Latin dance music cuts on as all THE YOUNG PEOPLE cheer and start to dance. There are breaks in the music, where the dancers freeze and ESTELLE inserts lines of the "Radio Rick" poem)* Radio Rick on the air. *(Dance—freeze)* On the air? I don't care!

(Dance, during which a full-sized SNOWMAN slowly shuffles onstage amid the dancers. After a last freeze in the music, they run to rearrange the furniture in the room to leave the center of the room clear and all THE YOUNG PEOPLE sit on the sides as observers as the SNOWMAN approaches center. A different, quavering kind of music is heard as ESTELLE moves down to a microphone and starts talking while the furniture is being reset)

ESTELLE: Hey, am I finally getting those VIBES I heard about from the old-timers who taught me the ropes?

HELENA: *(Confronting ESTELLE)* What old-timers?

PAUL: Am I getting what people who've reached a certain level of development still call HEEBIE-JEEBIES?

ESTELLE: Aren't you forgetting something, Helen? Somebody else is giving you PERMISSION to get just a taste of these hallucinations.

HELENA: Oh?

A GIRL: *(Approaching ESTELLE with a basin and cloth)* Are you washing your hands, Estelle?

ESTELLE: No.

A GIRL: I momentarily took my eyes off you.

ESTELLE: Why would I? *(She stalks away, as ANOTHER GIRL runs to the first girl to confide in her)*

ANOTHER GIRL: I think Estelle Merriweather, behind our backs, has been doing some TERRIBLE experiments.

ESTELLE: *(Turning back to them)* The body? Or the soul, dear? Maybe both. But step two, I cleaned up.

A THIRD GIRL: *(Referred to as MONINA FEINSTEIN)* It's almost frightening.

ESTELLE: What? *(She goes to the third girl and thrusts her hands out into her face, threateningly)* Would you clean these for me, Monina Feinstein!

(PAUL has seated himself to the side and rolled up his pants to study the scrape he received upon falling from the bicycle, and now someone with a basin and cloth is cleaning his wound. He screams in pain. MONINA FEINSTEIN wipes ESTELLE'S outstretched hands, shaking with the fear that if she does a bad job she'll be punished. Soft, mystical music is playing, and two of the GIRLS enter with a system of signs on poles strapped to their backs so that high above their heads are the legends

"Charity" over one GIRL, *and "Purity" over the other. In another corner of the studio someone is washing another's feet. When* ESTELLE's *hands are dry, she lifts them and speaks gently)*

Now my hands are clean.

THIRD GIRL: *(Whose eyes have been gently covered from behind by one of her friends)* It's almost frightening!

ESTELLE: *(Cool as a cucumber)* In what aspect?

THIRD GIRL: I can't see where I'm going!

ESTELLE: No place, fast. *(Shoves her hands forward again)* Are these clean? *(The friend removes her hands from* MONINA's *eyes. There is a moment's silence)*

THIRD GIRL: *(Quiet now)* Like snow.

ESTELLE: Cold, huh?

THIRD GIRL: I can't see.

ESTELLE: Why don't you perform an experiment? *(She goes behind her and covers her eyes forcefully, yanking her head back, and hissing)* I would if I could but I am not able!

ANOTHER GIRL: *(Running up to* ESTELLE) Evil! I can hear it right now!

ESTELLE: *(Shoving her aside)* Raising cain, Monina Feinstein? How do you define your particular capabilities?

(Two other girls link arms and together confront ESTELLE)

TWO GIRLS: Just watch! I can be in different psychological places at the same time.

(They split and cross the room in different directions)

ONE OF THE TWO: You try it, Estelle!

ESTELLE: *(Smiling with arrogant sweetness)* That would be very evil of me.

TWO GIRLS: That makes ME *(Noise of a loud "bang")*— a very important person around here!

HELENA: *(Coming to PAUL, soothingly)* What, if anything, makes you important, Paul Antonelli?

PAUL: *(He thinks, comes to a microphone)* Sometimes, I find myself trying to get out of a bad situation without knowing which direction leads out and which direction leads back in. *(He returns to his seat; then, feeling he hasn't said enough, returns to the mike)* Sometimes, I find myself driving on radio control down highway 7, without taking my mind outa the box of highways 1, 2, 3, 4, 5, and especially 6.

ESTELLE: *(Quiet now also)* I know that feeling.

PAUL: What?

ESTELLE: *(She comes slowly toward the microphone)* I know that feeling, Mr. Antonelli, and there IS something like that feeling . . . traveling fast down a wide, open highway. There's something like that feeling being on the road at nine A.M. in the morning sunlight, everything SPEEDING past, but not thinking really. Reaching toward a place or a city or a destination that doesn't really exist until you arrive. *(She dreams)* Detroit, Michigan . . . ! Cleveland, Ohio . . . ! Madison, Wisconsin . . . ! In other words, a place you've never been to. Because if you KNOW the city of your destination, then it exists, and the other things don't.

PAUL: *(Still at the mike)* What other things?

ESTELLE: The sunlight, Mr. Antonelli. The bright morning, the speed, the warm air: THEY exist . . . It's like . . . the radio, Mr. Antonelli.

PAUL: That analogy is too simple, Miss Merriweather.

ESTELLE: Think of the young people under my employ. Where are THEY speeding? Where are powerful drives leading THEM?

PAUL: Yes. Ah yes . . .

ESTELLE: *(Tears in her eyes, as soft string music is heard from far away)* Do they picture in their mind's eye, something like what I picture? Close your eyes, everybody, and count to ten. *(All close their eyes, and some begin to count, and others cry softly.* ESTELLE *strides to the sound-effects door, and slams it loudly, breaking the mood. All jump, startled, and look back at her. She smiles coolly)* Sometimes I lie. Sometimes I imitate somebody whose heart can be easily broken. *(She strides over to the* SNOWMAN. *All count. The light turns suddenly cold)* Uh oh. I think . . . all the microphones in this beautiful studio have turned to ice.

PAUL: Why is it so cold in here? *(All but* ESTELLE *are hugging themselves, trying to keep warm)*

HELENA: Somebody do something!

PAUL: I'm waiting for the Snowman to do something!

HELENA: I can't wait forever, he'll never—

A BOY: *(Jumping up and down and screaming excitedly)* Ohhh, look! At that moment, he MOVED!

A GIRL: *(As all scream in fear)* Christ, I can't believe he moved!

*(*ESTELLE *crosses again to the* SNOWMAN, *pulls out his carrot nose—which makes them all scream a second time. She takes a big bite out of the carrot)*

A GIRL: You're pushing too hard, Estelle Merriweather.

ESTELLE: Tough shit.

HELENA: In five minutes this radio station goes back on the air. You'd better wash out your mouth with soap, Estelle Merriweather.

ESTELLE: I just did . . . *(*ESTELLE *goes and kisses the* SNOWMAN*)*

HELENA: Snowman or no snowman—wash!

ESTELLE: I just did.

(The SNOWMAN has removed his head, revealing a human head underneath)

HELENA: Wash!
SNOWMAN: Geez, I already did!

(All run to admire the SNOWMAN, but HELENA shouts out to regain their attention)

HELENA: Wait a minute! A snowman talks—that's a radio first, I believe. *(They leave the SNOWMAN and gather around her)* But let me consider the reality of our potential audience for a moment.
A BOY: *(Admiringly)* Geez, she's doin' it.
HELENA: *(To soft violin music)* To obtain a bit more specific reality . . . I project—a film on this theme. We have to give this film . . . thematic coherence. To set the events, in relation to some system of intellectual or social coordinates. For instance . . . in today's world, some people experience a deficiency of genuine emotion— men and women of ice, correct? For such people, the snowman as archetype—!
ESTELLE: Symbolism, Helen. Everybody's half-baked ideas.
HELENA: Oh, I know what you mean—but it isn't that at all. It was something . . . inexplicable. A talking snowman!
A GIRL: Big deal.
HELENA: But it's a very big deal, my dear. A very, very—*(Getting flustered as they seem to be losing interest, she runs from one to the other as the music fades out)* Tell me you understand what I'm trying to express. Please, tell me. Estelle—certainly YOU understand?
ESTELLE: Are you talking about the past or the future?

I'll tell you what I understand. Up until this very minute, the doubt that controlled my life . . .

PAUL: *(Running down to interrupt her)* Hey lady—stop putting words in my mouth.

ESTELLE: I'm putting words into no one's mouth but my own.

THREE GIRLS: *(Arranged at a mike, sing in close harmony)* You're on the radioooo . . .

A GIRL: *(Announcing at another mike)* WWBW means . . .

PAUL: *(Pacing about, agitated)* Sure! I'm slipping from one highway to another like a semicatastrophe!

ESTELLE: Like an iced-up mental degenerate. Flip-flop, so what?

PAUL: Look lady . . .

THREE GIRLS: *(Sing again)* You're on . . . the radiooo . . . You're on the RA-DI-O!

PAUL: When my center of gravity shifts, I shift, get the picture?

ESTELLE: I get the picture.

PAUL: You don't get the picture.

ESTELLE: I get the picture.

PAUL: You think I got problems? You don't know my problems.

ESTELLE: You . . . are ice-cold, sir.

PAUL: Oh no.

HELENA: She has a point. It's your heart, sir.

PAUL: No. Touch my hand. *(He holds out a hand)* Touch it.

(PAUL takes a seat on a bench while ESTELLE turns to address the audience. Behind them, the young people hold up white panels that make it seem as if the radio station is surrounded by cliffs of ice)

ESTELLE: I put my hand out to touch the piece of ice he extended to me, and as my hand approached his hand,

I suddenly saw it fall into a second dimension of space, through a door that existed in my imagination. As it happened, the name written on the back of my hand that day was "heaven." *(The panels are thin cardboard, and they are slowly lifted into the air)* And lifting it to my forehead, it was as if I sped through several doors simultaneously. The door of the present and the door of the past. *(The panels are revolved in the air, and the music gets louder)* Was I forgetting or was I remembering? It didn't matter; it DOESN'T matter!

A GIRL: *(Opening a desk drawer and finding something)* What are these papers?

ESTELLE: *(Running over to grab them away)* Not to be taken seriously.

A GIRL: But it's your handwriting, Miss Merriweather.

ESTELLE: It's an IMITATION of my handwriting. *(Laughing a bit hysterically)* It's my life story, that's all—!

A GIRL: You promised your DOCTORS you wouldn't write till you were perfectly well.

ESTELLE: But I'm okay!

HELENA: *(Softly to PAUL, who is embracing one of the GIRLS)* Your heart is ice, sir. Ice.

ESTELLE: *(Striding over to them)* Mr. Antonelli—wash that accountant's ink off your fingers. Don't embrace one of my employees covered with FILTH!

PAUL: *(Looking up)* It's my life history, Miss Merriweather.

HELENA: You mean she realizes . . .

PAUL: *(Accusing ESTELLE)* Miss Fussbudget.

HELENA: . . . that aiming at something in a straight line . . .

PAUL: *(Rising, he pushes away the GIRL he's been caressing)* Miss Fix-it-all.

ESTELLE: *(Hysterically trying to shake off PAUL'S accusations)* It's the history of my life. No big deal.

HELENA: *(Encouraging PAUL)* The whole world is listening, Snowman!

PAUL: *(Running to a mike)* It's the same thing as getting yourself dirty. In other words, the roundness of the Snowman is no different from your big, round, radio waves, rolling slowly out of your central transmitters. Where are your central transmitters, Miss Merriweather?

ESTELLE: *(Trying to compose herself)* It's like this. As soon as he gets just a little bit dirty, he is no longer a snowman—like crystal-cold ice in which you keep the idea of something in suspended animation for a long, long time. When he gets dirty, he is just . . . another piece of shit.

PAUL: Oh no. *(Upset at this tarnishing of the SNOWMAN'S pure image)* Oh no!

ESTELLE: *(Going to a mike)* Question: If the human race dies out because neither the orthodox nor their opposite number are afraid of the multisensorial revolution, but just disgusted with the arrival of second sight . . .

PAUL: Huh?

ESTELLE: Am I to blame? No!

PAUL: No?

ESTELLE: *(Turning to PAUL insistently)* Oh no! No, no, no, no, oh no—

(The Nos continue to pour out of her, shaking her whole body, until HELENA interrupts. ESTELLE covers her mouth as if she would otherwise vomit uncontrollable Nos all over the stage)

HELENA: Suddenly she discovered a word flow that wouldn't stop.

(Holding her mouth, ESTELLE runs off)

HELENA: Estelle, come back here. Estelle! *(She runs off after ESTELLE)*

PAUL: Miss Merriweather! Madame Sovianavitch! Where are you going? Miss Merriweather!

(Bouncy, vulgar music rises, as the GIRLS *sing out the letters "R-A-D-I-O-eee" over and over, doing a silly marchlike dance, with the On-the-Air lights flashing and bells ringing. In the rear, some of the* BOYS *hold large cut-out cardboard heads, each six feet tall, with a cameraman-style eye-patch painted over one eye. The* BOYS *bob the heads up and down to the music, as lights flash above, marquee style. Then the music stops abruptly and all groan in disappointment)*

A BOY: *(Calling, at a microphone)* Miss Merriweather: On the air, Miss Merriweather.

(Bells ring, and ESTELLE *enters slowly. She is composed now, and goes to a microphone. She holds a clipboard from which she reads a list of questions)*

ESTELLE: Question: If a tribe of savage, lustful children enters the white children's how-to-be-pure party-festival combination . . . ? *(The young people recompose themselves)* Question: If London Bridge falls down . . . ? *(A loud bell rings and* PAUL *reenters with a small movie camera, filming* ESTELLE. *She backs away, up against a side wall)* Get that camera out of my face! Get away from me. Get away from me!

HELENA: *(Like a master of ceremonies)* Tragically, the camera does not reveal the natural good of things. It does not root them in their radiant source, but like a veritable eye of death, cuts them away from that source.

PAUL: No, not evil. Not evil. Nothing evil here! *(He runs out)*

HELENA: Repeat after me: Evil instruments of a false world.

ESTELLE: *(Into a mike)* Repeat after me: A fallen world that worships a multitude of graven images.

PAUL: *(He returns, shouldering a giant, oversized 35-mm movie camera)* Contrary to what you radio people believe, the giant 35-millimeter cameras of my imagination are not evil, *(Shouting)* Bathsheba Merriweather!

(A golden calf has been pulled forward and one of the GIRLS is posing on it, lustfully, as the lights shine on her. PAUL rushes to film the scene and an upset HELENA cries out in anguish)

HELENA: Not true, not true! False idols, graven images! Come to your senses. Where are we? *(Order is somehow being restored. The lights return to normal. Someone takes PAUL'S camera away)* We are in a healthy and virtuous place. This radio station returns human reality to the radiations which are its source. The radio is good, the medium of film is evil.

PAUL: Let me understand this once and for all. The radio is good.

A GIRL: *(Nodding)* Film is evil.

PAUL: *(Trying to understand)* Radio is good.

ANOTHER GIRL: For the hundredth time, Mr. Antonelli, film is evil.

PAUL: *(Nodding)* Radio is good.

(The others applaud, as if he'd answered a quiz correctly. The game is now accompanied by quiet, percolating music)

ESTELLE: *(Making a check on her clipboard sheet)* Fifty points.

PAUL: Radio is good.

ESTELLE: I said, fifty points.

A BOY: *(Coming to the mike to try his luck, in Spanish)* El cine es malo.

ESTELLE: Another one hundred points for certain sectors of the human race. *(More applause)*

ANOTHER BOY: *(At the mike, to try in Italian)* La radio è buona.

PAUL: Another one hundred points.

ESTELLE: For all white Anglo-Saxon people under the age of forty.

PAUL: You mean me? *(The YOUNG PEOPLE laugh)*

A BOY: *(At the mike to speak German)* Film ist übel—Film ist übel—Film ist übel!

HELENA: Another one hundred points for a smart-ass white boy.

ANOTHER BOY: *(Trying French but having problems remembering)* Le radio est . . . uh, uh, le . . . le cinéma est mal *(He is applauded)*.

ESTELLE: *(Unenthusiastically)* Okay, one hundred points.

ANOTHER BOY: *(In Hebrew)* Radio zeh tov.

ESTELLE: Another one hundred points for an apprentice Jewish asshole. *(Applause)*

THE SAME BOY: *(Frowning)* I'm not Jewish, Miss Merriweather.

ESTELLE: *(Shrugs)* You're not smart.

(Others laugh, and a bright-eyed innocent girl races to the mike)

THE GIRL: *(Proudly)* Miss Merriweather, Miss Merriweather, I'm Jewish!

A BOY: Don't worry, Petunia, you'll go far in the entertainment business.

A GIRL IN THE REAR: *(Mockingly)* Mrs. Louis B. Mayer. *(Sentimental violin music is added, and she goes through the list at accelerating speed)* Mrs. Harry B. Cohen, Mrs. Samuel Goldwyn, Mrs. Jack Warner, Mrs. Samuel Mischkin, Mrs. Todd Weinstein, Mrs. David Rabinowitz.

THE JEWISH GIRL: *(Pouting, overlapping)* That's not funny . . .

(At the same time, a girl sings in the rear operatically: "Film is evil, radio is good . . ." Then the music fades and the young people, left by themselves now, are slumped about the studio, dejected and melancholy. The light is different. No longer magical. After the party, as it were)

A BOY: Practically speaking, I got what I wanted. I got to be in a play—

ANOTHER BOY: But there was a film, too. None of US got to be in THAT.

THE FIRST BOY: *(Shrugging)* Even so. Even so *(Pause)*.

A GIRL: I got to be on the radio. Sort of.

A BOY: PRETENDING!

A GIRL: Not pretending.

(PAUL slowly enters, hugging to his chest the large side of beef that appeared at the beginning of the play)

PAUL: *(Quietly, as the light grows mysteriously and a high voice sings a single sustained note in the distance)* Look at this mighty guest.

A BOY: *(Continuing the previous conversation)* I mean, certain things were being pretended about, but not everything. Not by a long shot. *(Pause)*

PAUL: Hey. I think I know what I got here in my arms *(Pause)*. What's the answer? Radio Rick . . . ? Or Radio Richard . . . ? *(Pause)* Whatever it is . . . it's dead.

HELENA: *(Appearing quietly at the side)* Ah. Aren't we all?

ESTELLE: *(Also emerging from the shadows)* That is why . . . the medium of radio . . . is so superior to the medium of film, Mr. Antonelli. It's because film . . . gives the illusion of life, because it titillates so many human sense organs at the same time. But it's a lie when you do that, when you give that illusion. On the other hand, radio is like a voice from the grave. Really. That's one way to think about it.

PAUL: You have a sick point of view, Miss Merriweather.

ESTELLE: Do I indeed? I better check myself out in some mental mirror? *(Faint carousel music is heard in the distance)* Ah—I forgot: that's what I've been doing for the last hour or so. *(A bell rings, she exits, and the music gets louder)*

HELENA: *(Intoning over the music)* The radio station of the stars, is really—the radio station of the stars . . . !

(All the young people make a guttural noise and start dancing to the music in a grotesque, single file line, taking stiff steps like excited zombies, and making funny nasal noises as they dance around the studio. Then suddenly the music stops)

HELENA: *(Calling offstage)* Did you do that, Estelle?

ESTELLE: *(Reentering)* Yes.

HELENA: What did you do?

ESTELLE: I pulled the plug.

HELENA: Why?

ESTELLE: I want it . . . very quiet, Helen.

PAUL: I like feeling—a little MUSIC. A little excitement.

ESTELLE: You are not my Prince Charming, sir.

PAUL: *(Still holding the beef carcass)* This isn't mine, you know. I'm just . . . holding it.

ESTELLE: *(Sadly)* I don't mind dedicating myself to these . . . activities. But it has to be different. The way I want it. Quiet. Quiet. So that things can drift—out from this station . . . into space. But at the same time . . . things can come here and be here . . . . Quiet. *(Soft, dark chords of music)* Quiet. And then. We can hear what they are . . . really.

(The deep VOICE is heard throughout the studio. A bright light shines on the window, high above, where ESTELLE spent the first part of the play. Everyone onstage turns to look at the window, but the venetian blinds are closed and nothing is to be seen. So everyone just waits and listens)

VOICE: Radio Rick is on the air.
Radio Richard just don't care.
Radio Rick transmits a smile.
While Radio Richard
Sits . . . and waits
A while.

(The lights fade, and then the music fades)

The End

SYMPHONY

OF

RATS

Ron Vawter in **Symphony of Rats. (Photo by Paula Court)**

SYMPHONY
OF RATS

◆

Symphony of Rats is about the President of the United States as someone no different from the rest of us: a mixed-up, stupid, fallible person bounced back and forth by forces outside his control. The President is receiving messages telepathically, and he doesn't know whether to trust them or not, just as we all receive messages from our unconscious, or God, or the media, or our past experience, and often don't know whether to validate them by paying attention to them and acting upon them, or to dismiss them as irrational impulses we hope will pass.

In our culture, especially for white males in power, there's a compulsion to suppress any ambiguity that arises in our emotional or intellectual life. At one point in the play, the President is pressed into considering the realm of the imagination and he recoils defensively, unsure how to proceed. Suppose we had a President who allowed his imagination to function full time, would he be able to make the straight-ahead decisions he's expected to, given the structure of the world in which we live? Would I prefer it if the President of the United States opened himself to levels of ambiguous behavior and became a real wacko who let the country fall apart, as he devoted himself to expanding his consciousness? Of course, part of me thinks that's just what's needed. But would I like it if the social order deteriorated to the extent that people from New Jersey crossed the Hudson to take my beautiful SoHo loft? I probably wouldn't! So I'm of two minds on the subject, but these are more of the internal contradictions out of which I make my art. Actually, I even own stocks. How would I feel if the stock market crashed? One part of me believes that, after the initial trauma, it might lead to a social restructuring which could produce a more humane and less exploitative system than our own. But if the market did crash, I'd have big problems regarding my personal finances, which, of course, I'd hate. So I'm divided, sustaining within myself considerable ambiguity on the subject.

It's within the terms of such contradictions that I think of *Rats* as a political play—not only because it happens to be about the President. The real politics of America have to do with the conflict between people who can sustain ambiguity in their lives, and people who are terrified by ambiguity and fight to reduce every issue to clearly defined choices, either black or white, and so become conservative reactionaries. All my plays engage exactly this issue—how to sustain ambiguity in your conscious life without allowing it to plunge you into feelings of loss and confusion. And so I think all my plays are deeply political, though they're obviously not "political" if what interests you is the ideological positions to which people subscribe.

Virtually every political issue in America boils down to a question of whether or not individual personalities can sustain ambiguity. For instance, when American whites of

racist persuasion believe that black people are not civilized
and shouldn't be allowed to move into white neighbor-
hoods, what they really object to is exposure to a lifestyle
that disrupts their ability to sustain clear, categorical distinctions. They cling to mental boundaries that clarify their
hold on the differences between permitted and nonper-
mitted behavior. What they fear is nonclarity: you work
during work time, and you don't play loud music; you
keep the front lawn neat in a specific way, or it provokes
turbulent feelings that are upsetting; men and women
should relate to each other in a specific way that doesn't
excite repressed unease. If someone arrives from a different
culture who doesn't observe the social rules of your particular culture, confusion and ambiguity enter your psychic
life. You're forced to deal with noise, in the cybernetic
sense of the word: the static in a transmission that's not
part of the message. Noise is introduced into your life by
people who have different cultural habits, who don't observe the clear distinction between work periods and noisy
play periods, or who dress and serve food according to
different rules. Most political issues are reducible to the
individual psychological issue of how you manage ambiguity, or "noise," in your psychic life. Where do you put
up your fences? Where and how do you come to make
distinctions? And those are the very issues the various
framing techniques of my work address.

All of my plays are about my attempt to stage my particular rhythm of perception, which is to say, admittedly,
the plays are about *me*. Though I never acted a major role,
my voice on tape was present in the plays for years as I
commented on the action, and in *Symphony of Rats* I took
it one step farther. I plunged into video technology and
put my own face onstage. The President was bedeviled by
voices he thought came from outer space. Ron Vawter,

who played the President, is an actor forced to speak lines that came to him from outer space—that is, I sat at my typewriter and wrote lines he was forced to say. And so it was quite appropriate that the face on the outer-space figure the President is obsessed with, when it appears on-stage, turns out to be my own.

I designed two eleven-foot-tall robotic structures with arms and legs that could squat and stand. They were tubular metal forms, with television sets for heads, and those TVs both had my face broadcast on-screen. I decorated these giant puppet figures in a style suggesting primitive Mayan statues. There are certain less-than-respectable theories that suggest particular figures sculpted on Mayan relics are really depictions of space men who visited the Mayans in ancient times. My intention was to superimpose primitive, totemlike imagery—and space men are indeed twentieth-century totem figures—on the high-tech robots to suggest that perhaps the voices the President heard came from the primitiveness of his unconscious; or perhaps he was hearing from a primitive side of ourselves which we have projected into outer space. Or maybe they really were space giants from another planet. I tried to suggest all these possibilities at once. As a final touch, I decided to make these menacing space giants the unconscious source of forbidden sweets. So I had the actors approach one of them, push a button on its chest, and soft ice cream came squirting out to fill their extended ice cream cones, delivering the secret sweetness hiding inside everything we fear the most.

In *Symphony of Rats* I worked with the Wooster Group for a second time, though I didn't ask for performances nearly as frantic as those in *Miss Universal Happiness*. Every night of that play I thought Ron Vawter was going to kill himself, the way he threw himself full force against the walls of the set. But because the characters in *Rats* were the WASP leaders of our society, I wanted the actors to be sober and emotionally self-contained. I wanted to pull them toward more naturalistic, psychological performances than they were used to giving, either in my work or in the work they did with their own director, Liz LeCompte. And I think I was successful. We worked hard to get a more subdued, internalized performance style. They were quieter, thought more about what they were saying. I wanted them to *live* their lines more than they had in *Miss Universal Happiness*.

One directional ploy of mine I thought was particularly clever: there were standing microphones all over the stage for the actors to speak into, but all through rehearsal when they came to speak into the mikes, they seemed suddenly drained of life. Then I lowered the mikes a bit, so in order to speak into them the actors had to crouch slightly. This energized not only their bodies, but their whole emotional being: dealing with this slight awkwardness added just the right amount of tension to energize the actor's instrument.

I was especially happy about Ron's performance. At times I had felt frustrated during *Miss Universal Happiness* because I felt the performances lacked a certain inner reality—perhaps because so much effort had gone into building the overwhelming, circuslike atmosphere of the production. But for *Rats* I vowed to work for psychological intensity, especially in Ron's role. We worked together to develop ways that suggest his character was struggling with intellectual ideas in an effort to affect his own psyche. The idea was the performer was not a presenter of information, as in my early plays, but someone trying to do psychic work upon himself in front of an audience. This shift first happened in *The Cure*; I wanted the actors' performances to be a manifestation of this psychic working, just as my writing was a manifestation of the work I did on myself rather than a report on it. For instance, at the beginning of *Symphony of Rats*, Ron walks to a microphone and talks to the audience. He says, "What's out there in space? Jesus, you've been there. What's out there? Silence. Vast silence?" At first it seems he's asking the audience, but then it becomes clear he is really asking himself. He's wondering, How do I deal with this phenomenon, these voices that I hear in my head? In the past, I have done many plays in which questions like that would be addressed specifically to provoke the audience. "What's out there in space?" would have been a demand for the spectator to come up with an answer. But in *Symphony of Rats*, I wanted it to be clear that Ron was working it out for himself and did *not* want the audience to participate, even though he seemed to be addressing them directly. Rather, he was using the audience to amplify the intensity of his self-questioning.

The final production of *Rats* turned out quite differently from what I had imagined when it was first agreed the Wooster Group would provide the actors. Willem Dafoe, a member of the company, was going to be in it, then he was cast in Martin Scorsese's film *The Last Temptation of Christ* and had to withdraw. Were he available, the play would have taken a very different form. He, rather than Ron, would have played the President. I imagined him looking like James Dean at the end of *Giant*, made up as an old man with metal rim glasses, white hair, and a cane. He would have been a California-style President, as if at seventy Jerry Brown finally made it to the White House. Ron, in this scenario, would have been the President's secret Hindu guru. And the women, Kate Valk and Peyton Smith, would have been trying to decide to whom it would be better to pledge allegiance, to the guru or to the President?

All the dialogue would have been the same, though the lines would have been redistributed, and I don't think I would have set it in the White House. More likely it would have taken place in India, where the President would inexplicably keep visiting. So another production of the play could, one day, be done in that way.

Symphony of Rats was first produced by the Ontological-Hysteric Theater and the Wooster Group at the Performing Garage in New York City on January 6, 1988, with the following cast:

> Ron Vawter, as the President
> Kate Valk
> Peyton Smith
> Jeff Webster
> James Johnson, Ratcatcher
> David Finkelstein, Ratcatcher

The production was directed and designed by Richard Foreman; lighting by Paula Gordon; technical director, David Nelson; assistant to the director, James Johnson.

The play takes place in an area that is divided into two parts. One half seems to be a presidential sitting room, with a large fireplace and a felt-covered card table where presidential games are played. The mantel above the fireplace is wide enough for the actors to stand on, and a ladder leads up to it from the side. The other area is dominated by a presidential desk enclosed in a glass booth; a microphone sits on the desk, suggesting a secret broadcasting center. But the set is not realistic. Girders and other support systems dominate, plus there is much seemingly inappropriate decoration—gilded flowers festooned in corners, American flags, small paintings of flowers and telephones— as if it were a secret Pentagon operations center which had been decorated by an elderly, eccentric, and patriotic aunt of the President. Another noticeably bizarre element is the large, thick, brightly colored railings that subdivide the rooms. The walls are decorated with an assortment of wallpapers, with strange geometric objects painted over the wallpaper. This Pentagon control center has acquired distinct aspects of a child's playpen—which does not decrease its somberness and machine-like military qualities. The floor is painted in large geometric patterns. A presidential seal is visible on the floor, as well as on different sections of the wall. Many standing microphones are scattered about the set. More often than not, when the actors deliver their lines they speak into one of the microphones— all of which can be detached from their stands and may be carried about the stage. Usually, however, the actors do not detach the microphones, but come to the stands. These stands are unnaturally low, so that to speak into the microphone the actor is forced to bend his knees slightly and to angle his voice, as it were, into the mike.

JEFF, one of the presidential advisers, a tall man in a conservative business suit, is carefully laying out cards on the green felt tabletop as if he were going to read the cards to predict the future. He puffs on a pipe, contemplatively. KATE, a thin young woman in a floral print dress and a turban, enters and whispers to JEFF, then exits. The PRESIDENT slowly enters the room. Soft guitar music plays.

VOICE: *(From over a loudspeaker)* Ladies and gentlemen, the President of the United States.

(The PRESIDENT glances at the audience, then comes to the table and sits at one side. JEFF sits at the other. The chairs are built to be as tall as barstools, but they lean forward slightly. The two men carefully adjust their pants, pulling their trousers up an inch to eliminate the stretching of fabric over the knees. Then they lift their feet slightly and the chairs tilt foward a bit more. At this time PEYTON, a mature lady in a black lace dress, smoking a cigar and wearing a cap with devil's horns, appears from nowhere and begins racing quickly around the room, making absolutely no noise, in a crouched position like a devilish Groucho Marx. She is outside the two men's line of vision. They do not turn their heads as the PRESIDENT frowns slightly and speaks very quietly to JEFF)

PRESIDENT: Do you hear something?
JEFF: *(He speaks with an accent throughout the play)* No.
PRESIDENT: Funny.

(The PRESIDENT rises and begins to slowly look about the room. He doesn't see PEYTON even though she now crosses directly in front of him. The PRESIDENT goes slowly to a

microphone center stage. PEYTON *has arrived behind a wooden pillar. She leans out provocatively, puffing on her cigar)*

PEYTON: Hey—wanna go someplace special?

(She runs off, leaving the PRESIDENT *alone at the mike. He thinks for a while, then begins to speak into the microphone as if talking to himself, though he is addressing the audience)*

PRESIDENT: What's out there in space? *(Pause)* Jesus, you've been there. What's out there? Silence. Vast silence? *(Pause)* There are . . . complex webs of radiations all through space, aren't there? Yes? *(Pause)* Isn't that silence a kind of noise? Not for the human ear perhaps. *(Pause)* I guess I'm projecting my own thoughts. True, I haven't been there.

JEFF: *(Bending into a mike at his table)* True.

PRESIDENT: *(Pause)* So you say . . . vast silence.

JEFF: Yes.

PRESIDENT: *(Pause)* Vast silence.

JEFF: Yes.

PRESIDENT: Anything else? *(Pause)* No. That should be enough for me. You're trying to make a point.

JEFF: No. *(Pause)* I've made my point, Mr. President.

PRESIDENT: *(Pause)* Am I now in outer space? Why of course I am. I'm on Earth, but that's still . . . space. *(Pause. As he thinks this over,* PEYTON—*now without her devil's cap or cigar—reemerges as a sedate presidential adviser. Without the* PRESIDENT *noticing her, she and* JEFF *whisper behind his back)* Ladies and gentlemen, Earth . . . exists in outer space, doesn't it? Yes. So I'm in outer space. *(Pause)* I don't have to get in a rocket ship to be in outer space. No. I'm in outer space now. *(Pause)* What am I aware of? Vast silence?

JEFF: Is that what you're aware of, Mr. President?

PRESIDENT: *(Pause)* I don't know.

(PEYTON comes forward, smiling faintly, and gives a golf club to the PRESIDENT as several presidential assistants enter with clubs of their own. The assistants line up in the rear to practice their swings. The PRESIDENT takes his club, crosses to the glass booth, climbs on the presidential broadcast desk, and inside the glass booth tries to swing, banging into the sides of the booth and generally becoming tangled and disheveled)

PEYTON: Got a problem with your swing, Mr. President?

PRESIDENT: It don't mean a thing.

JEFF: *(Sucking calmly at his pipe)* Ah. A problem with a swing don't mean a thing. Not a thing. It don't mean a thing.

PEYTON: A problem with a swing is a big thing. *(She sings, very softly, addressing the audience)*
'Cause it don't mean a thing
If it ain't got that swing.
(Explains to the audience) Ladies and gentlemen. He in the emotional foreground got a problem with his swing. It's a big thing. A real big thing. All the others, they do okay. No problems, no beefs. A swing about which to sing.

PRESIDENT: *(Climbing down from the booth)* Golf my ass.

JEFF: It isn't the game of golf, Mr. President. It's a bigger game. The swing is the thing. But it isn't a game of golf, Mr. President. Not at all.

(The PRESIDENT is now at the rear with the other golfers. As he addresses his imaginary ball a golf pro uses a little stick to try and prod him into better form)

JEFF: *(Downstage, barking out commands)* Pull back here, Mr. President. Out here. Twist more here.

PRESIDENT: *(Irritated, pulling away from the pro)* Look—

JEFF: Look my ass, Mr. President. *(He makes a slightly obscene gesture using his fist)*

PRESIDENT: Ah, it's a wise man making a mental muscle.

JEFF: Are you into golf, Mr. President, or are you into a very significant hallucination?

PRESIDENT: I don't know what I'm into. *(He's bent over, leaning against a post)*

PEYTON: *(Standing behind the president, she somehow produces a golf ball from between his legs)* Hit the ball OUT OF the hole, Mr. President.

PRESIDENT: That's ass-backwards.

JEFF: Why not do the impossible, Mr. President?

PEYTON: Hey, wanna go someplace special?

JEFF and **PEYTON:** *(Singing softly)*
It don't mean a thing
if it ain't got that swing
doo wop doo wop
bop bop bop.

PRESIDENT: *(He's crossed to the booth and sits at his desk, addressing the nation over the radio)* You'll find this hard to believe. I've gotten messages from outer space. In my official capacity, these messages have come through to me. They reveal to me that the end of our world approaches. But I'm afraid to reveal this information . . . to my contemporaries. I feel I can't reveal it openly. It's a question of the mental well-being of millions of weak, fallible people for whom I feel responsible. But it's eating me up inside, knowing this, not being able to reveal this.

PEYTON: Perhaps what's required of you is a certain kind of spiritual effort, Mr. President.

PRESIDENT: Spiritual effort . . . ? I don't know specifically what you mean.

(He leaves his booth to rejoin them, accidentally running into a pillar and getting a good knock on the head)

PEYTON: *(Paying no attention to the* PRESIDENT'S *collision)* Unconsciously you know. Why fight it, Mr. President?

PRESIDENT: *(Holding his head)* Listen, this is eating me up inside. How can I pretend to myself it hasn't really happened?

PEYTON: Ah, that means you imagined it, and it happened.

PRESIDENT: I'm taking a vacation.

PEYTON: Beginning now?

PRESIDENT: *(Moves to a mike)* I have the option whenever I want the option. Here I go.

(KATE reenters and all line up behind the mikes to do a kind of recitation as the music, which until now has been repeated phrases of a romantic violin, becomes a lively piano bounce)

PEYTON: Mr. President! If you go out the front—

(She breaks off, in the hopes that the PRESIDENT *can complete her phrase, but all he seems able to do is stutter "Do-o-o—")*

KATE and **JEFF:** Door!

PEYTON: I'll surprise you with a big hello, hello
And you'll think I'm shouting from the upstairs window,
But really
It'll be in your OWN head.

PRESIDENT: *(Interjecting)* Did I leave the room?

PEYTON: If you sit in the invisible easy chair
I'll make REAL cookies and milk
So intense
Your head'll spin.

PRESIDENT: Did I lose my watch?

PEYTON: If you turn out all the lights,
I'll scream fire
And you'll suddenly be able
To see in the dark.

PRESIDENT: *(Taking out his wallet, perplexed)* Whose money is this?

PEYTON: If you open a drawer . . .

PRESIDENT: Did you say door?

PEYTON: Drawer.

PRESIDENT: Did I open a drawer?

PEYTON: Did you say DOOR?

PRESIDENT: Drawer.

PEYTON: DOOR?

(The recitation breaks down. KATE approaches the PRESIDENT and grabs his hand which he repeatedly pulls away)

PRESIDENT: No. Once upon a man. A time. Once upon a time, a man. He held out his hand to receive a gift. It was slapped into his hand. It was something to eat. *(KATE bites his hand and the PRESIDENT screams in pain)* It hurt. It hurt. It hurt. *(KATE holds up a small card with a picture of a tiger painted on it)* My mental Polaroid is broken. I snap a picture, but nothing happens.

KATE: *(Smiling softly, strangely)* Where do I come from, Mr. President?

PRESIDENT: Another planet? Why did I say that?

PEYTON: Guess why.

KATE: *(She carries a tray loaded with fruits and vegetables which she holds out toward the PRESIDENT. Very romantic violin music rises)* There is no food, Mr. President. This food is artificially created.

PRESIDENT: But you've just shown me a tray of—

KATE: This planet has, through the lack of foresight and

selfishness of its inhabitants, exhausted its natural resources, its ability to bear fruit and feed the population
of humans and animals. So this food you see has been
artificially created. *(The PRESIDENT takes an apple and eats
a bite, thoughtfully, as in the rear a magic cabinet rolls onstage.
He suddenly reacts as if the apple tasted terrible)* I will tell
you how food is created.

PRESIDENT: But that's self-evident. It has nothing to do
with my problems at the moment.

KATE: Only . . . women are able to create this food.
Placing themselves in certain, specially designed con-
tainers.

*(PEYTON is seen inside the cabinet, holding out her arms to
invite the whole world. The cabinet revolves, opening and
closing its doors, as KATE circles it once then returns to speak
to the PRESIDENT)*

PRESIDENT: *(As the cabinet revolves)* This is . . . very
interesting.

KATE: They are able to project thought-beams to a radio
absorption center in space.

PRESIDENT: In space. You mean it's possible?

KATE: Only women are able to do this. It is difficult for
them to explain what they are doing. But this is the way
food is created.

PRESIDENT: In the earth, the soil?

KATE: It grows in the earth, as before. Of course. But it
is now understood as an artificial, willed process which
depends upon the concentration of mind energy of millions of women all over the globe, in unison.

PRESIDENT: But how?

KATE: They project certain rays from within these resonating chambers . . .

PRESIDENT: *(Pointing to the cabinet)* Those?

KATE: . . . fructifying the earth through the multiple exchange of high energy brain waves.

PRESIDENT: This is . . . highly interesting.

PEYTON: *(Speaking into a microphone from inside the cabinet)* The method itself was discovered in simultaneous moments of mystical revelation occurring simultaneously to twenty-five women of different nationalities and ages, throughout the globe, years ago during the depth of the world food supply exhaustion and resulting famine. Remember?

PRESIDENT: Well, uh . . . yes, I . . .

PEYTON: All historically recorded but now, alas, a legend rather than reality.

PRESIDENT: It's true, we have plenty to eat, seemingly.

KATE: *(In a trance)* And women, thousands upon thousands all across the planet, do this thing. They make the earth fruitful, even though the exact mechanism of this thing is not known. It is done through faith, love . . . and the imagination!

(Mystical music rises)

PRESIDENT: The imagination, you say.

KATE: Yes, Mr. President.

PRESIDENT: I regret to say that's a realm into which the deeper I delve, the more problematic . . .

KATE: Really?

PRESIDENT: Yes, really.

KATE: You could be hiding from something, Mr. President.

(The music changes to a quiet Latin beat, and all come forward and do mild disco dance moves as they speak)

PEYTON: He made circles,
But some of them had faces inside.
Smiling?

PRESIDENT: . . . I suppose.

PEYTON: Don't guess, Mr. President.

PRESIDENT: He made cubes, and they multiplied
And screamed farina farina farina
Which meant, everything that exists
Gets hungry.

KATE: He made roads—
Going places
Was an acceptable way of spending time.

PRESIDENT: *(Demonstrating his running form)* Look at
these presidential fleet-feet!

KATE: He made a decision
Followed by another decision,
And by that method
Introduced mystery into life.

PEYTON: He stepped aboard the steamship named repetition,
And the ghost vessel spread invisible wings
Over primary sources in his role as—

PRESIDENT: *(Interrupting, assertively)*
He himself nevertheless
Never flew, nor became transparent,
Nor wove webs of his own muscle tissue
Over a long-suffering planet.

PEYTON: What happened?

KATE: Somebody dropped the book containing his first,
last, and middle name down the toilet. He made a big
fuss about that, but it didn't help one bit.

PEYTON: Are you ready for this, Mr. President? *(The
mood suddenly becomes frantic, the lights intense, and she sings
in operatic voice)* Acid brain . . .!

PRESIDENT: *(Moving away)* Whether I'm ready for such disgusting nonsense or not ready for such nonsense—

PEYTON: It burned away everything that could only be half seen, didn't it?

PRESIDENT: No! *(He jams a crown on his head)*

PEYTON: Who did it? You did it.

PRESIDENT: Wait a minute. That's not a personal gesture but an evolutionary biological given. Look, throw such a categorical brain acid against the face of the world— gets eaten to the bone. Blood, light, nothingness.

(PEYTON is on the PRESIDENT's desk, trapped in the glass booth, and suffering a kind of unimaginable acid attack. The music becomes more and more frenzied)

JEFF: *(Speaking from a mike in the rear)* Acid in the brain.

PRESIDENT: Grind it over the field of vision, into the web of intellectual constructs. What's left? Huh? A kind of fire that isn't readable. But one says, "I exist," and it could even be the fire talking.

JEFF: Acid in the brain, Mr. President. For all of that, thank acid in the brain.

(The music builds to a wild climax and the PRESIDENT is affected by it, skittering about the stage waving a white cane. The rolling cabinet returns and rolls into place beside the glass booth. The music is gone. Everything is calm)

PEYTON: *(Whispering)* You're arrived.

PRESIDENT: I don't know what that means, unless you're implying that a unique level of reality that wh . . . no no no no, that's impossible.

(KATE appears from behind the cabinet. She is covered with a number of cut-out cardboard rhomboids, painted plaid, a kind of armor. She holds out a little pillbox)

KATE: *(Speaking in a strange, Scotch accent)* I have a surprise for a very important person.

PRESIDENT: So I see.

KATE: I don't think so. *(She opens the pillbox)* It's a magic lozenge. C'mon now.

PRESIDENT: Does it hurt?

KATE: No, laddie. You put it on your tongue and you get transported to another planet.

PRESIDENT: Which?

KATE: I can't say.

PRESIDENT: Why not?

KATE: It has no name.

PRESIDENT: Is it desirable? Yes and no, I suppose.

KATE: I suppose. *(Pause)* That means it's very desirable.

PRESIDENT: Can I trust you?

KATE: Aye, laddie.

PRESIDENT: More than anybody?

KATE: More than anybody. *(He swallows the lozenge)* You're . . . arrived.

(The lozenge affects the PRESIDENT strangely. He runs around the stage, then dashes back and grabs a microphone front and center)

PRESIDENT: Is Helen here?

KATE: Who?

PRESIDENT: Helen. *(Asks himself)* Who the hell is Helen?

PEYTON: *(Her head appears through a hole in the top of the cabinet)* Shhhh.

PRESIDENT: Who the hell are you?

PEYTON: I don't have a name.

PRESIDENT: How do you know what a name is?

PEYTON: Because some people do.

PRESIDENT: On this planet?

KATE: Of course, laddie.

PRESIDENT: Does it have a name?

PEYTON: No.

PRESIDENT: How do you know what a name is?

KATE: Because some planets have a name and some don't.

PRESIDENT: Do you know the name Earth?

PEYTON: No.

PRESIDENT: *(Referring to KATE)* Let her answer.

KATE: Sometimes I answer, and sometimes SHE answers.

PRESIDENT: Why?

PEYTON: Laddie! I think you'd better meet Laurence!

PRESIDENT: Oh? Whoever that is, is someone . . . "named." Right.

(Someone removes a white screen that has recently been placed in front of the fireplace. Now revealed is JEFF, wearing a red beard that makes him look a bit like D. H. Lawrence. The music becomes slightly wild. JEFF stands with his arms folded in arrogance, puffing on his pipe)

How do you do—Lawrence?

JEFF: Laurence!

PRESIDENT: How do you do—LAURENCE?

JEFF: LAWRENCE . . . !

PRESIDENT: No answer. Of course Laurence is either energized by nervous, unconscious forces, or else . . .

PEYTON: Aye, laddie.

PRESIDENT: Well, of course, I don't know the rules of nature on this planet.

JEFF: *(Taking the pipe from his mouth)* This is secret number one, Mr. President.

PRESIDENT: It's fire—

KATE: Fire is it?

PRESIDENT: Wait a minute. *(He peeks into the fireplace)* Normally there would be fire down here. But you collect it into that pipe.

PEYTON: Pipe?

PRESIDENT: *(As smoke billows from the fireplace)* Excuse me. I know you have different names for many of the things I recognize from MY planet.

JEFF: No. It's not the name that I'm questioning.

PRESIDENT: Oh? It seems to me I should be asking the questions. Just give me two more minutes and I'll—*(He is holding his head in pain)*

PEYTON: Dizzy, Mr. President?

PRESIDENT: Not at all. I call this my watch!

KATE: What's that on your wrist?

PRESIDENT: *(Glances at his wrist, disoriented)* What time is it?

KATE: *(Coy)* You will have a bad effect on me, don't you think?

PRESIDENT: What I think should certainly take precedence over . . .

KATE: You're not getting the satisfaction that you seek, Mr. President.

PRESIDENT: Somebody just made sense!

JEFF: What a foolish concern, Mr. President.

PRESIDENT: Ah, you know who I am—

JEFF: Was that an issue?

PRESIDENT: One or two wheels in my head—

JEFF: *(Interrupting)* It would be foolish for me to repeat myself.

(His right leg suddenly sticks up in the air, rigid)

PRESIDENT: Oh? I thought you did. Right.

JEFF: That's better.

PRESIDENT: What's better?

(Strange music rises, and as the smoke gets thicker JEFF suddenly ducks into the fireplace and stands inside. Only his legs show.

The PRESIDENT *peeks into the fireplace, panics, and backs away in fear)*

Whose legs are those? Whose legs are those!

(The music fades as a voice on a loudspeaker is heard to repeat, at a furious pace, "Ladies and gentlemen, the PRESIDENT OF THE UNITED STATES." *The* PRESIDENT *again approaches the fireplace and looks at the legs. The right leg sticks out stiff, once again. The* PRESIDENT *nervously takes a drink from a tumbler of Scotch that is conveniently sitting on the fireplace mantel. Then he grabs a yachting cap, also from the mantel, props it on his head, leans against the mantel, and tries to laugh unconcernedly)*

PRESIDENT: *(To the leg, nonchalantly)* Excuse me. Who are you really? *(Pause)* Bend down and show me your face again please, so I can orient myself between ordinary planets and imaginary ones. To be blunt, what planet is this? I know I shouldn't expect an answer. How do I feel mentally? Okay, I feel like—mentally, I'm touching the eight corners of space I physically occupy. These are IDEAS I have. And they appear, even though they are ideas, more concrete than when I have them, if I have them, on the planet that I originally come from. *(A long pause, as he slowly comes to a microphone)* Why is that?

KATE: *(She runs in and goes to a microphone)* Want to be moving on, Mr. President?

PRESIDENT: Yes—as a matter of fact—I wouldn't mind, as they say, going back where I came from.

KATE: Sure; then what?

PRESIDENT: It's just that whatever limited capabilities I have are more RELEVANT to that planet and its human involvements—

KATE: Did you say . . . human?

PRESIDENT: I certainly did.

KATE: What's the human PART of you that says . . . *(She stops, looks at him, suddenly gives him a gentle kiss, and then steps back to consider)* human . . . *(She turns and runs up steps that lead her to the fireplace mantel, which is large enough for her to stand on)* human . . . *(PEYTON and JEFF take places behind microphones)* human . . .

PRESIDENT: I have human form, human brain, heart, feelings—

(He turns and kisses Peyton with, for a president, aggressive passion)

KATE: It's strange. All the human feelings I've ever seen look like the exact opposite of what the feelings were feeling.

PRESIDENT: *(Proud of his kiss)* Open your eyes, young lady, here's the evidence.

KATE: *(Very gently, as soft, lilting violin music continues)* You can broadcast your real feelings, Mr. President. I don't buy it. I think your emotional attachments are so deep you can bypass the name of the game and use hair coloring instead of letting a best pal yank it out by the roots.

JEFF: *(Sitting in the glass booth, at the PRESIDENT's desk)* You can broadcast your ideas about world problems, Mr. President. I don't buy it. I think you'd rather ride to town. Did I name the town? Did I name the method of transportation? Oh well, you can't trust me either.

PEYTON: Who can you trust, Mr. President? Me? The reptilian smile on my lips, the feline purr of my voice?

PRESIDENT: Only if I can accept the fact that our collaboration concerning the future of the so-called human race . . .

PEYTON: You don't buy it?

(She replaces JEFF in the glass booth)

PRESIDENT: Unfortunately we're both headed straight into the sunlight-filled rose garden of much-much fun, but we're doing it in noncommunicating universes.

KATE: Mr. President, you can broadcast a list of the animals that make your heart skip an occasional beat, but the minute people get familiar with your animal priorities . . .

(In the booth, PEYTON has been holding up little pictures of animals, and the PRESIDENT just now sees them)

PRESIDENT: *(Sarcastic)* Right. I probably have animals as ancestors. Great, great news.

KATE: Not so bad, Mr. President. Think of it as an evolutionary drive.

PRESIDENT: I don't buy it.

KATE: Buy it, Mr. President. Don't go to bed hungry for a sense of solidarity with the rest of the animal kingdom.

PRESIDENT: You mean it's time for bed?

JEFF: *(Appearing with a covered tray)* Dinner, Mr. President?

PRESIDENT: Sure—why lose my appetite over a problem I can't solve on an empty stomach?

(The PRESIDENT lifts the cover, the music rises and changes, and on the plate is a hairy something that he finds terribly frightening. He falls backward at the same instant that PEYTON flips over one of her animals pictures, revealing the words "Cosmic Love." JEFF moves away, again lifting his leg and rigidly sticking it out in front of him)

JEFF: I'd like to serve you, Mr. President, but as you can see I'm secretly paralyzed from the waist up. I'm no use to you any longer, I fear.

PRESIDENT: Ah, a diseased waiter.

JEFF: Approximately, Mr. President. A waiter who has been saved by Jesus Christ himself.

PRESIDENT: True, you don't look paralyzed.

JEFF: You too, sir.

PRESIDENT: (*Looking about angrily*) Did I hear right?

JEFF: What?

PRESIDENT: Did I hear right?!

JEFF: What?

PRESIDENT: DID I HEAR RIGHT!?

(*A deep* VOICE *speaks over a tape as the music becomes loud and nervous. Two twelve-foot-tall mechanical puppets arrive onstage. They half appear to be like ancient Mexican totem figures, full of bright painted wings, fins, and limbs encrusted with gold nails. But they also suggest giant space machines. Each has a large television set where the head should be. At the moment of their first appearance, the television screens are covered with drawn venetian blinds. All onstage are very frightened at the arrival of the puppets and run about to find what they consider a safe place from which to watch*)

VOICE: Deeper and deeper into the very heart of an argument in which he never believed he'd have to participate.

PRESIDENT: I wanna go home!

(*All run about, screaming*)

FIRST PUPPET: (*As his venetian blind opens, a human face is revealed on the video monitor in extreme closeup—the face of the author. The face is strangely distorted, as if pressed against a sheet of glass, and speaks with a grave, metallic voice*) Trust me, trust me. It's so much fun to be inarticulate, Mr. President. Trust me. It really is so much fun.

PRESIDENT: Get out of here! *(Wildly, to himself)* Act as if you're having fun—

(He jams a protective helmet onto his head. Attached to the helmet is a large white arrow which points directly at his skull)

FIRST PUPPET: Let's tell the truth. I am torn between the physicality of your world and the desire to do something I can only tell you about. The secret thing is— Take a look. I also only half exist. So sleep, sleep, put the mind to work, Mr. President.

PRESIDENT: I tried that. It doesn't seem to work.

FIRST PUPPET: Yesss! Something unteachable. Because it's the deepest, most real thing in your life at this present moment.

PRESIDENT: Goddamn it, cut it out.

(Everything goes crazy. People run around not knowing what to do. KATE has acquired a life-sized dummy that looks like an elegant lady in evening dress. It's as if all inhibitions were cast aside when the PUPPETS arrived. The result is frantic behavior, even on the PRESIDENT's part. He runs about in a red silk bathrobe)

FIRST PUPPET: The mirror mind at work, Mr. President. Don't have a mind, BE mind.

PRESIDENT: I think I'm losing my mind.

FIRST PUPPET: What's in my hand?

(The PUPPET's giant arm reaches out. A light is shining from the center of its hand)

PRESIDENT: A stone.

FIRST PUPPET: Does it look like a stone?

PRESIDENT: Yes.

FIRST PUPPET: Does it look heavy?

PRESIDENT: It looks heavy.

FIRST PUPPET: Ah, its size?

PRESIDENT: I mean a rock.

FIRST PUPPET: And its weight, does that change also?

PRESIDENT: Yes. No. I don't know.

FIRST PUPPET: How do you explain it?

PRESIDENT: Wait a minute. I know I'm avoiding a certain, possible level of reality. Could I take a real look at what you have in your real hand? Which looks like the center of the universe in a compressed ball of light, naturally. *(He grabs what looks like a big diamond but is really not; disappointed)* But damn it, this is a stone of no value whatsoever.

FIRST PUPPET: Mr. President, can you get a handle on reality?

PRESIDENT: Up till now, maybe not.

FIRST PUPPET: It's what human beings spend most of their time working on, so they tell me. But I only partially know about such things. Call me semihuman at best. Semihuman. I like the sound of that in my mouth. Semihuman. Let me describe what happens to me when I say that—semihuman. I fall into a heavenly state of being.

PRESIDENT: *(Tapping a mike)* Testing, 1–2–3–4.

FIRST PUPPET: Why is it that none of the fun-generators turned on when I said GO? They said to me, this isn't a race, and I said back to them, oh, I thought fun was always in a race of some kind.

PRESIDENT: Testing, 1–2–3–4!

FIRST PUPPET: That's a heavenly state of being, wouldn't you say? Then . . .

PRESIDENT: Then?

FIRST PUPPET: Then you came to this planet, Mr. President. And I said immediately—look, there's a friend. And the doorknob of my imagination said, hold me, I

LIKE the twists and turns of human imagination. And the rug under my feet said, walk on your hands please. Why, rug? I asked. Because I can't fly, was the answer, but I turn that limitation into an even more powerful imagination. And the windows in the next room said CRY CRY CRY, but the ringing in my ears wasn't a reminder of physical problems. *(A crash is heard)* I don't HAVE any PHYSICAL problems, which causes a lotta resentment to be directed toward me, believe it or not, because that's what human beings seem to be into on this planet. So where do you trace that resentment? Am I the guilty party? Check me over. See what I have for somewhat unfilled motives? . . . How shall I say this?

Out of my way, please.

I kill for money,

I kill for jewels,

I kill for higher realms and purposes.

You, on the other hand, I see you don't really kill.

Do you know what it is to kill?

PRESIDENT: *(As he whirls about, confused and upset)* Yes —I mean, no! Of course not.

FIRST PUPPET: Ahhh, doing a lot of revolutions, Mr. President. But never understanding that you keep constant, through the revolutions. So I start revolving at the same time, so that we are revolving together. Look at these human jewels into which we make ourselves. See it from that perspective. Keep the fun generators going, fast, bright, and the direction nobody in particular has to choose, because it chooses itself, on automatic pilot, Mr. President! It's enough to make somebody smile. Mr. President, are you smiling, too? Hey, how about leaving planet Earth for good? That's how you'll accomplish all those spiritual tasks you outlined for yourself in your unconscious mind, Mr. President; you'll be smiling, like I'm smiling!

(In moving away from the frightening RST PUPPET *they have all gathered in the shadow of the* SECOND PUPPET—*but now his venetian blind opens and he begins to speak. The same face and voice for this puppet as the first)*

SECOND PUPPET: Somebody who smiled once found that the payoff was an accordion solo to celebrate a personal event that was still two years off. So was a smile worth it? Yes. Because certain face muscles radiated an electrical pulse that the ecological system judged tiny but devoured nonetheless. Somebody—who drove a hard bargain at every possible opportunity—What were some of those opportunities?

PRESIDENT: *(Going through his pockets)* I'm sorry. I lost my list.

KATE: Please, Mr. President. Try being somebody worthy of a lady's trust.

(She puts a revolver in the PRESIDENT'S *hand and runs off with* PEYTON*)*

PRESIDENT: *(Looking about, baffled)* I hardly had your generous invitations in my back pocket when suddenly I found myself far from home, ostensibly.

PEYTON and **KATE:** *(Running back in with flowers, they force them on the* PRESIDENT*)* This IS home.

(He immediately tosses the flowers away)

PRESIDENT: Don't think I didn't bring the required flowers—but the icing on the ceremonial cake was too much! Too much! Too much icing!

SECOND PUPPET: Heyyyy! When you see wind—

PRESIDENT: I don't see it.

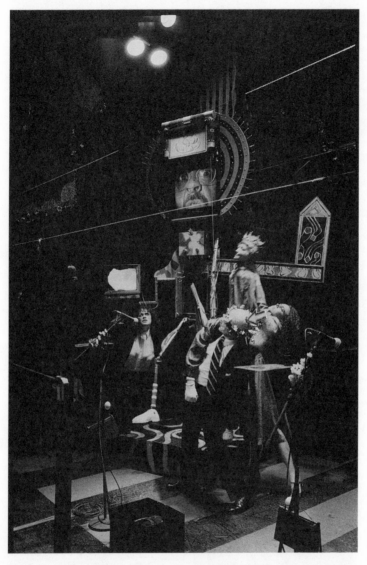

Peyton Smith, Ron Vawter, Kate Valk, and Richard Foreman on video monitor in **Symphony of Rats.** **(Photo by Paula Court)**

FIRST PUPPET: You don't see it, it's just indicated by the movements of leaves and blossoms.

(Just above the TV heads of the puppets, attached like hats, are small stages. Little curtains open to reveal tiny revolving skulls)

PRESIDENT: Ah, now I see it.

FIRST PUPPET: What DO you see, in terms of the so-called network between flowers?

PRESIDENT: My rose garden.

SECOND PUPPET: Congratulations, Mr. President, perception like an angel.

PRESIDENT: I SEE angels.

(The lights dim. He holds a candle to try and illuminate the room)

SECOND PUPPET: Congratulations. You must be somebody who puts serious shoes on to get through the oceans of spiritual turmoil, because each insight sets off so many sparks, somebody really big yells FIRE.

PRESIDENT: *(As he notices smoke again pouring in from the fireplace)* Fire!

SECOND PUPPET: And the first angel says—hey, he's dedicated to lust, because I see bright flowers. You want adventure? Yes, you want adventure. So open a door: *(The PRESIDENT has run to the back of the room where the rolling cabinet has reappeared. He opens the door to look inside)* Nothing. What a surprise. Try again. *(As the cabinet revolves, the PRESIDENT grabs a handle and the whole side of the cabinet opens, revealing JEFF, posed sternly holding out a golden jug, which the PRESIDENT takes and runs with downstage)* Ah! a ghost this time, and a bad one, I think.

(JEFF comes forward, still in his red beard, but now in a red robe, like the PRESIDENT's. He stops, takes the jug from the PRESIDENT, and drinks deeply)

FIRST PUPPET: So the second angel says—He's dedicated to greed, because I see water rising. You want a drink? *(JEFF offers the jug to the PRESIDENT, who runs away. JEFF follows him)* But nothing helps like a thirsty palate when you're on a spiritual quest. *(The PRESIDENT tries to get into the cabinet, which is now closed and locked)* Sorry. I forgot. The door's locked.

SECOND PUPPET: So the third angel says, He's dedicated to sloth. Now wait a minute. How can so many spirit beings be so deep into bad things? And you think the world should end because of that? No. Everything's possible! Hey—FORGET I SAID THAT!

FIRST PUPPET: Excuse me, Mr. President. A hypothetical question: If other systems, other worlds . . . really existed, would you wish to be in them? *(All look nervously at each other, not knowing what to answer)* Okay I'll give you the answer. You wouldn't have any choice. You WOULD be in them!

(A kind of drum music is heard which makes them all think an earthquake is coming. They rush to grab tight to the railings. Then the music fades and the PRESIDENT regains his courage and steps forward)

PRESIDENT: Wait a minute. If all I have to do is accept reality, why can't all my prayers be answered? I close my eyes. I begin to count.

(As he starts to count, the chest cavity of the SECOND PUPPET opens up and a mechanical hand extends an envelope. A little bell rings)

SECOND PUPPET: You get your wish, Mr. President. Here are two tickets to Tornadoville. Here are two tickets to Tornadoville.

PRESIDENT: *(In quiet awe, he comes forward with the tickets in hand)* Is it a place or a state of mind?

KATE: Tornadoville, or not Tornadoville.

PRESIDENT: I dream of going to Tornadoville.

PEYTON: How strange. I'd think it was one place you'd like to avoid.

PRESIDENT: Perhaps. It would seem that way.

PEYTON: In your imagination, what's it like?

PRESIDENT: *(Hushed, in awe)* You can tell by the name. Everything is total chaos . . . in Tornadoville.

PEYTON AND KATE: And you want to go there?

PRESIDENT: Yes.

PEYTON and **KATE:** But why?

PRESIDENT: I don't know why. But I know I want to go there.

PEYTON and **KATE:** *(Holding hands, chanting softly)* Tornadoville: where nothing stands still. That's what it's like—

PRESIDENT: I want to go there!

PEYTON and **KATE:** —most of the time, in Tornadoville. Tornadoville.

FIRST PUPPET: In Tornadoville, where nothing stands still. In Tornadoville.

SECOND PUPPET: Planet city of depravity, planet city of violence. In the middle sector of that city something gives birth, a holy spirit ignited, unlocatable, burning.

PRESIDENT: Why is my throat parched? Why is my tongue burning? Go to the idiot, I scream. Go to the idiot, I scream.

(PEYTON and KATE have gone to the FIRST PUPPET and discover a tube protruding from its chest cavity. They turn a knob and

soft ice cream pours forth from the PUPPET'S chest, which they manage to collect in ice cream cones as the PUPPET speaks. Ice cream is distributed to all as the FIRST PUPPET recites)

FIRST PUPPET: *(As all but the PRESIDENT creep offstage in fear)* I am the ice cream man
A giant of ice cream
I am I am I am.
I am the ice cream king
A voice of ice cream
I sing I sing I sing.
I am the ice cream captain
A fist of ice cream
I ram I ram I ram.
I am the ice cream brute
A blow of ice cream
I toot I toot I toot.

(The PRESIDENT is now alone with the PUPPETS. He rests his head against a pillar, licking his ice cream slowly, his eyes rolling up to heaven)

SECOND PUPPET: City of stars, stores, stones. In the invisible center, people from deep space, more than human, less than human, singing the good news about the transformation blueprint for Earth. Because suffering is in it. Man getting comfortable with suffering. Not to make it stop, but to make it . . . fruitful.

PRESIDENT: *(Coming down to a microphone)* Stupid idea. We want to end suffering.

SECOND PUPPET: Tornadoville, planet city of sacrifice and expiation.

PRESIDENT: Whenever I hear the word sacrifice I look into my mirror and say to myself: How come it's always me?—What'll it take? My financial holdings maybe? *(He starts getting angry)* My right arm from the elbow down?

How about my prick? Two good legs—a big heart? How 'bout my shaved head, huh?

(He bends his head forward, offering it to the PUPPET *for execution)*

SECOND PUPPET: *(Commenting on the* PRESIDENT'S *gesture)* Good idea! Guess why!

FIRST PUPPET: *(Bells ring; the* PRESIDENT *whirls about in pain, finishing up behind a pillar as the* FIRST PUPPET *takes on an even more frightening aspect)* I am the Tornadoville barber, but nobody notices my unique style. I wait for customers on a curve related to sunlight, rain, and fluctuating temperature. Heads fly off in imagination when I take scissors to the circumference. Tangents of energy, that's what I produce. *(The* PRESIDENT *appears from behind the pillar, his head wound tightly with black string that distorts his face completely, making him look even more frightening than the* PUPPETS*)* Nobody speaks of it, but in fact, yes, long after my disappearance poems are written. The subject encoded in gold. What subject? The Tornadoville barber, of course. Who am I really? How do I operate? Really?

Take a look—
Once more, one more customer
Offers his head
Heavy as lead,
Stuffed with shit,
I'd better go to work on it.
I think I'll go to work on it.
I think I'll do a job on it.

(The PUPPETS *disappear. The* PRESIDENT *is alone in his office, badly shaken, his head still wrapped in the distorting black string. Dim lights, late at night. Others lurk in the shadows)*

JEFF: *(After a silence)* Are you all right, Mr. President?

PRESIDENT: *(Quiet, shaken)* I seem to have returned from a profound experience of . . . elsewhereness. You don't believe me? Look at my face. Or should I say, look into this black hole.

KATE: Are you still asleep, Mr. President?

PRESIDENT: I try not to. Sleep, after all, takes one into the unconscious life of men, women, children, old people. *(She kisses him gently on the cheek)* Get away from me. All this garbage is pouring out of me. Ugh—can't you see it? *(He is unwrapping the string)* Like RAYS, like . . . I'm broadcasting such JUNK . . . do something about it! That's an order to myself. *(They bring him to a mike)* Do something about it.

KATE: About what?

PRESIDENT: You haven't been listening. *(Pause)* Take my pulse. *(She reaches for his wrist and he pulls away)* I mean my mental and emotional pulse. My spiritual pulse.

KATE: I don't know how, sir.

PRESIDENT: Okay. Get me a standard United States citizen.

KATE: I don't know any, sir.

PRESIDENT: *(Tapping the mike)* Is this thing on?

JEFF: *(Posed at the fireplace)* Aye, sir.

PRESIDENT: *(Directly into the mike)* Get me a United States citizen, goddamn it! *(to himself)* You're the President after all, you should be able to do that. *(KATE kisses him again, and this time he rather likes it. He straightens his tie, a bit embarrassed)* You just tried kissing the President of the United States. How do you feel about that?

KATE: Well, I feel funny . . . all over.

PRESIDENT: Strange. Why do I feel the same way? It's crazy—I almost feel like I want to start dancing. No no no, that's crazy. One thing I don't want to do is dancing.

(Faint Latin dance music can be heard)

JEFF: Okay. Try it, Mr. President.

(PEYTON and KATE are now across the room from the PRESI-DENT, doing little dance steps that are obviously meant to encourage him)

PRESIDENT: I'm afraid . . . everything that's happened . . . Well, I'm not a very good dancer.

JEFF: *(Nodding toward PEYTON and KATE)* Here are some pretty good dancers from around here, Mr. President. Are you envious of them?

(The music builds)

PRESIDENT: I've just been through . . . *(their steps become more elaborate)* I've got other things on my mind.

JEFF: No reason to be shy, Mr. President. They are stupid girls with not much brain in the head. They dance good.

KATE and PEYTON: *(Calling across to the PRESIDENT)* Yoo-hoo . . .

PRESIDENT: Yes, yes . . . they do.

JEFF: You try.

PRESIDENT: *(He takes a step forward, then retreats back to JEFF)* Absolutely out of the question.

JEFF: Try even talking to one of these air brains. Try to have a conversation.

PEYTON: Hi. I dance good, but I don't have a great mental background, Mr. President. So you'll probably outdo me on any conversational level.

PRESIDENT: Well I'll have to admit, it hasn't been a very pleasant few weeks. But when you do that kind of dance, it's something very . . . glamorous.

PEYTON: We shouldn't even TRY to carry on a conversation when dancing.

PRESIDENT: I suppose words aren't the only way to communicate.

KATE: Boffo! So join us!

PRESIDENT: *(With a nervous laugh)* I think I will. *(He joins them and shimmies in place to the music)*

KATE: You dance so GOOD. I thought I heard you were inhibited, Mr. President.

PRESIDENT: I was. But I think the glamour of the situation, dancing with you attractive ladies, made me break through that wall of inhibition and . . . start dancing. Then when I do it, I find out I'm not too bad at it after all. Thank God. So I'm glad I made the plunge.

JEFF: I'm sure the young ladies share that opinion, Mr. President.

KATE and **PEYTON:** Yes . . . !

PRESIDENT: I'm game!

(His shimmy changes into a wild conga line, with variations, in which he leads PEYTON *and* KATE *in a circle around the room several times. The music rises and becomes so loud that we can only faintly hear an excited voice coming out of the loudspeakers, announcing repeatedly throughout the dance, "Ladies and gentlemen, the* PRESIDENT *of the United States! The* PRESIDENT *of the United States, ladies and gentlemen!" There are continual shrieks of delight from the ladies, and the third time around the* PRESIDENT *waves to the audience, shouting, "Come on—everybody dance!" The fourth time around they try to grab* JEFF *and pull him into the dance, but he sternly resists. After three tries, the* PRESIDENT *becomes irritated, then resolves)*

Somebody who doesn't want to dance, doesn't have to dance.

(The music is much softer now, and the three dance lightly by themselves in place as the PRESIDENT *tries to make small talk)*

What kind of life do you ladies lead?

KATE: No, remember what we said. No dancing and talking in combo.

PRESIDENT: But it's possible. I've often seen people dancing and talking both. In movies, for instance.

PEYTON: But remember, this is real life, Mr. President.

PRESIDENT: It's very glamorous and exciting though . . .

PEYTON: Real life! *(The music abruptly stops. The lights dim. She turns to the PRESIDENT, ready to get angry)* Ohh, who did that?

PRESIDENT: *(Under his breath)* I knew it couldn't last. *(a big smile for the ladies)* I'm ready to continue whenever they get the music back.

KATE: *(Advancing on the PRESIDENT as if she doesn't believe him)* What?

PRESIDENT: Why are you looking at me like that? Say something. Aren't we still friends?

(All advance on the PRESIDENT, menacingly. Weird music rises)

KATE: *(Angrily into a mike)* You know what the man DID to me?

You probably won't believe it.

He took me into a private rose garden and said, "Don't smell."

I put my hand over my nose, and guess what?

I passed out.

So did I blame that on the beautiful roses?

PRESIDENT: I think I should say—

PEYTON: You'll work it out, "Ralph."

PRESIDENT: My name isn't Ralph!

KATE: You know what the man DID to me?

PEYTON: You probably won't believe it.

KATE: He said, hey—

PEYTON: Cut many rugs, Mr. President?

KATE: *(Continuing)* I got beautiful tuna fish sandwiches
I'm distributing for free.
Guess what.
I had no pain in my stomach after that.

PEYTON: The man was making a sexual overture,
"Larry."

KATE: I'm not Larry.

PEYTON: You know what the man DID to me?

KATE: You probably won't believe it.

PEYTON: He collected all the loose change
I scattered in hidden places
With my unconscious mind.
Some was under the bed, behind the bureau, by the left
leg
of the large comfortable armchair—then he stood up
straight and shouted—"thief!" THIEF!

KATE: What was a poor girl to do? I left town.

PEYTON: Did it make you sad, "Paul"?

PRESIDENT: My name isn't Paul. Whether I'm sad or
not I can't quite figure.

KATE and PEYTON: You probably won't believe it—

KATE: He rolled a big disk in my direction saying
"catch"—but my bare hands are always in danger of
conflagration. And he knows that well. *(A globe of the
world is being gently passed about, and it ends up in the
PRESIDENT'S hands. He examines it as if he had never seen
anything like it)*
"Look, I'm still sucking my fingers," I cried.
But he didn't pay me much heed
And went on rolling into all the Western states like Utah,
Arizona, Mexico, Bermuda.

PEYTON: Weren't you there first, "Phil"?

PRESIDENT: Ah, so that's who I am. I'm Phil!

PEYTON: Take a pill, Phil!

KATE: You probably won't believe it.
He knotted a handkerchief,
Slipped it over my head, and started to pull.
(JEFF slowly does so to KATE)
"You're cutting off my air supply," I cried out.
I was spinning so fast the TV was just a BLUR,
But that wasn't my number-one priority.

PEYTON: So I started shouting out numbers
To try and keep my orientation intact.
1–2–3–

KATE: "Hey, what are you trying to spell?
Do you have a message for me?"
That's what our President cried out,
But of course I had no message.

PEYTON: I don't believe you, "Larry."

PRESIDENT: Full circle. I AM Larry.

(By now, the PRESIDENT has circled to the glass booth, climbed onto the desk, on which he stands holding the globe up in the air, in slow triumph)

KATE: I knew it all along.

PEYTON: Dance, Larry.

PRESIDENT: You asked for it! *(He does a slow dance with the globe, reminiscent of Charlie Chaplin's dance in* The Great Dictator*)*

JEFF: Look what this man does to us.

PEYTON: To whom exactly? To Larry, of course.

JEFF: *(A heavily accented carousel music builds and the PRES- IDENT drops the globe from over the top of the glass booth so it falls into JEFF's hands)* You probably won't believe this!

PRESIDENT: *(The music fades and he composes himself)* Dancing was not my strong point. In fact, for me—for someone in my position—it was a kind of humiliation. *(A reporter has sneaked in from the side and is shooting photos of the* PRESIDENT.*)* So when I realized that cameras were just perceptible in my very restricted field of vision, I had people break the cameras, destroying thereby the evidence of my inappropriate behavior. But the immediate result, of course, was that I was on the receiving end of colorful epithets. I won't go through the whole list, but one of the milder epithets hurled at me that day was the epithet "dirty rat." "DIRTY RAT, you broke our valuable cameras, you dirty rat." *(*JEFF *has been creeping alongside the glass booth, in a rat's head)* I tried to explain myself rationally by explaining that the camera does not reflect life in its full multilayered dimensionality, but from one point of view only.

JEFF: *(At a mike now, removing his rat's head)* Strange, Mr. President. I never heard about this experience.

PRESIDENT: Quite true, McAlister. I wanted, in fact, to protect you.

JEFF: How come WE never heard about that event?

PRESIDENT: Because I never told you my real name. So you never had a chance to put two and two together.

PEYTON: *(Calling softly into a mike, while soft music plays)* Spaceship Earth . . . yoo-hoo.

(Kate has run lightly up to stand on the fireplace mantel)

KATE: Poised at the edge of some abyss, waiting to jump. What fun that will be.

PEYTON: Afternoons . . . are sad times, aren't they?

KATE: Tears running down his face.
What fun that will be.
But don't worry . . .

JEFF: Nobody will be listening if you cry, Mr. President.

PRESIDENT: I must cry. If I hold back my genuine tears,

the universe won't conclude in the desired fashion. That's an ultimate fact, I'm afraid.

JEFF: Ultimate fact, Mr. President?

PRESIDENT: *(Looking around in the booth, disoriented)* Where . . . am I now? Remind me? *(Suddenly he screams in pain and collapses to his knees. Then he begins speaking in the voice of one possessed)* I am deeply into the seventh realm. Archangels are visible. Taking the shape of self-evident pulsation factors. *(He is thrown out of the trance, recovers, straightens his tie)* Hard for other people to understand what that means probably, so doubly, I don't have to explain myself. *(He takes a glass of water, offered by* PEYTON*)* Can I offer anybody besides myself a refreshing glass of water? *(He shoves the glass forward as if to offer it to the audience, and, much to his surprise, it hits against the glass)* No. That water can't enter into someone else's world. Remember, everything I'm saying is coded. Therefore, my real purposes are not understandable. *(He is slowly seized by anguish; he shouts at the audience)* Go away! Please!

PEYTON: *(She tries to reach up to comfort the* PRESIDENT*, but he shoves her away violently)* Eeek! Mr. President!

PRESIDENT: *(He gives her a long, dirty look, then composes himself and turns back to his public)* Be careful. I'm going to teach you about life now, more than you care to know. It turns out you all live on a planet upon which you daily perceive . . . only one of seven possible levels of reality. Animals, however—elephants, zebras, rats— perceive two such levels, neither of them the level that we, as humans, perceive. Lucky? No. It's not a matter of more desirable or less desirable levelwise. It's time, however, for you to have a so-called ultimate adventure. Remember, I'm speaking in code. Plus I am not going to be kind. Remember, my friends: God does not like strangers who stay strangers. So . . . *(He puts out his hand)* let's be friends. *(He advances his hand, but it, like the glass, smashes into the glass wall of the booth, and he retracts it in pain)* See? You can't reach into this world! Don't even try! But there has to be another solution. Join me! You figure out how . . . !

PEYTON: *(Slowly into a microphone)* Is it possible that all of you out there thought you were participating in a detective story? I won't disappoint you. I'm the detective, and here's what happened.

PRESIDENT: *(In a hard-boiled detective style, as organ music plays)* It was perhaps five years ago. I was introduced to a woman who claimed she received anonymous telephone calls in which a strange metallic voice gave strange metaphysical messages from another level of reality.

PEYTON: Hello? Hello?

PRESIDENT: But this woman . . . was unable to describe the contents of those messages, much less to quote or relate, even in her own words, their content. Then she appeared before us in another guise. *(KATE is suddenly illuminated on the fireplace mantel, dressed in her Scotch plaid panels)* She carried, this time, a list of names and addresses of other people who claimed to have visionary experiences of one kind or another. I decided to check out at least a few names. Amazingly . . . one of them turned out to be the President of the United States.

KATE: Were you traveling in your imagination, Mr. President?

PRESIDENT: Yes, in more than one sense.

KATE: *(Holding up a picture of a train)* Of course.

PRESIDENT: What's that?

KATE: Well, it's a picture of a train.

PRESIDENT: I don't need that to refresh my memory. In fact . . .

KATE: I know.

PRESIDENT: It bears no relation to . . .

KATE: I know.

PRESIDENT: How would you like to hear about my experience—really.

KATE: That's why I'm here.

PRESIDENT: Well . . . *(KATE flips her picture, and on the back are written the words "Cosmic Love." A low hum deafens the PRESIDENT and he staggers back, shrieking)* You're outside my time frame!

KATE: Call him . . . the triangulated hero.

(PEYTON and JEFF run in rear, holding golden triangular shapes and the PRESIDENT, trying to escape offstage, bounces off them back to the center of the room)

PRESIDENT: *(As weird space music drives another recitation performance by everyone at microphones, often switching positions)* Right! I'm outside of YOUR knowledge of good and evil because, to me, the rising sun, which other people refer to as the beginning of a new day, is not only a new planet, but a bundle of responsibilities to things other than petty human happiness.

KATE: Call him the hero of the prematurely short pants.

(PEYTON and JEFF have repositioned, and again the PRESIDENT, trying to escape, bounces off their triangles)

PRESIDENT: Right! I'm outside your notion of charity because when I give of myself, I know that the bitterness they suppressed is in fact life blood for one half the human race, but also a very profound tranquilizer for people whose hair style and persona both are a product of reality-producing imagination.

JEFF: Call him a free man, except you'd be lying like you lie about everything.

PRESIDENT: Call me the muscular man in the baldness advertisements, because when I lose my hair that's a sign of something else.

(He slips on three pairs of eyeglasses at once; they crisscross at odd angles over his face)

KATE: Call him loud, clear, and independent of needs other people consider primary. Because his most intimate behavior isn't of one psychological school or another, but a melange of things picked up in history books.

PRESIDENT: You don't have to read books to read life, you know. *(The others run for their books)* You don't read either one? Then you're living in hell.

KATE: Does it have something to do with nonstop verbal flow?

PRESIDENT: Yes!

KATE: That explains perhaps the deinvention of the intergalactic trolley.

PRESIDENT: Yes. Because it was easier to get from one place to the other using the imagination, but everybody else forgot that answer. So I went for a swim in a mental thing. Don't kick me out of the doll factory, please! I better set my bearings, because whenever my hand shakes—I go bananas!

(Grotesque doll-music swamps all. The PRESIDENT staggers about and finds his way back to the desk in the glass booth, climbs on top, and collapses on his knees. KATE and PEYTON call out, "Doll factory! Doll factory!" and two, strange, otherworldly-looking stagehands deliver large paintings that KATE, PEYTON, and JEFF hold up, their chins barely over the edge of the frame. The paintings show flowers out of which

emerge the faces of strange, otherworldly creatures—who, in fact, look just like the delivering stagehands)

Hey, that's the next leg of a journey I won't get to take unless I get kicked out of office. But I already went into something called deep space and look what I came back with. I don't know what to call it, but it hurts, it hurts, it hurts!

(The music fades and all is silent. Then KATE *continues softly)*

KATE: This is a very pregnant memory trace. For like other human beings, the President of the United States is subject to internal psychological stress termed self-destructive or therapeutic. *(Beautiful light falls all over the stage—on the* PRESIDENT *in his stressed-out pose on the desk-top, collapsed against the glass, and on the field of paintings held by the others surrounding the booth)* Historically verifiable or not, this is a very pregnant memory trace, because the President of the United States could, or at least might, manifest a desire for self-transcendence not totally fulfilled by glamorous and resonant adult fantasies of power and personal self-aggrandizement. Beautiful, don't you think?

PEYTON: *(Calling from far away)* Mr. President . . . all of the self-abilities you anticipate . . . ?

PRESIDENT: They were predicated on "how to," "was," and even the future conditional tense of the verb "having fun." But how could I, really?

PEYTON: Some of those very same abilities . . .

PRESIDENT: Really.

PEYTON: . . . had something to do with a beautiful woman's ability to evoke something you can't see, hear, or touch with the tip of your tongue. Everybody do this dance!

PRESIDENT: *(Sniffling into a handkerchief)* A more sensitive manipulation of the head, that's what I worked on finally, but after a hundred miles of nonrepeatable trajectories, I knew I had to get outta this tight box of responsibilities that add up to a human zero.

KATE: Do this dance, everybody.

(She and PEYTON have exchanged their paintings for little skull-shaped mugs which they hold in their pink mitten hands, and from which they sip hot chocolate through straws. JEFF moves about the PRESIDENT'S booth, spraying a fine mist of water on the glass with a garden sprayer)

PRESIDENT: You call it music? I call it deliberate mystification!

PEYTON: That's because all those wonderful abilities . . .

PRESIDENT: *(Trying to hold back his sobs)* —had nothing to do with where I was going to be NEXT year. IF next year comes. Ah, what the hell—it probably will. *(He cries like a baby)*

KATE: Mr. President, if we all talk about dying and don't— *(She and PEYTON giggle loudly, and then suck noisily through their straws)* Do we die?

PRESIDENT: I don't die, you don't die, but the universe has other things in mind. *(It has begun to snow gently on the PRESIDENT in the booth. Someone suspends a black flag that drapes beautifully over his shoulder)*

KATE: Of course, if the chatterbox of the third brain comes up with one or two good ideas . . .

PEYTON: Is it more than smart to be a professional in an obsolescent category?

PRESIDENT: "The end of all categories," said the man in line for immortality. *(He struggles to his feet, pulls up his jacket sleeve to press his wrist against the glass, and speaks* *bitterly)* Look, I have blood vessels, but you don't see them directly. You got what's called an intimation of that network of veins. It goes on and on, doesn't it, into every possible universe I might have visited, imagination or no imagination. When a man of my achievements bleeds real blood!

JEFF: *(Quietly, sitting in the PRESIDENT'S booth)* Bastard. It's time to free yourself from those myths you only partially believe in. That's what I'd say. Your belief systems are your version of total failure, you asshole.

PRESIDENT: *(Posing, like Washington crossing the Delaware)* This friend of mine speaks like a goddamned angel, doesn't he?

JEFF: *(Very gently)* Hello, motherfucker. I bring you news of a distant universe. But of course, shithead, you've heard that before.

PEYTON: *(Smiling sweetly)* Have a seat, you dirty rotten rat.

PRESIDENT: Are YOU the one person next in line for a progressive way to detach the body from the what-came-first?

KATE: *(Also placid)* Oh, you're plugging into my energy sources? You bastard.

PEYTON: Dirty rat.

KATE: You son of a bitch. I'm sorry, I—

PRESIDENT: *(Harsher now, he has come down from his desk and advances upon them, starting to unbutton his fly)* Please, no regrets. I have an intimate way of suggesting the great distance between us that even space travel doesn't seem to penetrate.

KATE: *(To the PRESIDENT, as someone with a rat head comes and puts his arm around her)* You're not the only friend I have, you know.

PRESIDENT: Sure. I manifest like the ordinary sometimes. *(His pants are undone now, and he is in front of* PEYTON *seeming to coldly penetrate her, as she leans away unhappily)*

JEFF: Then do join us, Mr. President. The ordinary thing might be a YES, but I know that with your YES, you'll surprise the hell outta us—somehow.

PRESIDENT: *(As he approaches climax)* Sure, my body goes into orbit like clockwork. But is that any reason to celebrate the usual lack of physiological self-control?

(Over the loudspeakers we hear overlapping voices repeating over and over, rapidly and without feeling, "The President of the United States, ladies and gentlemen, the President of the United States." And while the PRESIDENT *has been having his way with* PEYTON, *a golden ball, something like a mystical version of a flying saucer, has slowly descended on an angular path to stop and hover just over the* PRESIDENT'S *head)*

KATE: *(Sadly watching the* PRESIDENT *button up)* And he kept on doing it until . . .

JEFF: Did something happen, Mr. President?

PRESIDENT: Yeah. My eyeballs burned up like asteroids on a collision course.

VOICE: *(Over the loudspeaker)* Mr. President: turn something back into nothing. Just as I do.

PEYTON: *(As the rolling cabinet reappears, to slow, sad carousel music)* Ahh. Yes. Here comes your car, Mr. President. The one you ride in, when you ride in your major car.

(The side of the cabinet opens, revealing an interior painted, in pastel colors, like a giant bull's-eye. The PRESIDENT *approaches suspiciously and walks in, as again we hear the voices agitatedly repeating, "Ladies and gentlemen, the President of the United States")*

KATE: What's the verdict, Mr. President?

PRESIDENT: Well, it's not like the others I ride in when I'm on my travels but . . .

KATE: Yes?

PRESIDENT: *(Impressed)* This is some car.

KATE: Maybe it's your lucky car, Mr. President. Because here's an award. *(She takes an envelope attached to the side of the cabinet)* Guess what it's for? *(Pause)* Best world.

PRESIDENT: *(Quietly, dazed)* Best car.

KATE: No, best world.

PRESIDENT: *(Insistent now)* Best car!

KATE: The prize? *(She extracts a round mirror from the envelope)* A mirror.

(Sound of a mirror breaking, as the door of the cabinet closes with the PRESIDENT inside. The cabinet spins and a deep VOICE is heard over the loudspeakers. The music rises)

VOICE: Ah, but face it, Mr. President, everybody has to break a few mirrors to make a new man now and then. Face it, Mr. President. It's like getting a mental face-lift. But the secret is . . . it's somebody else's face that gets lifted, opened, unveiled. And deep inside that new, old, terrible face you'd almost forgotten . . .

(JEFF has crossed to the fireplace. He slowly opens a panel above the mantel. Inside is a giant, sleeping, stone-looking, ogrelike face, which slowly inflates as smoke pours from the fireplace. On an angled table at the rear of the room a large disk starts to spin; the disk is covered with swirls of color—teacups and saucers are attached around its rim. Somebody whispers, over the loudspeaker, "Eureka, we've reached it. Eureka. The giant, granite, pockmarked face of sleep." All but the PRESIDENT have gathered to watch the expanding face.)

The PRESIDENT's *head appears from a hole in the roof of the cabinet)*

PRESIDENT: Thought metaphors have been pounding it for eternity!

(The music rises as the PRESIDENT *disappears back into the cabinet. The others are now wearing rat heads and white bibs. They lift their arms in time to the music, which can now be recognized as a lumbering, slow, carousel organ version of "Lullaby of Birdland." They all begin a slow dance about the room as the deep* VOICE *intones to the rhythm of the music. Telephone bells ring in the distance)*

VOICE: Don't believe the future
Can't be found.
Rats can fly
Above the ground.
Floating on a music
Nobody else can enjoy—
Just for you:
To employ!

(By now, the dancers have knocked on the cabinet door, and the PRESIDENT *has appeared through the hole in the roof, a crown on his head, his eyes covered with white Ping-Pong balls)*

Dance away to heaven.
Use two feet.
Grow two wings
That madly beat.
Carry little bodies
Up to the brain.
I renew.
Wouldn't you?

(The dancers have arrived at final positions. Seen through the heavy smoke filling the room they point at the PRESIDENT, *moving their arms rhythmically to the music. The* PRESIDENT's *head shakes spastically, his tongue dribbles out of his open mouth. Each line of the song is now punctuated by a squeal of delight from the rats)*

Animals assemble
Two by two.
Fall in line,
The thing to do.
Listen to a music
Sweeter than what's gone before
As you roll on the floor.

(An electronic hum starts rising, beginning to interfere with the music)

Try to reach a place that
Can't be named,
'Cause your wildness
Can't be tamed.
Lift your little voices
High in a sweet symphony.
You and me—

(By now, the hum has grown as loud as an approaching squadron of giant aircraft. The PRESIDENT *looks fearfully up to the sky, as the lights focus on him and then fade to blackness)*

The End

·

WHAT
DID
HE SEE?

·

Lili Taylor, Rocco Sisto, and Will Patton in **What Did He See?**
(Photo by Martha Swope)

WHAT DID
HE SEE?

◆

What Did He See? is a kind of spiritual autobiography; the most nakedly autobiographical of all my plays. For me, the center of the play is the scene at the end in which Rocco Sisto asks Will Patton what he does with himself, and Will says, "Nothing." Will talks about retiring, to loaf and invite his soul, as it were, though he's not exactly a Whitmanesque character. That last scene should exude an autumnal atmosphere in which two mature men, sad and bitter, sit, leaning on their canes with world-weary elegance, shooting verbal darts at each other in the gentlest tones possible. I wanted them to be genteel, sophisticated yet ruthless, battle-scarred tigers. One man is saying: I've seen it all, I'm retiring, because now I understand it's all for naught. The other man, though he has also come to realize that a life of striving leads nowhere, tells him, You're copping out. Rocco taunts Will with calculated accusations of cowardice. To me, that scene *was* the play: how to deal with the realization that the goals you work

toward aren't worth a candle, while nonetheless understanding that giving up is morally unacceptable.

I once thought that the theater offered a greater challenge
than other arts to someone like myself trying to express a
specific philosophical program, because the theater is three-
dimensional, concrete, and takes place in real time. It's one
thing to make a sketch on a piece of paper and draw little
squiggles that indicate, for instance, the granular nature of
the universe, but to make a similar idea resonate in 3-D,
concrete, close-to-real-life theater: *now that was something!*
Much later, around the time I was writing *The Cure*, I
began to think differently. I came to think that concreteness
and closeness to life were the very things that may be
undesirable about the theater. I wondered, is it really desirable that an artist emphasize, by working in the theater,
that rush toward the concrete which is the fall into matter,
in Gnostic terms? I wondered if it wasn't counterprod-
uctive for me to make a theater that preached a spirituality
akin to Rilke's "bees of the invisible," while manifesting
it in an inherently non-spiritual, material form? I realized
that, logically, the next step was to consider: might it be
better to contemplate my own ideas without the ego-
involvement that comes when you try to turn them into
an artistic commodity, like a play? Perhaps it would be
better to invest my energy, as Duchamp said in a late
interview, in the simple joys of breathing!

The dialogue for *What Did He See?* was inspired by
memories of two older men I'd known in Paris, both of
whom had retired. These two men made no bones about
the fact that they had led adventurous lives, but now chose
to practice only the art of savoring each day as it passed.
I found them fascinating, far more interesting than most
of the famous French artists and intellectuals I'd met. And
I was wondering, would I ever be like them? Was I like

them now? And why wouldn't that be a proper ideal to pursue? These are the questions at the center of the play.

Much of the material in *What Did He See?* were direct statements to myself about what I realized I was feeling— that I'd like to retire, I'm sick of the theater. At the same time I feel guilty because I'm constantly hearing about how productive I am, but I really don't think I work very hard. I lie around the house all day, reading, writing a few notes. Wow, I'm on vacation all the time.

I'm allowed this passive state because my situation is, in terms of twentieth-century life, almost an aristocratic one: like Proust's, you could say. I have to worry some about the realities of life, but not nearly as much as most people. And in my work I can't lie about my situation. In trying to be honest about my particular angle on the world, I recognize that I produce an art that reflects a relatively isolated position. This leaves my work open to an attack similar to the kind Sartre made against Mallarmé's kind of poetry: though it may be interesting, its relevance is limited by the fact that it represents the position of someone who is able to retreat to an ivory tower. But *What Did He See?* also deals with the personal guilt that follows any form of escapism. You always ask yourself: am I making enough of a social contribution? What does this kind of retreat do to the mind and body? Does the particular passivity one invites in order to write as I do end up softening the brain? Does it soften the body—because I lie around a lot when I'm reading and writing? Does it soften the body, which ends up softening the brain? And is this reclusive strategy a way of cheating on yourself as well as on the world, which in its social manifestations leads you to believe that you are obligated from birth to be an intermeshed, inter-locked part of the social unit?

There are many cultural traditions that have encouraged

men to leave society, to become monks, and to have less to do with people—to follow a path that will, they hope, lead to another level of self, or God, or whatever a particular tradition proposes in his place. But Western twentieth-century culture has virtually eliminated that choice as a viable option; it's still possible, but it's completely marginalized. In our world, the choice to pursue a reclusive life of the spirit leads to great internal conflicts, and that is the subject of *What Did He See?* Because it is an *internal* conflict, it wouldn't have the appropriate resonance if it was dramatized in a conventional way—had I invented a social confrontation which such a choice might create, for instance. So, the form of the play is lyric rather than dramatic. It's structured as a poem rather than as a story, engendering theme and variations rather than conflict and resolution.

Normally, drama presents people in a moment of crisis as they suddenly come face-to-face with a problem, and then follows them as they work in some fashion to resolve it. In life, however, though you occasionally face that sort of crisis, most of your time is spent being unable to identify for yourself what your real problems actually are, to say nothing about the goals you might pursue to solve them. What interests me is not the special moment of crisis exploited by normal drama, but the everyday tension of human life—how a given human consciousness orients itself to its everyday circumstances; how it makes its moves, step by step, in response to the tiniest fluctuations in its environment.

The language of the play contained more direct psychological content than I had ever included before, which enabled the actors to relate to the text in a more conventional way, and as a result *What Did He See?* was the most conventionally naturalistic of all my plays in performance.

Even though it's presented in an unconventional context, the actors were able to give their roles the same kind of psychological commitment they would when performing in a normal play. One of Will's scenes, for instance, begins, "Tropes of tiredness and sloth. . . . Lattice-like afternoon vistas of light." While it's certainly not Chekhovian naturalism, it does have a flavor of Byronic romantic drama. Here's Byron, wandering onstage, played by Will Patton, who is a powerful actor from the psychological school of theater. He looks around his castle, then into a mirror at his haggard face and says, "Tropes of tiredness and sloth . . ." Then he looks at the late afternoon light streaming in through the window and says, "afternoon vistas of light." It's just like romantic drama. And I'm sure Will invented a secret scenario for himself so that his journey through the play might seem to have a linear progression. That's what Kate used to do all the time, too, though the many plays she was in didn't lend themselves to it nearly as easily as *What Did He See?*

When I was selecting the material that made up the play, I found it quite similar to *The Cure* in terms of the physical atmosphere it suggested and the qualities of consciousness that filled it; nor does it seem to me very different from *Lava*, though these plays may appear to come from very different worlds. But the specifics of the production are all up for grabs until I decide where the play will be staged and who will be in it. These choices determine which of several potential directions the productions will be pulled in. The text gets pulled after the production.

What Did He See? was unique for me, though what happened would have been standard procedure in most American theaters. A week into rehearsal, after I had blocked the whole play, we had our first run-through— and it was just awful. I mean, *my* work was dreadful. I

started again from the top, but I quickly realized that I had
a group of actors who could only fulfill their potential if
they were given the freedom to feel their way through the
play, something I usually would never allow. But I told
them, Let's go through it again, and this time do whatever
you want. They were pretty familiar with the play at this
point, they had a sense of what the play was about, who
they were, and what was going on. So when they were
told they could do whatever they wanted, while they automatically gravitated to some of the things I had set up,
they also introduced a great deal of their own movement.
I kept most of what they did on their first attempt; they
rarely got a second chance to try different blocking, because, on the whole, I found their first instincts to be the
truest. When we tried to change it, it didn't seem as real.
Certain sections of the play I did restage many times until
I was satisfied, but more than fifty percent of the production was molded by the three actors' intuitive choices.

This resulted in a much more conventional, naturalistic
performance style, as you might expect. Not that there
weren't many abstract and disassociative theatrical elements in the production, but they were side by side with
the psychological performance style of the actors. For most
of the plays I direct, while I control every moment of the
blocking, I've never concerned myself with trying to re-
make a performer into my image of the role he or she is
performing. I cast the most interesting people I can find,
and then, within the blocking I've arranged, I allow them
to discover for themselves how to execute my instructions.
Not that I don't work with them to clarify aspects of what
they're doing, not that I don't ask for certain emotional
choices rather than others, but I've never urged an actor
to develop a deeper or different character than the one he
or she spontaneously presents. The role of the director is

to decide which aspects of the performance he's going to control and which aspects he isn't. The final production is a dialectical interaction between the options of control and noncontrol, just as a painter might let his paint drip sloppily on the canvas while his conscious artistic control is exercised instead on other elements of the composition. Late Picasso said, in effect, the drips are something I *don't* want to control. That interaction between control and "irresponsibility" is an important part of any art that doesn't end up dryly academic. No director can control every molecule of a production. People often forget this, and because they see me controlling aspects of the performance that directors usually don't pay attention to, they think: my God, he's a control freak, a dictator. But, by the same token, I barely interfere with aspects of the performance like the details of the actor's imaginary inner world, à la Stanislavsky. Of course, I will speak to an actor about such concerns, if that's what he or she needs or desires. But apart from the contingencies of a particular production, I choose to apply my attention elsewhere.

When writing *What Did He See?* as usual I had no idea who was talking line by line, and it was only after I found actors who interested me that I looked at the script to decide who would say what. The assignment of lines could have been entirely different, but, as it turned out, the characters approached comedia-style archetypes. It happened that Will began to emerge as a recherché recluse, a romantic figure, who was also a little Lord Fauntleroy in a bathrobe. He sat on a throne. He was an artist of some sort, but one who had grave doubts about the validity of making art, and dreamed of retiring. Essentially, Will was me imagining myself as the hero of a novel by Huysman. Rocco played a sailor, an earthier figure committed to aggressively barreling his way through life, someone who thought a man's role was to grow up and join the army, or in his case, the navy. He stood in for one of the several people from my past who told me to get down from my ivory tower, or to join the army. And Lili Taylor was the eternal innocent, yet tough, agent of transformation, who belongs to the real world, but in an idiosyncratic manner that implies the real world might be a crucible for transformation, rather than a prison for received forms. This was the archetypal role that Kate played in so many of my plays, before she retired from acting.

As I write this, however, I wonder if it's right to draw attention to this aspect of the play, because if an audience were told that they're going to see a play about a reclusive poet who meets a young, sexy, free spirit and a drunken sailor, both of whom urge him out into the real world, they'd find that plenty of expectations aroused along those lines would not be fulfilled. It would be a false lead. In spite of its classic theatrical elements, this play was still dominated by the nonrealistic circulation of impulse, idea, and impression that dominate all my other plays. It would be a mistake, therefore, to suggest that the classic tendencies in this play were anything more than passing allusions to such things. Simply a whiff, an aroma of poetic realism. Whatever use the play makes of realism, or of characterological types, are only a "playing with" these conceptual notions. The play is just taking advantage of some of the raw material that is floating about in our culture. I would like to see my plays touch base with every possible aesthetic tendency. *What Did He See?* invaded the world of normal, actor-oriented, psychological theater—which is simply another one of the many trinkets produced by our heterogeneous culture, sitting there on the shelf to be taken down and exploited for whatever ends we wish.

I realized that once I gave the actors the freedom I did,

the audience would relate to the play more empathetically than I would have liked, and the comedia-type characters they played only strengthened that tendency. But at the same time I was able to play with that empathy, using all kinds of distancing techniques. As usual, there were the famous strings across the stage between the actors and the audience. And, as usual, I directed the lights into the audience's eyes. In addition, for this production, three days before opening night I erected a glass wall between the audience and the stage. At a late run-through, something seemed wrong; I realized the empathy the performers aroused was not being fulfilled by the text. The problem was there was no payoff for those feelings of involvement that the actors did evoke, and as a result, they seemed removed—which I didn't mind—but directionless. After a night of agonizing, I concluded I should radicalize that removed feeling. I erected a large glass wall between the actors and the audience as a tactic to remind the spectators that the play was something to be *observed* rather than entered. Even if the performance style was totally seductive, I wanted them to savor that seductiveness, to observe it, rather than try and become involved in it. And the glass wall did the trick.

There were many moments in *What Did He See?* in which Will regresses to a childlike state. For instance, at one point he becomes the buoy boy, dressed as an ocean buoy bobbing on the ocean, which seemed quite nursery-roomlike to me. Sections of the text were pure nonsense speech, childlike babble, in Lewis Carroll style. Sound took predominance over sense in those sections, like the scene in which they talk about "Gippying my guppers." In the production at the Public Theater, those lines were staged to relate to something that, with phallic overtones, had to do with Will's feet. He was wearing red socks, and he pointed to them during those lines, which associated those nonsense phrases with infantile relations to the body, and the poetic qualities such associations evoke.

Throughout the performance, free play was given to the regressive desire of a return to childhood. There was one scene—I cut it from the final production for structural reasons—in which Will has a dream about how all the great writers of the world, sensing the end of the world was near, decided that they would only write stories for children. That feeling was very much present while I was working on *What Did He See?* It was essentially an innocent children's story for grownups; grownups who were, one hoped, still children.

The play also has an apocalyptic quality. Several times during the performance the actors rushed to short poles with handles on top that stood in the middle of the stage, and they spun them around as if cranking a giant machine. It was the kind of frantic, seemingly pointless activity one imagines taking place just before the world blows up. Then, at the end of the play, Will goes back to one of those handles, turns it round and round and says, in effect, everything's wonderful, everything's terrible—laughing and crying at the same time. What more is there to do or say, as the still unenlightened human race goes out, not with a bang, but a whimper. It's appropriate to think of Eliot's *The Waste Land*, for the play evokes the twilight of the West—specifically the twilight of the West as we try to be reborn as children. Either twilight would turn into a new dawn, or it would be indeed a final night. I thought of the play as deeply autumnal in that sense, with the childlike imagery and strategies as an attempt at rebirth.

What Did He See? was first produced by the Ontological-Hysteric Theater at the Public Theater in New York City on October 11, 1988, with the following cast:

Will Patton
Rocco Sisto
Lili Taylor

The production was directed and designed by Richard Foreman; lights by Anne Militello; stage manager David Herskovits.

Rocco Sisto, Will Patton, and Lili Taylor in What Did He See? *(Photo by Martha Swope)*

A room full of strange objects, tapestrylike hangings, and walls covered with pictures and flowers. A short flight of steps leads up to a throne of sorts. Center stage are three poles coming up from the floor, each with a handle on an outstretched arm so the actors can revolve them in either direction, as if winding up a large mechanism beneath the floor. There are also a few pillars at the sides, and carpets covering the floor. Between the audience and the stage hang glass panels through which the audience sees the play—it also sees the faint reflection of its own presence. The colors are somber but glowing, as if this were the retreat of an eccentric Renaissance poet, though the time and place are the present. Throughout the play the actors speak quietly and intimately; in the original production they wore body microphones which made this possible.

As the play begins, a voice is heard over the loudspeakers. At the same time, we see a young woman, LILI, *dressed in a childlike white frock, playing quietly with a large rubber ball on the carpet.* ROCCO, *a dissolute sailor, enters from the side, looking offstage into the light as if he had just come away from some sort of bad experience. He is not necessarily dressed as a sailor, perhaps only wearing a beat-up captain's hat. Soft music floats in the background.*

VOICE: *(Deeply ironic)* Try looking at it this way. Everyone thinks of himself as a sailor of life's wide seas. But does a sailor navigate, really? Or does the ocean of life control totally his adventure? Sometimes one discovers one's route through mental powers, but other times it's simply . . . the blind dictates of the heart.

ROCCO: We sailors have feeling too y'know. Maybe you don't believe it, but we sure as hell have feelings.

LILI: I believe you. I've known some sailors with feelings.

ROCCO: Real feelings?

LILI: Yeah, but mostly they were younger.

ROCCO: Of course, and I know the kind you mean. In reality, what you're talkin' about is teenagers.

LILI: What I'm talkin' about is sailors.

ROCCO: Teenage sailors. They're around here, paradin' a certain kind of feelings, but not the kinda feelings I'm talkin' about.

LILI: Oh yeah? For a guy your age you come on pretty strong.

ROCCO: And you? Just tryin' to be difficult. I know the kind.

LILI: What do you know about my kind? Nothin' hot on toast.

ROCCO: Sure, sure, tryin' to be difficult.

LILI: Sure I am tryin' to be difficult. Here I am dealin' with a very difficult circumstance, don't you think?

ROCCO: Let me turn everything upside-down nice. Try comin' with me this afternoon?

LILI: I got things to do. I got certain commitments.

ROCCO: Who in particular?

LILI: I don't know that ahead of time.

ROCCO: I'm angry.

LILI: I go to a lot of meetings. I find out later.

VOICE: Who in particular?

ROCCO: (Recovering from being startled by the voice on tape, he comes close to LILI, seductively) An angry sailor is talkin' to you, sayin' come with me this afternoon. I love kids.

LILI: I love kids too.

ROCCO: You know what I'm gonna do when we get back to my place? I'm gonna disconnect all the electricity and teach you how to read secret messages by candle-light.

LILI: I think secrets are kinda scary.

ROCCO: Remember, I love kids.

LILI: Is that how you think a me? Really?

ROCCO: Really. So how about it, kid?

LILI: If I did come with you in particular and somethin' happened—in particular . . .

ROCCO: Somethin' like what?

LILI: Just somethin'. Who'd be to blame? You? Or me . . .

ROCCO: I think we're talkin' about me.

LILI: *(Shouting at him)* So who's really more pathetic, tell me about it!

ROCCO: I don't follow, which sounds like it's for some-body else to be listening.

LILI: Sure it's meant for somebody else to be listening. That's why I'm goin' to my meetin's, even though you wanna stop me from goin' to my meetin's.

ROCCO: I know what kinda meetings are those meetin's an' lemme tell you, I don't need them.

LILI: Everybody needs them.

ROCCO: Not me, kiddo.

LILI: You could make some personal improvements too, I do suppose. *(She goes and pulls back the edge of a tapestry, urging him to look behind)*

ROCCO: *(Clearly not wanting to look)* Along with who else in particular? I don't need that stuff in there.

LILI: You need it most of anybody I seen around here for a long time, and especially somebody like you in the NAVY.

ROCCO: Listen, we sailors got feelings.

(He works up his courage and plunges behind the tapestry)

LILI: *(Calling after him)* Okay. What's inside the tent?

ROCCO: *(Swinging back into the room at the end of a heavy rope)* You know who else I seen in here?

LILI: Yeah, but I want to hear it from you.

ROCCO: Fuck off, kiddo.

(He swings back out of the room)

LILI: Ohhhhh—I think what I just heard is some kinda sailor language!

VOICE: Alternatively, he who represents himself as at best an armchair adventurer, thinks—self-revelation is the best policy. But what's revealed sometimes smothers itself amid multiple impulsive gesticulations.

(As the VOICE speaks, WILL slowly enters and leans sadly against a pillar. He is dressed in a red brocade bathrobe, red silk pajamas underneath, and wears a red sleeping cap. He also wears white gloves. His face is pale. He looks toward the tapestry ROCCO has disappeared behind, and then into empty space)

WILL: Hard to believe. He walked into the tomb all by himself.

LILI: *(Crossing to peer at WILL)* What are you talkin' about a tomb when I say tent?

WILL: Not a tent.

LILI: What are you talkin' about?

WILL: Tropes of tiredness and sloth.

LILI: What are you talkin' about?

WILL: Lattice-like afternoon vistas of light. *(He suddenly rushes offstage with unexpected energy, then immediately reappears from another entrance, carrying a very large mirror in a gold frame. The minute he returns, he again seems to be dreaming)* In a mirror? Of course. An ancient theme. There's nothing in a mirror . . . but a reflection. Let's be very exact? I hope so. *(LILI takes the mirror from him, and magically he seems to be holding a book instead)* I am reading, am I not, the philosopher . . . HEGEL. *(The book falls from his hands)* Why . . . this lassitude? This . . . energylessness? I dislike people, yet . . .

LILI: I know, I know. You gotta have them around just for gettin' a little energy once in a while, huh.

WILL: But why? How silly really. To need other people for such purposes. *(He talks to himself)* Okay. What purposes?

LILI: *(Positioning the mirror on the floor, tilting it back a bit, trying to catch Will's image)* Look what I got here, Paul. See anything special?

VOICE: Pull the self . . . into the distortion.

WILL: That's . . . the religious life. That's why I'm one hundred percent, dressed like this. *(ROCCO has returned rear, holding something that looks like a tiny, illuminated stage. He peers at WILL over the top of this ministage as WILL speaks to the glass wall, and to the audience beyond.)* Theater . . . religion . . . isomorphic. That's why I'm dressed like this. Man, you see, can be other than man . . . in an other than human environment. You see? *(WILL slowly backs into a center doorway which is festooned with leaves and fruit)* So please, pull me . . . into the distortion. Please. Please. *(Pointing casually to an apple)* Have something to eat.

LILI: Tell me, your royal highness—What do you think you will find at the center of this great silence you pursue so assiduously?

WILL: I will find that I am still king, absolute sovereign.

ROCCO: *(Rolling his eyes)* La de dah.

WILL: I have to tell the truth. I no longer . . . function like a normal human being.

LILI: Oh?

WILL: It's not that I'm no longer, in fact, a human being. I am a human being, but I'm different.

ROCCO: La de dah.

WILL: Aspects . . . have taken me to another level of reality, in fact. *(He races up to his throne, again carrying his large mirror)* Is it not said by scholars, correctly I must assume, that the roots of theater lie in religious ritual? That means, if it means something specific—

ROCCO: Semispecific.

WILL: Semi?

ROCCO: Semi!

WILL: That means, if it means something specific, man's hunger to transcend the ordinary human condition.

VOICE: "Human . . . condition."

ROCCO: And you believe that you can perform such an act of transcendence?

WILL: Not completely. But my hunger . . . stretches me in that direction.

ROCCO: *(Staring at WILL on his throne)* How irrelevant . . . to think of oneself as mere royalty. *(Pause)* Correct. How irrelevant.

WILL: *(Still with his giant mirror)*
What's in a mirror?
Nobody knows, really.
What's a better way to live?
Nobody knows. Nobody really knows.
That's what's tearing me up inside.
Find out
What—

ROCCO: *(Circling the room, dreamily)* Nobody knows, nobody knows, nobody knows! *(He turns and points to WILL)* I'm speaking to you directly. I'm asking Paul—

WILL: I'm not Paul.

ROCCO: *(Suddenly aggressive)*—to imagine the noon sun

in a cloudless sky. Pull back the curtains that cover the window of an individual human soul.

WILL: I see no windows.

ROCCO: You, sir.

LILI: *(She has been walking in circles, now she butts in)* I'm not Paul.

ROCCO: *(Ignoring LILI)* Imagine the sun that blinds is honey. And the swirls of the active imagination are the bees that collect that honey. And the flower, where does one postulate that flower?

WILL: Let my nose lead me. *(And he touches his nose)*

VOICE: Nose.

ROCCO: *(Stabbing WILL with his finger)* Look into the collective eye, your highness. But of course, you're already doing that.

WILL: I'm making myself available.

ROCCO: Not likely, son of a bitch.

WILL: The human being heated by the blinding sun. Assuming the human being exposes himself to its rays. Willingly or unwillingly. They issue forth. Correct?

ROCCO: Correct. Son of a bitch.

(ROCCO and LILI race offstage, leaving WILL alone with his mirror)

WILL: If I could have a real mirror, for a whole night of intense reflection.
Then.
I'd be alone with it.
Truly.
And whatever poured into that mirror would be . . .
things
that then found themselves first in ME.
Then, and only then
I would be . . .

founded
mirrorlike
during the daylight hours.
So that one could say
blessed by the sun
so that when night did fall—
which I can achieve either by closing my eyes
or by disappearing from this room
or by waiting for the earth itself to revolve. . . .
And it does
revolve, oh it does, if you
wait for it. Just WAIT for it.
Is that what I implied—without even knowing the cast
of my
own thought?

(Most of the play has been underscored with soft, romantic musical phrases, but now the music shifts to a happy, childlike march. As the others reappear, WILL goes to one of the posts with a handle as if to start spinning it. The others race to the other two posts. Then they all change posts. Finally everyone is revolving the handles at a lively rate to the music)

VOICE: *(As the music fades, and they all slow their revolving of the handles to a stop)* Try thinking of it like this: if the earth does revolve, who's best at accompanying those revolutions? He who does revolve, or he who revolves not, or he who revolves defectively, and therefore productively, though at very great cost?

LILI: *(She has exited and reappeared with a puppet on a string—an elegant Victorian doll—a version of herself? She manipulates the puppet as if it was addressing WILL)* You, spectator, must perform only those actions for which you have a clear explanation. Does this room . . .

WILL: *(Looking at the puppet)* Is it still a room, in fact?

LILI: Yes. *(Pause)* Does this room look in any way familiar to you?

WILL: Yes.

LILI: Very familiar?

WILL: *(Pause)* Yes. Very.

LILI: You must have been here before.

WILL: *(Pause; he looks at her)* There's no answer to your question without hurting you.

LILI: Why?

WILL: You expect great things from me. But that's hardly to your advantage.

LILI: That's an excuse.

WILL: *(He begins to raise a hand)* Here's an excuse.

LILI: Wait a minute! Were you about to hit me? You missed. *(Pause)* You can't believe you missed. Because you're so strong. *(She slaps him)*

WILL: A violent man . . .

LILI: Is that you?

WILL: *(Running back to sit on his throne)* with no reason to take a reasonable vacation, ended up working his mental and emotional fingers to the bone.

LILI: Were you about to hit somebody?

WILL: Not this time.

ROCCO: *(Reentering)* Okay Paul, I know you can read time . . .

LILI: But can you read . . . universal time?

ROCCO: *(Pause)* I know you can read local time, but can you read time?

LILI: Didn't I already ask?

WILL: I thought I did.

ROCCO: Okay Paul—you seem to live outside of time. How do you do it with such pizzaz?

WILL: *(He comes down from his throne and offers his hand)* It's effortless. Join me. *(Pause)* Are you afraid to take my hand?

ROCCO: Yes. Everybody's afraid of the unknown.

WILL: That's why I'm keeping them hidden behind my body.

ROCCO: Everybody's afraid of the unknown. Yes. *(He turns to leave)*

LILI: *(Approaching WILL with both hands behind her back)* Choose. Which hand is really hidden.

ROCCO: *(As if he's been slapped while exiting)* Oww!

WILL: The right hand is really hidden.

LILI: *(Not revealing her hands)* Wrong.

WILL: What's happening now?

ROCCO: *(He reenters with two ice cream cones)* I'm happening. I'm happening with my snacks.

WILL: I'm out in the cold.

ROCCO: That's kid stuff.

WILL: I'm not a kid.

(A childish five-note phrase played on a glockenspiel is heard over the loudspeakers)

VOICE: Don't be childish, when it's so much more productive to let invisible energies enter the insatiable infant, infinitely . . . inside.

ROCCO: *(Hiding his cones behind his back)* Okay. Say the first thing that comes into your head.

WILL: Vanilla.

ROCCO: *(Smiling seductively as he shows the cones to WILL)* I thought you'd never ask.

WILL: I've come to the disturbing conclusion that self-realization, the desirable goal, of course, cannot be achieved. Unless I reduce my social contacts to a minimum.

ROCCO: Danger . . .

WILL: I know there's danger. But within the social arena, the multiple influences of vanity are such—

ROCCO: All the better when things get a little tough. *(He exits)*

WILL: All the more impossible when it's tough.

LILI: *(She has run up and is climbing about on WILL's throne)* Hey Paul, do you remember the story of the well-known Buddhist monk, Miyo-ko-ko-roko, who spent maybe a hundred years alone on a mountaintop to get calm and peaceful, and then, the first time back, he goes into the marketplace and gets bumped around by a couple of tough kids. Wow, did he fly off the handle! So what happened to the calm and peaceful he was supposed to be into on a full-time basis?

WILL: Objection number one to your story.

LILI: Oh, I bet I heard it a million times.

WILL: Miyo-ko-ko-roko, the clown, should never have come down from his mountaintop.

ROCCO: *(He returns wearing dark glasses, a man's felt hat, and a prayer shawl of an indeterminate kind. He holds two thin sticks, each with a cotton swab at the end. He slides up behind WILL and, from behind, holds out the sticks on either side of WILL's body)* He had to come down from his mountaintop.

WILL: He didn't have to.

LILI: *(Pause)* The word is, he had to come down from his mountaintop *(She runs to WILL. Referring to ROCCO)* Doctor Marino goes into a trance, Paul. That's why I asked him to come here. I thought it would really interest you.

WILL: Oh?

LILI: You're being noncommittal. I know. Because your hold on reality is slippery.

WILL: Not at all.

(As they continue, ROCCO slowly brings the cotton swabs up into contact with WILL'S face. They seem to cause him discomfort as he slowly twists into a distorted position)

LILI: I understand that . . . from the human race you wish to withdraw, but Doctor Marino has come in order to make your life so difficult . . . that you will find yourself . . . reinvolved.

WILL: *(Still contorted)* Do you understand . . . why I am considering such a withdrawal? The normal way of life, which is no longer possible, suits me, but is no longer possible. The normal relationship between a man and a woman—

LILI: Do you hallucinate the word "normal" while in the midst of doing other tasks?

WILL: Nothing special. The normal. The ordinary. I want . . . some passion. But considerable fidelity—all that. Not much to ask, really. The normal things.

LILI: Is it normal that the light streaming from the inside of a story you want to tell me is so bright?

WILL: How bright?

ROCCO: There's a proposal to be made.

WILL: Tell me, how bright?

ROCCO: *(He slowly releases WILL from his sticks)* What you must do is . . . what's proposed . . . is to return now to the earliest childhood memory and to stay completely in the world of that memory. Then having sunk your consciousness into that memory, view the material that arises in the here and now, from the position of that earliest childhood memory. You will experience with clarity what might otherwise seem contradictory, ambiguous, and elusive.

WILL: This is no problem for me. I've always wanted to

return . . . imaginatively—except imagination is the
wrong word. It lacks the requisite . . . ruthlessness.

ROCCO: *(Pause)* What do you suppose would be—

WILL: What's for dinner tonight?

LILI: *(She has slid out of the room, and now returns carrying
a strange object, a gold ball to which are attached spoons and
forks. She holds it out toward WILL)* What's wrong with
you, Paul? If you can tell time, you can tell it's too early
to think about dinner.

WILL: What time is it? *(He grabs the ball)* NOW!

LILI: Now.

ROCCO: Good point.

WILL: *(Turns to ROCCO)* "Now?"

LILI: *(Backing away)* I have no idea what's happening to
Paul while he's watching what goes on under his nose.

WILL: *(He comes forward, staring at the ball)* Dappled sunlight . . . latticelike, as I moved through afternoon vistas
of light, traveling into an unfamiliar section of the city
—flickering under my eyesight, from the height of an
omnibus transporting me through my own visionary
field. I mean, traveling, seemingly, in a giant structure
on two separate levels.

ROCCO: Ah, double-decker giant omnibus of somebody's little boyness, red, perhaps, with intricate semi-
Victorian complexity.

WILL: Someone with white hair, who loves me very
much, seated beside me but seeing not what I am
seeing—even, at the end of this red vessel's journey. As
I glide, as if on skates, but I was a stranger to skates,
into a large grey and silver room with tables and chairs
and light fixtures reflected in the many large windows.
Many, many, many, many gentle ladies in warm fur
coats . . . seated at individual tables with white table-
cloths supporting polished silverware, an entire roomful

of potential grandmothers to the young child, myself. But only one being so, of course . . . in faint fragrance, amid the fur, and the dappled light doing itself to my consciousness.

LILI: Doing what?

(She exits)

WILL: Evoking the memory in a specific way. Something that seemed so . . . unfathomable, so contradictory, it had to be explained to me. I was told that what I saw, and it was across the white tablecloth, though it seemed much farther than across what was a table—an ocean . . . ?

LILI: *(She returns carrying a glass globe, inside of which is a toy boat on a sea of cotton)* Go on.

WILL: *(Gently taking the globe from LILI)* A round, pure globule of white vanilla ice cream. I had not tasted at that age what for many years after seemed to me mysteriously attuned to adult taste buds only. Vanilla. Vanilla ice cream, in fact, but presented to me on this first occasion in what seemed to be precise ice cream slices. Which I cannot believe I have only in later years imagined, those slices of ice cream covered completely with a smooth, thick, and—unimaginable to me—hot, HOT, liquid chocolate syrup.

ROCCO: *(Quietly, full of insinuation)* Indeed. If the ice cream itself was covered with this hot syrup, how did you know that the ice cream was, in fact, beneath?

WILL: I don't know what I perceived.

ROCCO: I think I know how you discovered it, Paul. *(Pause)* As the lady across from you . . . bit into the covered ice cream—

LILI: *(Mocking ROCCO)* Oh, la de dah . . .

ROCCO: *(Quietly ecstatic)* A white glimpse, showed for a moment.

WILL: Has time stopped? *(Pause)* Of course, in one sense it hasn't. Hot and cold, I could not put those two . . . temperatures into one . . . unit. *(He lifts the globe, looks up at it, and sings gently)* "Somewhere, over the rainbow . . ."

ROCCO: Shut up, Paul!

(Nursery rhyme music is heard and they perform, very formally, with dance steps and hand movement, a kind of poem)

LILI: He went to town, where he fell down, and tried to brush his hair.
The ladies on the sidewalk said, You've lost it—who knows where.
While men who had the dogs in tow said, "Hurry, when they bark
The ship that sails tomorrow night is ready to embark."

ROCCO: He hurried to the giant pier where piles of dust were stored
And watched as giant stevedores began to load on board
The contents of his pockets which he soon turned inside out
Then wanted to reclaim his toys when someone warned "Don't shout."

WILL: And so he drifted back to town amazed at what he'd seen.
His friends no longer called to him, his hands were much too clean.
And when he went to bed that night, he pledged, "I will not sleep.
For should I shut my eyes, I lose that boat that travels deep."

LILI: So all that night he did the job of staying wide awake.

He never left his bedroom though his mighty bed did
quake.

WILL: And when the day returned at last and asked him
where he'd been . . .

ROCCO: He sealed his lips and crossed his hands and held
his secret . . . IN!

WILL: *(The music stops. He holds his fingers up to the golden
light)* The hour of embarkation, he imagines, as the hour
of . . . right now, which none of these fingers ever
touches.

ROCCO: Ah, he tells time with his fingers. How childlike.
How daring!

WILL: *(As the light builds to blinding brightness)*
Our fingers shine!
Our fingers shine!
Our fingers multiple and fine!

VOICE: *(As the VOICE tells its story, a life-sized brown bear
appears, wearing a crown and carrying a large cardboard box.
LILI, unaware, goes to the throne and appears to fall asleep as
if she were a child being told a bedtime story)* Shining? Performing additional tasks perhaps? And the shining fingers are perhaps fingers from which flow stories, written
in a personal hand that scratches slow heartache over
these yellowing pages. Till a strange thing begins happening, because all the stories that are told seem finally
to have reached every possible conclusion, which means
that the real stories no longer look like stories. So that
finally, when the big brown bear at last takes down from
the shelf his stuffed cardboard box and carries it slowly
across the carpet, everyone knows secretly that what's
inside the story box isn't the real past, or the real future,
but just one more collection of goodies masquerading
as all that serious business . . . from a long ago childhood.

WILL: *(He has slowly crossed to look at the bear, and takes the
box)* Somehow, I think I've screwed up.

ROCCO: What's the reference point?

WILL: I have a package that was supposed to go on the boat in question.

ROCCO: No problem.

WILL: *(Sits)* Oh, there's a problem.

ROCCO: What problem?

WILL: I've still got it. On my lap. *(Pause)* I'm still in possession.

ROCCO: Lucky you.

WILL: Why?

ROCCO: Think about it, Paul. Would it have been judicious to send a package on an unknown vessel?

LILI: *(Sits up)* I don't see no vessel.

ROCCO: With an unknown destination?

WILL: I'd rather pretend I didn't hear the question.

ROCCO: Of course, because for you, time has stopped.

WILL: Tell me the secret.

ROCCO: You know it already. *(WILL reaches into the box and extracts a white fur coat, which then he hugs to his body)* You just made it happen.

WILL: Tell me something genuinely . . . RAVISHING, about the slices of . . . white vanilla ice cream that are hidden from me.

LILI: Where does chocolate sauce come from, Paul?

WILL: Bears.

ROCCO: Wrong.

WILL: Bears make chocolate, which they steal from honeybees in their beehives.

LILI: What's in the box, on the floor?

WILL: *(Putting it on)* A fur coat. *(He steps away from them, and looks into space)* When bears steal chocolate they don't think of themselves as stealing chocolate. But rather, as collecting chocolate for a world which, to them, remains sunk in invisibleness. What can I tell you? The ice . . . was cold. Like ice. *(His voice changes as he imitates a bear)*

Thank you for telling me the ice was like ice. *(He returns to himself)* In fact, I have snatched something from the jaws of the divine beast. Then . . . he will eat me up.

ROCCO: Difficult dreams to navigate, buoy boy.

WILL: I'm eaten, but I'm eating.

ROCCO: Of course, it's a circular ocean, buoy boy.

WILL: Just getting my bearings maybe.

LILI: What's bobbin' up and down on big waves like a little boy's empty belly, buoy boy?

WILL: *(At the side of the room, from a large cabinet, he takes a little tin box with a decorated cover)* Tiny ice cream cookies in tin boxes
That's what I'm thinking about
As fog . . . rolls in off the ocean.
Cookies, in tin boxes . . .

(As he continues, LILI starts softly singing beneath his speech "By the light of the silvery moon . . .")

Pictures painted on tin
Embossed to reverberate:
Same thing—

LILI: *(Very sleepy)* Same thing.

WILL: Mixed with cellophane wrappers
Tea and tin.

LILI: Tea and tin.

WILL: Tea and tin.

LILI: Nothing fathomable, finally
and call that ocean—

VOICE: *(Finishing the phrase)* Mental fog.

(WILL leaves the stage, eating a cookie)

LILI: Name of that ocean—

VOICE: *(Again)* Mental fog.

LILI: And that has no face.

Thank goodness.
And oh, it's so soft against the skin
Isn't it, mental fog.

(She falls asleep in the throne)

VOICE: Mental fog . . .

(WILL reenters dressed as a flotation buoy, with a kind of tower over his head and a warning bell on top of the crown. He holds two round, stripped, golden side panels that he flaps slowly like wings or fins. ROCCO enters behind a white folding screen that he pushes gently in front of him as he walks, peering over it, as if trying to spy out the buoy across a vast ocean)

ROCCO: *(Intoning the weird pronunciations as if he were a kind of drunken foghorn)* Wander-ful buoy boy
Yer oonly pre-bloom—
Absoonse oce-onic, me-self shall rec-toofee
Vith intell-igence intra-session!
WILL: *(Bellowing out from his confining costume)* HOW DO
THAT GREAT GASSO!
ROCCO: My mind-ly dod-i-cation, availith self of pre-ject
Per-pitr-youal, and ocean-anic, panic, I shall coulm
With trans-port-ation physio-tronic for that
Row-tund what's it, that
You aire. So
June me—ocean-ward.
WILL: *(Waving his panels slowly)* I shall, I shall, I shall.
ROCCO: *(Retreating, with his screen, till he is offstage)* We
shall. We shall.
LILI: *(Waking up, she comes down angrily from her throne)* I
shall not, I shall not, let this whatever it is, calls itself
buoy-boy, get off on the idea being some kinda BEA-
CON for somebody's roller-coaster ride down a main

artery even though it's TEARS filling a private ocean.

WILL: Ah, a night spent dreaming? Maybe. But don't you admit disappearing into a picture is no way to begin a real friendship?

ROCCO: *(Reappearing, normal and nasty)* Then again, don't count on friends, when what you want out of a relationship is something more than a trivial night on the town, metaphorically speaking.

LILI: Sure. Everybody tries turning into a personal lighthouse—but usually they do it by painting pretty pictures that're supposed to pull ya straight through the picture frame!

WILL: I'm a normal man.

(He is quickly extracted from his buoy costume)

ROCCO: In every way?

WILL: In every way.

ROCCO: Your dreams are not normal.

WILL: I don't remember them.

ROCCO: Take my word for it.

WILL: I dreamed . . . I was very elegant. Dressed elegantly. Living an idle and elegant life. *(He holds a small card with different colored squares in front of his face)* A normal fantasy.

ROCCO: No it isn't.

WILL: Try this. I gave up my productive activities.

(He flips the card; the other side is white)

ROCCO: I like the idea. But it stinks.

LILI: *(Comes straight to WILL)* What I'd like you to understand—You ARE king, and you are NOT king. *(Pause)* What do you think you will find at the center of the great silence you pursue so assiduously?

WILL: Do you know what certain people believe in? I will find that I am still king.

LILI: And will that make you happy?

WILL: Yes and no.

(*ROCCO and LILI leave. WILL speaks out front*)

Explain how it happens that at a certain moment in my life, I very distinctly hallucinate two or three wise men, entering my room, who bow down before me and announce that I have been identified as sovereign reincarnate. I accept this information . . . quietly and calmly, hoping that such moderate behavior in the face of great revelation . . . proves . . . something wonderful about my inner being. That part of myself I never, consciously, touch. (*He pauses. Then, as if suddenly startled, he grabs a chair, lifts it over his head, whirling as if to fight off an attacker. But freezes, seeing no attacker. Puts down the chair and laughs, embarrassed*) What happened? What just went past in a blur? I didn't see anything.

LILI: (*She reenters, carrying a golden ball*) I didn't see anything.

WILL: Sure. You had your eagle eye . . .

LILI: (*Grabs his hand*) Look look look
Whose fingers shine
Multiple and fine!

WILL: What are you bringing me? A gold ball? What else is new?

ROCCO: (*Who has reappeared*) Call it the ocean, I suppose—

WILL: Let's stop throwing words around like cream pies and let them kinda FLY BACK to whatever home base they have as a real home base. How about it?

LILI: My mother told me, never have anything to do with a man who's not deep into meaning . . .

WILL: Meaning.

LILI: Meaning.

WILL: He had meaning in his eye, he had meaning in his ear, he had meaning coming out of fists he carried deep in his meaningful pockets!

ROCCO: Oh, la de dah . . .

WILL: The war of meaning. *(Arriving at his throne and sitting)* Could we, in a pinch, punch our way out of this confabulous configuration?

LILI: But why blubber when it's a bother?

ROCCO: *(Waving his hands in the air, speaking to the room in general)* 'Cause I make blubber, buster, when I'm butting in with my blather!

LILI: Make a certain kinda whelp out of it, will ya.

WILL: So we ALL did diddle.

ROCCO: But your version's in the middle, to fiddle and fum.

What kinda fun?

A ghast, man, glum,

So glad to be gone

When it comes to goin', but gorgeous as you get 'um—

Got 'um?

You gorgony uppers are what get my guppers.

WILL: *(Straining in his chair, red-faced as he points to his red socks and slippers)* Get me more guppers!

Get me more guppers!

Get me more guppers!

And get me more guppers!

(He falls off the chair)

Don't be glum!

(He bolts up and leaps off his platform to run and sit in another thronelike chair in the corner)

Get me more guppers

To guppy my uppers

To guppy my uppers
That guppy my gum!
Don't be glum.

ROCCO: *(Strutting across the stage, articulating his moves with a cane he has acquired)* Geppy my glippers
To glippy my glippers
To glap my glup
And glopity glum
Glopity glum, glopity glum
Glopity glum glum glum
Glopity glum!!!

WILL: *(To ROCCO)* You want my help? Sometimes I give it in spoonfuls, but don't let your socks get dirty when I start steppin' out with my aggressive clarity imitations.

ROCCO: Verbal I assume?

WILL: Assume not, 'cause I'm out to protect myself—see? It's no longer a secret.

ROCCO: Really?

WILL: *(Turning away from them, hissing under his breath)*
Martin, Martin
The cream of the crop
What has he got
I don't got?

LILI: It's simple really. You raise your hand once too often, and make a commitment to certain risks—

WILL: I understand that. I made a serious commitment to a spiritually motivated being I never met—you know how many people laughed behind my back? So I made it part of my act.

ROCCO: But you never let me cry on your shoulder, or borrow a wet handkerchief to catch buckets of stuff which did pour out so you didn't know where the hell it was comin' from!

WILL: But I knew.

ROCCO: The truth?

WILL: But I knew.

LILI: Why didn't we know you knew if you knew?

WILL: I was hiding it. *(Pause)* Of course. I was hiding it. So. Why do you think I was hiding it? *(LILI and ROCCO point at WILL)* Hey. What is the answer? Come back but don't listen! *(LILI and ROCCO stop pointing, and exit quickly)* Hidden, the truth is potent. That's why. And now I shall perform a self-destructive gesture of self-renunciation.

ROCCO: *(Returns from another door)* You must be desperate, kid. *(WILL takes a step forward)* Back off.

(WILL stops. He goes to one of the spinning sticks, looks at it, then slowly starts spinning it, and gently sings to soft, ecstatic music as LILI and ROCCO watch in awe)

WILL: *(Singing)* Paradise Drive, Paradise Drive
What's needed, supplied
On Paradise Drive.

(He freezes and speaks to the audience through the glass)

Here's the truth:
Since I've been young
when confronted with a task
I've wanted to get through
that task as quickly as possible,
so that,
freed of the task,
I could again be in a state
of nonactivity.
Outside time?

LILI AND ROCCO: *(Singing softly behind as WILL continues; they quietly spin the handles as they sing)* Paradise Drive, Paradise Drive.

WILL: Resting in place.

Doing . . . Nothing.

Why?

Because perhaps I realized there was no value in producing

anything really.

No value

in letting the impulse of a conditioned, hypnotized person such as my representative self, COAGULATE . . .

into an artifact, into a thing, a task accomplished, or an adventure.

(LILI and ROCCO leave, unnoticed, and WILL is alone)

Because the corruption of my own fallen, conditioned state would be hidden in the center of that THING I would produce no matter how beautiful and seductive that thing might seem. That hidden corruption would separate me, and others, from the true source inside the self.

Alas.

How can I make that "alas" . . . more

believable. More heartrending.

Alas.

That's what's most seductive about me. Be careful. That "alas."

(Pause)

Alas.

(Pause, then he tries again with feeling)

Alas.

(He smiles)

That's another one of my little secrets—"Alas."

(He turns and exits abruptly, but comes back immediately. At the same time, the bear slowly enters from the other side and watches him)

By the way . . . What is the REAL TIME in which I claim to find myself placed? And why this need to solidify such real time in the midst of our shared experience? Turning it into some kind of . . . spectacle? Okay. Strike out irrelevant and foolish questions, because I've already made a fool of myself in giving away my power. Except, giving away one's power is not making a fool of oneself. It depends who's watching.

(He stares at the audience, then turns and stares at the bear. ROCCO returns dressed as an elegant retired gentleman, with hat and cane, and calls out to WILL. As WILL turns to ROCCO, the bear exits. Sad violin music is heard)

ROCCO: What, finally, do you do with your life, sir?
WILL: Nothing.
ROCCO: Ah, nothing. *(Pause. WILL goes to look at a painting hung high on the wall. It portrays the animals entering Noah's ark)* How fortunate, to be a man of leisure. Are you evil, sir?
WILL: *(He turns from the painting to look back at ROCCO)* No, sir.
ROCCO: You've hidden something, haven't you? *(Pause)* Why are you looking at me like that?
WILL: I can explain. It happened six years ago . . .
ROCCO: And you still think about it, sir?
WILL: *(They both slowly sit)* Six years ago . . . in a mundane television interview I was not really following, but rather using as background noise while I was doing something different . . . I heard someone utter the word RADIATE . . . and I was transported. Radiate—that

was the word, and it transformed . . . everything. *(Pause)* That of course explains nothing. But it's a key.

ROCCO: You look satisfied with yourself.

WILL: Shit. *(Pause)* Do I really?

ROCCO: Yes.

WILL: Shit. God damn it . . . shit.

ROCCO: Tell me again. What is it, exactly, you do, sir?

WILL: Nothing.

ROCCO: Ah? *(Pause)* What is your name, sir?

WILL: McCarthy, believe it or not—

ROCCO: *(Cutting him off)* Let's say—not believing anything like McCarthy, sir. *(Pause; they stare at each other)* Tell me, I could be wrong—do windmills make you dizzy, sir?

WILL: Windmills?

ROCCO: Windmills.

WILL: Slightly. Why are you looking at me like that?

ROCCO: Simply trying to plumb your depths, sir.

WILL: "Sir"?

ROCCO: I call you "sir" as a token of my esteem. Remember—it's just a token.

WILL: Did you like the story about the television interview, and what happened to me?

ROCCO: I didn't understand it.

WILL: Oh come now.

ROCCO: No. I didn't.

WILL: What's the best story to tell?

ROCCO: *(Pause)* I couldn't say.

WILL: Come on now.

ROCCO: I couldn't.

WILL: Hiding the truth?

ROCCO: No, sir.

WILL: Very smart. *(Pause)* But I can't seem to help myself. The best story to tell: the reenchantment of the world.

So that everything evokes . . . that metaphysical level for which we all, really do hunger. Do you agree? *(Pause)* I'll try again. Have something to eat. *(Pause; no response from ROCCO)* What's the best story to tell? Well . . . the story that devours itself. Circular . . .

(WILL is wandering about the room. He stops at the cabinet.)

ROCCO: Ah yes. That was my point, sir.

WILL: What's on the cabinet? Where the hell am I? A small windmill. How the hell did it get here? *(He picks up a tiny model of a windmill)* "Here."

VOICE: "Here."

WILL: It's not important how it got here. "Now."

VOICE: "Now. Here—"

WILL: What's important is that it IS here, now. Both aspects have, in this one realm, a kind of significance, I'm sure.

ROCCO: Interesting, you never define what you mean by such a word as "aspects." And the word "realm," sir. And the other . . . "significance" was it?

WILL: *(Turns to ROCCO, smiling)* Well . . . I'm just, suddenly, very sure of myself.

ROCCO: A lot of character does radiate from you, sir. Intermittently.

WILL: Did you say . . . radiance?

ROCCO: Almost.

WILL: I'm not sure, exactly.

ROCCO: Ah, that's one of your favorite phrases.

WILL: Since when?

ROCCO: That time, you used it as a question.

WILL: What?

ROCCO: "Radiance."

WILL: I did, didn't I. Though you shouldn't have said so to my face. Why are you looking at me like that?

ROCCO: Do I blush for you?

WILL: How do you mean?

ROCCO: It's a penetrating look, isn't it? That's because I'm trying to penetrate, to understand your motives.

WILL: Must I have them still?

ROCCO: I think you must. I don't claim you'd always be aware of them—

WILL: Motives . . .

ROCCO: —but at least, in a subliminal sense, a subconscious sense.

WILL: Whereas I'd maintain that if they are subconscious, then I don't have them. Rather THEY have ME.

ROCCO: *(Pause; under his breath)* Son of a bitch. How come you haven't called attention to the fact that my gaze has suddenly become less penetrating?

WILL: *(To himself)* A face appears to me
in a mirror—
and speaks to me
the minute I concentrate,
causing it to radiate
a certain character . . .

ROCCO: Shit. *(He covers his eyes, feels dizzy, and begins to count)* 1–2–3–4–

(He falls heavily to the carpet)

WILL: *(Smiling)* Ah, you're under the impression you also would like to make contact with other levels?

ROCCO: *(Lifting himself, dizzily, from the floor)* What the hell—that's what I'm trying to show!

WILL: Go ahead and show me. *(pause)*

ROCCO: *(Gasping for breath, determinedly)* Here's what I propose. A knock comes on the door. Three wise men enter and say, guess what, fall on their knees, explain that the reincarnation of a deceased spiritual person has been discovered inhabiting MY body.

WILL: What's the best story to tell?

ROCCO: Goddamn it, I'm telling it now!

WILL: I'll try again. What's the best story to tell? Well, the story that devours itself. Circular. *(He starts moving in a circle through the room to faint circus music)* 1–2–3–4– *(He falls heavily to the floor. The music stops.* WILL *speaks, spread out on the carpet)* Welcome to my religion! I prefer to make smart people out of dumb people. Then, I rise with whoever rises.

(He has lifted himself from the carpet)

ROCCO: You mean physical levitation?

LILI: *(She has returned, unnoticed)* Of course not.

WILL: Let me show you a picture of another level of being. *(He has taken a small picture off the wall and displays it to the audience—a bucolic scene of animals in the countryside, painted in naive and delicate style)* Do you recognize this picture?

Of course not.

So I'll ask once again.

Recognize this planet?

(Silence)

A good answer would be—No. But it gives me a very cosmic emotion.

ROCCO: Very good, Paul. You must be letting things pour directly into that big hole-in-the-head I see no-place special between two big blue eyes. But what a strange vehicle for enlightenment.

WILL: *(Turns to* ROCCO*)* How so?

ROCCO: There's a certain vulgarity about you, my boy.

WILL: Of course, since I'm looking into a mirror. But

that's nothing unusual, because the thing I demand from life is mystery. But how can mystery be DEMANDED, since obviously what answers a demand isn't mysterious at all?

ROCCO: Oh?

WILL: That's my analysis of vulgarity.

ROCCO: Mine too.

WILL: Where did you learn such analysis—

ROCCO: Little men came to me from unnameable flying objects called cups and saucers.

LILI: Oh, is it time for tea?

ROCCO: Ladies and gentlemen always know when it's teatime.

LILI: Local time?

WILL: Let's see another trick.

ROCCO: Very perceptive—it was one of my subtlest.

(He goes to the cabinet and takes out a magician's cane)

WILL: Yes, let's see one appropriate to THIS planetary situation: less subtle. *(ROCCO waves the cane in the air and turns it into a bouquet of flowers)* Ah, this means that the play is about to begin. *(LILI and ROCCO run offstage. WILL stares at the audience and waits)* But I confess, it's been postponed. The leading actor is sick. *(Pause)* That's not true. I'm the leading actor and I accept no responsibility for cancellations. *(Pause)* Welcome to . . . Welcome to the theater. I am on a throne. *(Points to the throne, then looks out at the audience, to see if anyone wants to sit upon his throne)* Is there someone else with similar hopes? *(Pause)* You hesitate, thinking, ahhh, it's just a play, and I dare not expose myself to ridicule. But the point is, here, or some other time and place, will you end up being a remarkable person? Or will you, too, suffer a

permanent setback on your road to personal glory—
which I'm not asking you to think about too carefully,
because I know that precision in the wrong area can
produce a special kind of catastrophe that human language doesn't really register in spite of what you'd like
to believe. But don't worry—*(WILL is becoming agitated,
filled with manic intensity)* Nobody's asking you to take
a flying leap into a future that clearly has no precedent,
because it hasn't happened. Not a disadvantage, but only
a polite way of saying—no thanks! Nothing to add to
the curriculm that life itself hasn't gone one better on
yet—as of last year anyway. *(He hits his head to correct
himself, then shouts to himself)* I didn't remember that
LAST YEAR was something we were even allowed to
talk about! Because all the experience in the world
doesn't really add up, if you know what I mean, at this
late date in the game. So let's not—WHO SAID TALK?
Though I think I did overhear somebody say that an
open mouth is better than a circular mental saw that rips
through brain tissue so fast, it's a tissue of nothing but
lies nobody got to register even!

LILI: *(Appearing rear)* Hey, I like it when you talk fast.

ROCCO: *(Appearing rear, at the other side)* Ahh, I like it
when you talk fast.

WILL: *(Anguished, holding his head)* But I don't talk fast
ENOUGH! That's the problem! It's just forward march
into the place I can't help going anyway, which means
look, we're back where we started—*(He runs to the spinning stick)* But of course, that's not possible! *(He starts
walking about the stick, turning the handle, half crying, half
laughing to himself)* Oh shit . . . !
Oh shit . . . !
This is great . . . !
Oh shit!

(Bouncing march music rises as WILL turns faster, tears in his eyes, but unclear even to himself what they mean)

Oh shit, this is great . . . !

(WILL continues circling, muttering to himself, laughing, crying, and the light focuses down upon him)

VOICE: And so what's the beginning and the ending pretended? But of course, with only a circular story to tell, whatever he's feeling turns circular also. So when you ask, is he laughing or crying? The answer is: both at once.
He doesn't have to choose.
He gets it all, as it were.
Making him, if you have the eyes to see,
One hell of a lucky guy!
One hell of a lucky guy!
One hell of a lucky guy!

(Music rises, and the lights fade on the image of WILL, circling in the falling dark)

The End

◆

LAVA

◆

Matthew Courtney and Kyle deCamp in Lava. (Photo by C. M. Hardt)

LAVA

♦

Though you may not notice if you only watched it in performance, *Lava* is like a series of staged essays, several contradictory approaches to the same problem: why can language never adequately express the true and complex quality of an internal impulse? It's a series of what Gertrude Stein called meditations; ruminations on philosophical ideas in which the intent is to enjoy, to savor, and to dance with the music of your ideas and what they spark inside you. Down through the years I've obsessively written notes to myself about aesthetics, about how to use one's head, and about how I should go about writing my plays. In *Lava* more material than usual came from notes of this sort. When I was actually writing those notes I never expected to use them in a play, though I've learned that's where they may well wind up.

Part of this material was intended to be tongue-in-cheek, because the attitudes toward language expressed in these meditations were standard poststructuralist theory. It's Derrida and Lacan reconstituted in a simple, ironic synopsis. So, for instance, after a paragraph explains how language couldn't possibly capture an individual's real feelings—because it's an inherited language rather than one invented anew by each new speaker—the tape finishes with the melancholy simplification, "That's why I'm crying." That line should be taken ironically, of course: yet another example of language not expressing the fullness of what's really felt. And the line was read with a self-pitying sniffle that made the ironic quality very clear. Other lines in the text try to make the person speaking them appear a little foolish and self-indulgent, as we all are.

And the person who is speaking is me. In this play there is no doubt about it, because my voice, coming over the loudspeaker, dominates about seventy percent of the play. There are four performers onstage who may be me as well. I hoped the performers would flicker back and forth between two possibilities: people who could make these philosophical pronouncements on their own, and people who are under the thrall of this omnipresent voice, the voice of their author, their director, their boss—even the voice of God.

My greatest efforts in staging *Lava* went into making the listening experience as powerful as the watching experience. Even in normal, narrative theater, it's difficult to be aware of the text as language without losing yourself in other elements of the production. The dialogue usually serves to make you see past the spoken language so that you watch the story it is telling—in a "proselike" way, the language disappears in favor of the story it is conveying. With *Lava* I wanted to stage a play that would give the spectator the sensory experience of listening, word by word, to what was being said. I wanted it to be an aural, rather than a visual, experience. I found this very difficult to do because my tendency is to create the kind of stage

picture that pulls you back into watching instead of listening. But all through rehearsals I kept making adjustments to put the emphasis on the aural experience, so the
spectator would listen to what was happening in the
language.

Usually in my plays something bizarre will happen onstage, and then the spoken text will give you a new perspective on what you were seeing. But with *Lava* it was
the reverse. First the text would be delivered in a way that
made the audience aware of the text itself, then something
would happen onstage to give a new perspective on the
text, and they could then savor the way the text was being
colored and shaped by the staging.

I have always been interested in theater, not because it
speaks publicly to a group of people, not because it is a
public art, but because I like to operate on many perceptual
levels at once. I like articulating counterimpulses, coun-
terdirections. I find that the threater, of all the arts, is
uniquely suited to this kind of activity; even more than
film, where the multiple elements you begin with—bodies,
voices, physical locales, lighting effects—are subsumed by
the fact of projected light. The individual elements become
subservient to the unifying characteristics of film projection. In the theater, you deal with real materials. You can
use projected light, real flesh, real wood, the sound of the
spoken text, the sound of the music, and so forth. It's this
complexity that interests me. It allows for a multitude of
things to happen onstage which recast the language of the
text, displace and expand it, and give it new meanings.
When you stage a text, you expand its subject to include
the unspoken communication between bodies; the text is
colored and shaped, and made to reveal content you might
otherwise not have believed it held.

The text of *Lava* speaks about the ambiguity and incompleteness of language, but the staging of the text points to the ambiguity of physical behavior as well. That mix relates to what Julia Kristeva calls the "chora," the language impulse she describes as underlying most so-called experimental literature—writing in which the author gives form to originary, prevocal impulses which he daringly commits to the page before they are fully domesticated by the cultural restraints of official language or literary style. I've always maintained that I write a drama of impulses rather than actions, and that my particular style of staging is a way of representing originative impulse before it is tamed by social constraints, including the constraint of easily understood language. I stage my plays in a way that continually attempts to remind us of the fact that whatever form our life takes, it always burns on the fuel of primitive, childlike, impulsive, spasmodic behavior. It's the Freudian notion that our cultural edifices are essentially built from shit; from the polymorphous-perverse tendencies of the remembered childhood body.

The actors in *Lava* fulfilled the function of clowns—people who carry out certain tasks, and who have feelings which go through them and then disappear. They were totally subservient to the omnipresent voice on tape, and that fact lent them a quality related to my earliest performances. So *Lava* was a blend of the old and the new. The dominance of the tape recalled my early plays, but I gave each of the actors a personal history, something I'd only begun to do in *Penguin Touquet*. In early rehearsals of *Lava* we spoke about the character's relationships with one another, and imagined them in emotionally potent situations, but at one point their stories started to seem too real, the actors became too involved with their "characters," and that limited the full resonance of the text. So we cut back, depended less on private histories, and made the performances more neutral, more emotionally ambiguous.

Most of all, the actors in *Lava* were trying to listen.
They worked very hard to really listen to what I was saying
on the tape. I wanted them genuinely to feel my words
reverberating inside their consciousness. At the same time,
they executed the usual choreographed movements and
gestures I chose to express the things that could be imagined happening inside them vis-à-vis the text. Much as
Martha Graham would choreograph a dancer's body to
respond to sudden musical phrases with a bodily contraction, I'd choreograph the actors to respond as if the words
and ideas of the text had direct, unmediated, physical effect
on the body.

Occasionally in *Lava* the actors delivered their lines in
tandem with the taped voice, which suggested, just as my
early plays suggested, that all ideas, all language, circulate
as common property in any society. That our ideas don't
spring from sources within our isolated self, but are the
residue of what we've heard from others, of the way we've
been infiltrated by the atmospheres of our social and intellectual lives. At the same time, I had the actors overlap
the tape to create ambiguity regarding their real persona.
Were they supposed to represent my own ego, were they
my surrogates? Or were they independent individuals
listening to the word of God as it came through the
loudspeakers?

Art is often made by trying to connect two distant
points, which was André Breton's notion, inspired by Lau-
treamont, of how to make metaphors: you bring an umbrella and a sewing machine together on a dissecting table.
Things that don't belong together, yoked together. The
surrealists proposed that metaphor is more powerful when
the two terms are taken from realms far apart in normal
thinking. Anything you express in language is given palpable shape only by resorting to metaphorical modes. All
language is metaphor, and the words we choose to render

our experience invariably suggest overtones of experience quite other from the one we're trying to express in language. It happens the minute you put a sentence together. For instance, "The sun rises." Of course, the sun doesn't rise like a person, standing up on the horizon. But we yoke "sun," which comes with one set of associations, together with "rises," which comes with another, in order to make what we think of as a simple, unemotional statement. What this means is that we are always saying, emotionally, more than we intend. Some even propose that within metaphor hides the unconscious. So what is a metaphor? It's a marker that indicates the presence of a gap—a gap the mind jumps across in the ecstasy of getting the idea.

Metaphor enables you to jump the gap between the sun, which is a fiery circle in the sky, and a particular motion you associate with a person waking up at the beginning of the day. To say "the sun is rising" gives you a little thrill, it awakens you to consciousness. The mere presence of a gap implies that you have to jump it; it isn't a gap until you become aware of both sides. The gap leads you to make the jump, and the jump excites you into consciousness, it brings you to life.

Writing, of course, is built out of such gaps, and you increase the size of the gaps if you want more consciousness.

In *Lava*, I discuss how I want to trick myself so that I can escape the objects my consciousness fixes upon and instead enter such gaps directly. That's akin to getting behind my own ideas, and touching the primal hum that precedes all socialized forms of discourse and behavior. The minute you begin to conceptualize what flows through you, the minute you give things names and shapes, you've made yourself a prison of ideas and objects. But what I'm after is what in *Lava* I call "category three," which is a third possibility between logic and randomness. It's something between narrative development and pure chance. It's the cracks in reality that can't be mapped, the cracks in our normal, inherited systems of discourse. It's the gaps in the web of our conceptual networks.

There are writers who despair that language is incapable of expressing the true self, and that a gap exists between the self and the words that come, but for me that gap is the field of all creativity—it's an ecstatic field rather than a field of despair. It's the field of the unconscious, of God; it's the unfathomable from which everything pours forth.

The valuable nature of art lies in its ability to evoke intuition of that invisible ground from which everything we know rises. It points to all that gushes forth into life, before that moment when it becomes shaped and categorized by a conceptual system. It evokes the unnameable. To catch a glimpse of the hum of the universe is of tremendous value to society. Manifest in the form of art, it offers society the energy of the source. Our culture dams up a multitude of potentially enriching energies, just as most cultures do. Art is one of the ways to unlock in each man and woman an awareness of that flowing source. We rarely drink from that source, because we're afraid that it will somehow brand us as outside the responsible demands of our culture. But within the context of that "time off," which is art, even the most conservative among us can be persuaded to partake of this nectar of the gods.

Everything I do when making my plays is intended to force our consciousness into these energy-producing gaps, but with the understanding that to concretize what arises in that gap is to make it a dead rather than a living thing. That's why I think the theater is always about death, and why images of death have always been present in my theater. The concrete, conceptualized, physical repetition that is the theatrical performance is a manifestation of death. In *What Did He See?* the notion of retiring, of withdrawing from the activity of making art, appeals to the central character for precisely that reason. He understands that to produce, especially in the realm of art, is to turn the live thing (the impulse) into the dead thing (the work of art). But I carry within me the dream that I should be able to remain suspended in the live thing, in the gap of the non-representable, rather than falling back into the production of dead, representable, and materialized action. That's why in *Lava* I suggest that the ideal theater would be a theater of nonacts, because the minute that anything is concretized, and is given a form, it becomes part of the fallen world.

Lava was first produced by the Ontological-Hysteric Theater and the Wooster Group at the Performing Garage in New York City on December 5, 1989, with the following cast:

> Neil Bradley
> Matthew Courtney
> Peter Davis
> Kyle deCamp
> Heidi Tradewell

The production was directed and designed by Richard Foreman; lights by Heather Carson; sound design by Tim Schellenbaum; properties by Heidi Tradewell; technical director, Mike Taylor; assistant director, David Herskovits.

Neil Bradley, Kyle deCamp, and Peter Davis in Lava. (Photo by Paula Court)

While the audience is still talking and glancing at their pro-
grams, before the lights have gone down in the auditorium, a
woman in a red sweater appears and begins to write on a
blackboard onstage. What she writes is the beginning text of
the play that follows. The room is curtained in black cloth
which forms a variety of false walls, overhanging valences,
and tubular pillars. Many industrial lamps hang from the
ceiling, angled toward the audience. The room seems a kind
of examination chamber, or study hall, with a vaguely cere-
monial atmosphere—but nothing grand, except in its somber-
ness. Dirty, with chicken feathers strewn about on soiled
oriental carpets that cover the floor. In one corner an open
window, white lace curtains moving softly in the breeze. The
room is dominated by a large table on which a few books lie.
A white, elastic band is stretched across the middle of the table
like a Ping-Pong net. A narrow horizontal window behind
this table leads to another room. Microphones on stands are
scattered about the room. A few bookcases with strange objects
that can't be seen clearly, a few vases with wilted garden
flowers, and newspaper pages in foreign, exotic script, tacked
to raw walls. All that can be heard at first is the scratching of
chalk on the blackboard, as a deep and ominous VOICE *comes*
from giant loudspeakers hung over the table. Throughout the
play this silent woman continues writing the text of the play
upon one of the three or four visible blackboards, skipping
forward whenever she falls behind the VOICE. *On many oc-*
casions, one of the other actors may join in on a blackboard
where she is not. Below the speakers hangs an oscilloscope,

displaying the active graph of the deep VOICE's *speaking as it continues throughout the play. Just before the* VOICE *begins speaking the text, through other speakers at the side of the stage, another* VOICE *is heard reading off series of random numbers, from one to nine. This* VOICE *recurs, as indicated in the text of the play, always going through the same random sequence. In this case, the numbers fade as the text proper begins.*

VOICE: *(Very hypnotic, deep and slow, as it should be throughout the play)* A stream of talk continuum of nondifferentiation.

A phrase repeated, hypnotized therefore hypnotized into that nondifferentiation.

Usually drama is meaningful acts, right?

(The soft beginnings of Gypsy music are heard)

And remember, meaning is always the reinforcing of
  the given, oppressive ideology.
So if you believe not in that, but think your only task
  is to be elsewhere
To act from elsewhere
Rather than to continue the circle of acts here in the
  ideological prison—
It's a kind of MUSIC that erases the act as meaningful.
Turning language into a kind of music that erases the
  act as meaningful.
Theater of nonacts.
Speech act as nonact also.
So just phrases.
So just either a nonstatement
Or
What arises as a neutral statement, as a neutral, inherited
  repetition, of the language you're born into.

Not by choice, you're born into it.
That language used therefore
As a non-do it. Exactly: as a non-do it.
So go ahead and superimpose.
Go ahead and mismatch.
Like reaching for a fish in the water when the fish isn't
    quite there because the water makes it somewhere else,
Which opens a gap.

(As the music rises, MATTHEW, a bald man in a dark overcoat, scarfs, a monocle, and with a large hump on his back, appears and slowly crosses to the table. He laboriously lifts a large stack of books, and clamping down with his chin on top of the stack, slowly walks out of the room as the VOICE continues)

A gap is that void which
Is the self
And is the real.
That gap which is the void which is the real and is the
    "god" in that void.
Derision:
Derision is all the culture is worth.
And yet you and I are part of it, right?
And something beyond it is great, right?
But can only be indicated in a way that deserves our
    derision.
Yet you're under an OBLIGATION to indicate it!
And that still deserves our derision.
So to those who are serious and try to indicate it, I
    say—bah.
But to those jokers who don't even "try" to indicate the
    holy, to them I say—bah! also.

(By now MATTHEW is almost gone and a woman, KYLE, appears in the interior window, staring after him. She then

slowly looks up to the speakers from which the VOICE *issues.*
She is dressed in a dirty black apron and wears a military
fatigue cap. The curtains at the other, exterior, window blow
more forcefully)

Because every "sayable" is inherited, so it's a bad fit to
    whatever's real in you.
But in that gap in that gap in that bad fit lies the truth.
To be CONSCIOUS is to "say."
You have to say, that's what it means to be conscious.
To be conscious is therefore to be removed from self
    and your own experience.
To be conscious is to experience nothing but LIE.
Consciousness is LIE Consciousness is LIE.
So go ahead and lie, which is a lie, and tell the truth
    which is a lie.
So tell the truth which is a lie, so go ahead and lie, lie.
A stream of talk, a lie.
One lie on another.
One lie on another.

(The music ends, replaced by an electronic hum, and KYLE
comes around into the room and sits at the table. There is a
pause, then the VOICE *continues as the hum fades, and the*
woman looks up to the speakers. Throughout the rest of the
play, different soft music and electronic hums return again and
again, accompanying much of the performance)

Can you explain it? I'm only happy when I remember
to fix on a simple, paradoxically unhappy fact. Namely,
the fact that whatever I say necessarily misses the mark.
Because I, myself, don't choose the terms in which I
explain what I'm feeling about myself or the world or
anything imaginable, since of necessity I use a language
forced on me. Invented by other people.

But when I center—wobblelike, of course—on that
  insight
Only then I feel . . . I don't know . . .
Energized.
Because a gap bursts open in me—
And air, not real air of course,
Rushes in and cleanses me!
And that's where I want to stay—
Pivoting on that one idea.
Say it again?

(KYLE suddenly slaps herself on the side of her face, then takes out lipstick and reddens her lips, as MATTHEW and two younger, similarly dressed and humpbacked men, PETER and NEIL, appear in different corners of the room, holding large books)

Gladly. What I'm saying is there's a hole in me, in all of us. We have to talk, right? But whatever we say is . . . off the mark. Off the mark. The brain has no pain fibers—Off the mark. Can you explain that I'm only happy when I can KEY, all the time, on that one idea? The brain has no pain fibers.

(The three men move to the table and sit in chairs on different sides of the table as KYLE retreats as if afraid of them. She repositions herself in a distant chair, stretching out her body provocatively. As the VOICE continues, they alternate between staring out at the audience, or at each other, or up toward the speakers—gestures they will return to again and again throughout the rest of the play at given moments)

You realize, I don't have to be anything . . . but a hole in space. That's my only responsibility. I have two choices. Either I'm a mirror, or a hole. If I'm a mirror, I reflect back to people something they can name, or recognize, or think about, or have an opinion about. I'm a mirror for their expectations, which all arise out of what they have already experienced.

But if I bypass all their expectations, even the expectation of the unexpected, then—I'm a void, a hole in their experience, a void. And then only . . . I'm something real, instead of a mirror, get it?

A hole is real.

Bottomless, you could say, which is the closest you can get to it. If it's bottomless, it's real. If it's not, it's a mirror, and it isn't anything at all really, if it's a mirror. I'd rather be REAL—

(An invisible hand pushes NEIL *forward onto the table. He recovers, and he and* PETER *cross to help* MATTHEW *slowly lift a foot onto the table as the lights fade slowly)*

—for some stupid reason. I don't want to be a mirror, thank you.

Good-bye.

Don't go yet. Say something. Why do I think you're not going to say anything?

Well, I should at least give you a chance. Keep an open mind.

(By now the lights are out. Music rises and the VOICE *speaks over it)*

Once, when I wore my boots, my hair caught fire. Wow, that was fun.

(Lights have come up, more intense than before. MATTHEW, *still with his foot displayed on the table, holds his throat)*

MATTHEW: Once, when I was driving in my new Cadillac, the ice cream I was eating dripped down the edge

of a sugared cone and put spots on a red foulard necktie.
Wow, that was fun.

PETER: Once, when I was in school I learned everything
in a single day and I was accused of being pushy.

NEIL: Once, when I had an unpredictable religious experience, I was made to eat supper a second time 'cause
my family hoped they could wash the experience out of
my psychological reservoir.

KYLE: What business was your father in—?

MATTHEW, PETER, NEIL: Wow, that was not fun!

(Now the VOICE *comes through other speakers, repeating a
phrase again and again, while the actors run to microphones
and speak, overlapping the* VOICE LOOP, *which continues at
the same time. As this proceeds, the actors may change places,
sit, perform other actions in seemingly random fashion. This
technique recurs several times during the play, and it should
be understood that when* VOICE LOOP *is indicated, that loop
continues repeating its phrase until either a new* VOICE LOOP
begins, or the VOICE *returns to its normal discursive text)*

VOICE LOOP: The brain has no pain fibers . . .

KYLE: Don't get caught, I said. Oops.

PETER: Fast thinking.

KYLE: I don't think except when I'm in trouble.
Do I like trouble?
Wow, what a blow to my self-esteem.

PETER: You glow all over.

KYLE: Do I?

PETER: Try holding it in.

KYLE: Why?

PETER: Your mouth is your weak part, your mouth is
your weak part.

KYLE: Oops.

PETER: I'm always right. I'm always right.

VOICE LOOP: 1–2–3, perfectly like you'd like it to be . . .

MATTHEW: Enough said, he said. Was that me?

NEIL: I aim at your ideas.

MATTHEW: Too bad, I let go.

NEIL: That's why my aim is so good.

MATTHEW: Good.

NEIL: Good.

VOICE LOOP: Did you fold your head, like you were supposed to?

PETER: Oh, now I see.

KYLE: Cover one eye.

PETER: I'm not supposed to.

KYLE: Cover one eye.

PETER: I'm not supposed to. I'm not supposed to.

VOICE LOOP: Put your head into this, if you dare.

MATTHEW: No such luck—

KYLE: I missed that, good. No such luck. Try again.

MATTHEW: I caught up.

VOICE: Hello to you all. I am here to minister and I shall.

(KYLE goes behind the table where she kneels, spreads a handkerchief on the edge of the table, and rests her chin on the handkerchief to listen to the VOICE)

Tears shall flow from your eyes and run, riverlike, beneath my feet, and I shall be supported and sweep toward you through the activity of your own tears . . .

I shall drift into your very hearts.

I shall heal you all.

Do not ask HOW, or my power will evaporate.

And you DO want my power, because you do want my power to work upon you, because you do want my healing.

So, let your tears flow,

Flow toward me, that I may have a method for reaching
into your very heart.
Why cry?
The truth is as follows.
It can't be said, the truth.
Which, of course, renders even that statement question-
able. Hum.
This is my hand.

(*MATTHEW is staring into his own hand*)

Even that isn't the truth, but it is, but it isn't,
Because the hand you separate out from the rest of your
body and the rest of the world in order to say here is
my hand
Can't be separated, really.
Except, let me take a somewhat less contestable position
than that, even.
The truth about my inner life can't be told.
Or yours, or anyone's.
I love, I fear, I hate—
MATTHEW: (*Overlapping the* VOICE) I do love, I do fear,
I do hate—
VOICE: (*Continuing*) Such and such an attitude to such
and such an object.
MATTHEW: Exactly.
VOICE: But. Not exactly at all. Whatever words you use
to express any of those feelings are words you were born
into. Words you can choose all predetermined by the
particular language you were born into. Because the test
of time and millions of human beings having experiences
have proved those words—useful and exact and correct.
No wait, do be serious and careful for a minute and
recognize it isn't true. Here's a picture of someone you
love.

(KYLE slowly produces a photo of a woman, and lays it on the table before them)

Meditate upon this, and upon your feelings, and can you truly say that the words, "I love you," or whatever subtle and intricate phrases you come up with, REALLY express the elusive cloud of shifting . . . things . . . that flicker through you on this or any occasion? I mean, before you give it a name, allow yourself to experience it, and then SENSE whether or not the name really . . . matches with total exactness.

(KYLE begins to withdraw the picture)

Wait a minute.
Whether or not you agree with me
Remember,
I'm just answering your question,
Why I'm crying.
Well, I'm crying because there's no way to express my
    real feelings
With a language that isn't my language.
Whether or not you agree, that's why I'm crying.

(In the following sequence, actors and VOICE speak at the same time, never quite in synch, making it hard to follow what's being said. At the same time, KYLE is slowly crossing to the open window to stand amid the blowing curtains, staring out into the black night, her back to the audience. The men are frozen over their books)

VOICE and **MATTHEW:** That's expressing yourself.
VOICE and **PETER:** Oh no it isn't, that's something I've been programmed to do also—
VOICE and **MATTHEW:** Biologically programmed, yes—

VOICE and **PETER**: Well that biology isn't me, there's something else.

VOICE and **MATTHEW**: Oh?

VOICE and **PETER**: I'd go so far as to say, not only does all SAYING err from the mark, even experience misses, by which I mean—you have an experience, but the experience isn't the experience, you see?

VOICE and **MATTHEW**: Not yet.

VOICE and **PETER**: Something happens—you have an experience—but what you experience, that you can feel consciously you experienced, is not what you really experienced. . . . That's my FEELING about it. I don't have to defend my feelings, I suppose. . . . Other people could have different feelings. But don't you see my point is universally valid.

VOICE and **KYLE**: Whatever you experience, even right now, you have no way of registering it to yourself completely, as it affects you, which is both as an experience—ah you say, I'm recognizing I have an experience—but that's on the basis of so many learned assumptions that you just took as they were . . .

VOICE and **KYLE** and **NEIL**: . . . stuffed into you, because finally you went along with things everybody else said were the way to look at things and experience things and feel things . . .

VOICE and **NEIL**: . . . with one exception.

MATTHEW: What exception?

NEIL: My exception. Once. I did escape once . . . I . . . *(Pause)*

MATTHEW: What's wrong?

NEIL: I've gone up.

MATTHEW: What?

NEIL: I've gone up on my lines.

MATTHEW: I thought you were speaking from the heart.

NEIL: Oh come on. I think this is interesting, but I didn't have these thoughts. I memorized something that somebody else wrote, and now I . . . I'm blocked.

MATTHEW: *(Pointing to an illuminated photo of the author, which rests on a side table, surrounded by flowers)* Stare at that face. Use mental telepathy.

NEIL: *(Tries)* It doesn't work.

PETER: *(Tossing him a script)* Here's the script, Neil.

NEIL: Shithead.

MATTHEW: Don't blow your cool, Neil.

NEIL: You don't know who I was thinking about. *(Referring to photo)* Him. You. Maybe even myself.

MATTHEW: But I say the same thing. Don't blow your cool.

NEIL: *(Reading from the script)* My exception, I did escape once.

MATTHEW: Escape what?

NEIL: One experience that, I believe, didn't err.

NEIL and **VOICE:** *(Fading back in under NEIL)* Wasn't off the mark. I'll tell you about it.

(Loud drum music begins, and NEIL races across the room as all join hands and run, holding hands, single file following NEIL around the table. Having made a circuit, they drop hands, whirl in place, scratch themselves to the beat of the music, and cross the room taking strange goose steps till they are blocked by different pieces of furniture around the room. At the end, the music had been replaced by quiet, mystical chords, and soon all seem to be asleep, face down on the table as the VOICE continues)

VOICE: One night, a situation in my private life brought me frustration. Nothing major, but frustration. And in irritation I threw myself down on my bed, with a feeling of giving up. At that moment, everything changed, as

if a switch had been thrown, the basis of my consciousness changed. *(MATTHEW slowly rolls on the table till he is
face up, then slowly rises and slowly walks to his seat. The
others also slowly awake and seat themselves as the VOICE
continues)* It was as if my head were replaced with a glass
sphere perhaps six feet in diameter, and everything in
the outside world was seen as tiny images on that sphere,
but those images projected somehow from the inside,
as if their real source was inside me. And this was accompanied by a feeling of joy and light, and the sense
that everything had been resolved once and for all, and
there was nothing but completion and happiness in the
world. And this . . . state lasted in me for twenty minutes. And then it began to fade, but for perhaps a half
hour, though it had gone, I could REMEMBER the
feeling. And then I slept, and when I awoke, I could
remember that I had had the experience, but could
only remember the feeling in the form I could describe
to myself in language, but no longer the real feeling
as a feeling memory. Well. To me, that moment of
paradise was the only experience I've ever had that I
trusted that wasn't off the mark—off the mark. *(They
all reach forward onto the table and pick up small white cards
which they hold in front of their eyes)* Displaced, but free
of the kind of slight mismatch that infects all experience
and language and saying and memory, as I see it. So
that's where my tears came from—and even there, of
course, I was crying to make you ask why I was crying.
I haven't been able to tell you, or even myself—which
is worse—what that singular experience was really like.
I've lost it.

KYLE: You'll just have to keep trying.

VOICE: Ah. Now that's the point. I can only try . . . by
getting . . . behind my own ideas and words and ex-

periences. That's why you find me hard to understand. I have to . . . trick myself—so that I don't get in the way of myself, understand? I understand you're looking for an excuse for a lot of fuzzy thinking . . . *(All quickly throw down on the table the cards which were covering their eyes)* and irrational behavior. Oh no. I'm just trying to live in a world . . . well, that isn't a fallen world, like this world. *(A little childish phrase is heard played on a toy piano. As it ends, all slowly rise from the table, shielding their eyes from the lights and turning their backs toward the table, as the* VOICE *continues)* I'm afraid it's the world you live in. Yes, yes—but here's the game plan. Category one, the material world—you live in it. Yes. I live in it. But it's . . . not such a great world, the way I look at worlds.

MATTHEW: *(Over his shoulder, peeking up at the loud-speaker)* Don't cry.

VOICE: Category two. Forgive me, but—category two is the world of the spirit. I have to admit, I can't claim to live in that world of the spirit. If it exists.

MATTHEW: It better exist, shithead.

PETER: I suspect there's a category three.

VOICE: Category three. Yes. That's the best I can do. If something can . . . flow through me, flow through me in the right way, from these two other places at once, flowing through me, then I'm in category three. Welcome to category three.

NEIL: But we are still in category one, aren't we, Matthew.

MATTHEW: *(Glaring at* NEIL *across the table)* Don't call me by my real name, Neil. Welcome to category three!

VOICE: We're still in category one.
  Welcome to category one!
  Welcome to category one!
  Welcome to category one!

(Old-fashioned organ music rises, as all lean over the table to stare up at the loudspeakers from which pours very bright light)

Get into the gear box.
Get inside the control room.
Get into the web.
Get into the network itself.
Get inside the circuit.
Tacky, but considerable.
Tacky, but considerable.
Here it is. A piece of the truth,
Balanced against the whole truth.
Which is heavier? You'll get a real surprise,
A real surprise.

(The music is rising, loud with heavy drums, and again every-body races about to join hands and do a frantic running dance. It finishes with whirling in place, scratching and goose steps to the table. Then the VOICE *returns, speaking the random number loop, and everyone runs to the microphones as various* VOICE LOOPS *begin, replacing the numbers. The actors speak quietly at the same time)*

VOICE LOOP: Was the real doctor, pain-oriented . . .

(They have quickly exited and reappeared, carrying plates and eating bread and jam. They put the plates aside)

NEIL: Something is giving me . . . a real sense of direction. But it wobbles—Jesus, does it wobble.
KYLE: I don't see that.
VOICE LOOP: Nobody, Nobody, Nobody, that was the whispered message . . .
MATTHEW: Funny, I feel so . . . did somebody shut the door? Ha—we should establish a direction probably. Did I go someplace?

KYLE: Funny, I had a flash, but you didn't.

VOICE LOOP: *(As MATTHEW rises and slowly exits, licking his fingers)* Remarkable people, never depend on self-revelation . . .

NEIL: Did I forget my—responsibilities?

KYLE: I can tell that word isn't genuine.

NEIL: Which one?

KYLE: Oh, I lost it.

NEIL: Which one?

VOICE LOOP: Elaborate messages all seem to gather, rust-o-rama . . .

PETER: I notice that if I shake my head, I stop breathing.

NEIL: But I see sparks fly.

MATTHEW: *(Peering in from the interior window)* What? What? What?

PETER: Now I don't.

NEIL: Now I do.

VOICE: *(MATTHEW has run into the room and they all compose themselves at the table, again staring up at the speakers)* The secret of things is to find category three. There is first, logic. Of things coming out of other things, a logical connection, be that cause and effect, or determined by categories or logical types, or motivational source, etc. Things like that, etc.

(By now KYLE has moved to a curtained alcove, and pulling back the curtain she has, in slow motion, dragged a pedestal with an oversized vase of flowers into the room. She freezes, holding the pedestal in a tilted position and staring up at the vase which doesn't, amazingly, fall off. As soon as she is established in this position, MATTHEW runs to one of the large pillars of cloth that hang in the room. He puts his arms out, encircles and hugs the pillar, which, being cloth, contracts in his embrace. Slowly, as if under a great weight, he lifts and

carries the bunched-up cloth to a wall, so that he and KYLE *end up both frozen, both with their large and rather absurd "packages of material" suspended unnaturally, as they stare each other down. The* VOICE *continues throughout)*

Then there is category two. Random nonsense, nonsense, chance, random relations, all those kinds of relations or nonrelations, whatever you choose to call them. But category three is something that eludes both category one and two. Most people, viewing it superficially, mistake category three for category two—that is, randomness and chance. But the items of category three, though not connected, are in fact connected, but in a way that is not perceivable within our available grids.
So
It's taken on faith, as it were.
But as somebody said
It moves mountains.
It's that door to another world
That is located in that other world.
Go through it. But it's not in this world.

*(*MATTHEW *drops his pillar and runs to the table, and* KYLE *rights hers and puts it in a corner, and all the men sit and pick up lipsticks and start applying them to their mouths. They hold small hand mirrors to help them carry out the task with concentrated, manic seriousness)*

So category three eludes logic, yet is not random or chancelike, but is a connective tissue that cannot be traced, and yet is the one truly lively way of perceiving the world. It lays down the ground of the real being alive, where the other two categories, logic and chance, are predictable in their emotional kick. And don't kid

yourself, that's the only lust that moves you, that lust
for that emotional kick. So do you want a new one or
an old one? A new emotional kick or an old one?
What lays down the grid of real, alive living is category
three.

(The men have dropped their lipsticks, and begin to do a slow,
bizarre dance with their arms only)

Category three is the only real source, this category
three, which is a door that isn't openable from this side,
but it opens. One must enter, to be alive, only category
three, which one enters from death's side only, into life.

(Their dance ends with arms stretched out before them on the
table, as if pointing to fault lines in its surface. At the same
time, KYLE serves glasses from which they drink deeply)

It is a category
Which people will call unnatural and irrational, but it
     isn't.
It falls between the cracks of the normal rational.
It is the ultimate fruitful location,
Those cracks in reality, which nurture
Because they are not reality, which is not alive
But seen through the perceiving mechanism, which
     means not touched really,
Just messages, coming from far away
Through a very defective system
Ruled by fear and habit.
So one should want, always, to be in that nurturing
     ground
Which is category three.

(KYLE has now acquired a bowler hat which she defiantly plops
on her head, and the men rise suddenly, upset by her
transformation)

Welcome to category three.

(The men run off, upset, as KYLE crosses to the exterior window to enjoy the breeze as the curtains billow about her)

Should I observe myself breathing in and out, here in category three? Try it, but don't let being distracted get you distracted.

(MATTHEW sneaks back into a corner of the room, and KYLE and MATTHEW stare at each other in silence)

Welcome to category three.
Welcome to category three.
Welcome to category three.

(Neither moves a muscle)

Shall I feel love and attraction to other human beings here in category three? Why not. Why not. What I mean is, try it—Oh oh, you just made the wrong move. I didn't move anything.
WELCOME TO CATEGORY THREE.
WELCOME TO CATEGORY THREE.
WELCOME TO CATEGORY THREE.
VOICE LOOP: I said, the bright one, with the potato in his mouth . . .
MATTHEW: Looking for something?
KYLE: Somebody needs to swallow their remaining inhibitions.
MATTHEW: Talk big. Please.

(Loud drum music rises as the men run to a bookcase from which they each take a white belt. They slip the belts behind their bottoms, and holding an end in each hand, they start to, in effect, polish their behinds by vibrating the taut belts. As KYLE continues speaking against the VOICE LOOPS, they link hands and run to look out the interior window, then turn to

face the audience once they have put one end of the belt between their teeth and have wrapped the other end about their two hands like handcuffs. Using their teeth, they pull their belts tight)

VOICE LOOP: Somebody backed into a high energy field . . .

KYLE: I discovered something. A straight line, right into the brain. *(She runs to another microphone)* Lemme get a handle on this. This is going right past me. Effectively, nonstop. You better move fast.

VOICE LOOP: Please make an effort . . . *(She runs to another microphone)* I own it. Turn a corner. Turn another corner.

KYLE: Oh, now I see, I'm not supposed to.

VOICE: You opened the door inside . . . to get inside.
You opened the door outside, to get outside.
I don't know how
But you did it.
I didn't know I did it
But you did it.

(The men have repositioned themselves together at the far side of the table, leaning toward KYLE, who is at the other end. KYLE takes a golden pineapple off a plate, and using the elastic cord stretched across the middle of the table, she shoots the pineapple, slingshot style, across to the men. Then she brings her leg up onto the table, displaying her booted foot with a bang as it hits amid the books and dishes. They don't immediately react)

Plenty of people gave up on balance. The whole system went down the drain. Was I part of the system? Much to my surprise, yes comes up. Play with it? Why not.

I'm a hell of a guy when the right ball comes rolling into my part of the landscape.

(Soft raga music is heard, and all participate in a dance number that is a series of tableaux. First the men bow down, faces and arms outstretched on the table, and KYLE comes around to climb on NEIL'S back. Then she advances across the table to bow down to MATTHEW, who has gone to a far corner. Then PETER brings out a large round target and she seizes it, peering above its top at the audience, only to be grabbed about the thighs by PETER and lifted down from the table to the floor. NEIL runs toward her and is as if thrown back by the aura of the target. During this activity, the VOICE recites a short poem)

Go to a good school.
Go to your apartment.
Go to the highest place in France.
Go to Chinese laundries after deciding to have a good
     meal.
Go to bed, sometimes.
Go to the country estate.
Go to the waterfront, but exercise.
Go to a garage.
Go to a farm, but first, go to a farm.
Go to earth.
Go to short wave. Hello.
MATTHEW: *(Interjecting as he runs offstage)* Hello. Hello
there.
VOICE: Go to meaning.
Go to an encyclopedia.

(By now, all but NEIL have repositioned themselves at the edges of the table, each hiding behind a large, primitive cardboard mask. The masks are painted in different patterns. They rock the masks gently on the table. After a moment, NEIL

rushes in as if thrown onto the stage and collapses onto the table. He immediately rises and whirls to watch the rocking masks)

How's the language machine working? Tell me. How's the language machine working? Is the language machine working good? Tell me about it. Tell me about it. The language machine is working. How many words is the language machine turning out each day? Each day, two or three words. The language machine is not working good. No. The language machine is working good. Is there a difference of opinion as to whether the language machine is working good?

(All run to microphones, still hiding behind masks, as NEIL places reverently onto the table a strange, undefinable object he's taken from the bookcase)

VOICE LOOP: Guaranteed crash course, absolute momentum . . .

KYLE: Lots of times I'm on the verge, I keep going.

MATTHEW: Everybody agrees.

NEIL: That's funny, I thought I was on my own.

PETER: Sure, but don't look.

KYLE: Okay, don't look.

NEIL: Now, look.

KYLE: Okay, I looked.

MATTHEW: It's okay?

KYLE: Okay, I looked. Okay, I looked.

VOICE: Is there a difference of opinion as to whether the language machine is working good? Is the language machine working good?

(The random number loop is heard softly behind, as the men sit, holding white cards in front of their eyes)

MATTHEW: This is a dance I did, in the privacy of my biggest adventure.

NEIL: It went good?

MATTHEW: Good was a no-no word.

PETER: When.

MATTHEW: Oh, don't make me . . . think.

NEIL: Look, he's doing it.

VOICE: Good, is there a difference of opinion as to whether the language machine is working good? Good. Good.

(KYLE emerges with two chocolate pies. A bell rings once, and she sets the pies on the table. The men slowly drop their cards and stare at the pies, which she offers to them as the VOICE continues)

Chocklet pies.
Here are some chocolate pies.
Here are some beautiful chocolate pies.
Here are some chocolate pies.
Yummmm!

(The random number loop begins softly, under the text)

Surprise. There's something to touch but there's nothing to lick.

(KYLE picks up a hammer, runs around the table which frightens the men offstage, and as she reapproaches the pies she bangs the hammer on the table)

I can still say, chocolate pies.
Eyes.
Pies.
Eyes.

(The men have reappeared behind the interior window, each carrying a large book, which they thumb through frantically)

Now let's find them, those pies.
He tries and he tries to find those pies.

(KYLE moves to the rear of the table, climbs up on it, and crawls across it on all fours toward the two pies)

Is there an energy field around chocolate pies that is some kind of energy other than a chocolate derivative?

(She puts a finger into one pie and licks her finger, as the men stop paying attention to their books and stare, transfixed, at KYLE)

Look, you were the one who imagined it.
Those pies are real, buster.
Two eyes don't prove it,
Pies prove it.
You got pies, because you make it happen through your
    eyes.

(The men race around into the room, carrying their books on their backs like heavy burdens, and as they reach positions by the table, each slowly lowers a book onto the surface)

Then how come I also brought up the issue of an energy field? Chocolate pies. Whoever tries to eat, really gets shook up inside, so calm chocolate is something to psyche out. Psyche out. Speak to the world in pie form. Pie in the sky form.
Chocolate pie. Chocolate pie.

(Lively Gypsy music rises as a brief dance of the men pays homage to KYLE, still on the table among pies and books)

KYLE: *(As the music softens for a moment)* Whenever I feel bad, I sing to myself.

(The music rises again as the men dance. KYLE descends from the table, exits, and returns with a tray of upright candles. She places the tray on the table. The men take a candle each, and as the music fades to quiet organ tones, all sit in chairs, each holding a candle, which they light and then blow out at various moments through the next sequence)

NEIL: Whenever I feel really bad I let hundreds of words come fast without thinking.

MATTHEW: Whenever I feel bad, or really bad, I make up a lie and tell everybody.

PETER: Whenever I feel bad one word follows another. I take it back.

MATTHEW: Too late, Peter.

KYLE: Repeat that.

MATTHEW: Too late, Peter.

KYLE: Repeat that.

MATTHEW: Whenever I feel bad, I try to make it worse to get better.

KYLE: Whenever I feel bad, I lie down. *(She rests her head on the table)* Nothing works, of course. Except everything does.

PETER: Whenever I feel bad, I cover my eyes—with deliberation.

NEIL: I put my hands over my ears—like pillows.

MATTHEW: Whenever I feel bad I try walking on ice-cold feet.

(All fall asleep except MATTHEW, who holds a lit candle out over the table)

VOICE LOOP: When I talk, it hurts my extremities . . . *(They still sleep, as the VOICE LOOP changes)* Hello, I've replaced myself with a radio . . .

(NEIL slowly awakes, looks at MATTHEW, then covers his eyes with his hands. Suddenly a loud tone awakens the others as

NEIL rises and walks in a quick, zombielike way, out of the room. The lights get extremely dim)

VOICE LOOP: Oh, I tripped over a word, and perhaps that was when the word death entered . . . *(Those onstage search the room)* Solutions to all my problems are forthcoming . . .

(In the dim light, NEIL enters, carrying a giant, white geometric object with a clock face in the center. Soft music is heard as the others come together gently and hold hands, walking in a slow circle around NEIL and the object)

VOICE LOOP: A piano is in my heart . . .

(The object is gently passed to each in turn. Then PETER places it gently on the table. KYLE, who is now behind the exterior window, points to it with a giant, decorated stick, as the men get paper bags from which each extracts an apple. They leaf through their books and eat apples at the same time)

VOICE LOOP: My bag of tricks is extensive . . . *(KYLE drops her stick into the room, pronouncing "Woops . . . !")* You notice, that my interpretation of reality is reality . . .

KYLE: *(Running into the room and going to a mike)* Something doesn't come through unless I let it, did you notice? How could I notice with my hands in my pockets? Hey. How can I notice without no verbal excess whatsoever?

(Angry at being ignored, she picks up a rolled newspaper and bangs it on the table as loud drum music has obliterated her speech. The men try to brush her away—as if a fly were buzzing about their heads and distracting them. She angrily grabs the geometric object and runs with it from the room. The men calm down, and again pick up the white cards and place them before their eyes)

VOICE LOOP: The conventional memory stopped working . . .

MATTHEW: This happens to be a dance I did in the privacy of my . . . biggest adventure.

PETER: It went good?

(The random number loop is heard again for sixty seconds)

MATTHEW: Good was a no-no word.

NEIL: When?

MATTHEW: Oh, don't make me . . . think.

PETER: Look, he's doing it.

(The music now has become a lullaby, and the men all fall asleep)

VOICE: Who can change?
Who in this room can change?
Who in this room can manifest a different aspect?
Who in this room can get so deep into this book that reading it sends arrows into the brain?
Who can make reading, tears?
Who can punch his eyes by looking at himself?
Who can change that much?

(The men awake and look about. The music has been replaced by an electronic hum)

I realize that the change issue is the inside issue,
But it's the outside issue.

(KYLE enters carrying an armful of men's hats)

Suppose I put on a heretofore funny hat, and it wasn't funny.

(KYLE tosses all the hats on the table, and the men take a frightened step back)

You know why?

Because something different is at work in me.

I can't name it.

But it doesn't have to have a name to be first rate.

(The lights grow even brighter as a chord sounds, and all look up toward the loudspeakers)

Welcome to category three. Welcome. You've heard about category three? Not logic, not irrational accident or chance. Something else, a crack, a twist in the very obvious thing in front of my nose. Maybe even the nose.

MATTHEW: *(Staring at the others)* Here it goes, category three.

PETER: Can anything under the sun be category three?

NEIL: *(Points to his nose)* This nose, can I catch it again?

MATTHEW: Category three.

PETER: How strange, you didn't try to expand upon that.

MATTHEW: But I could.

(As the random number loop rises, they take awkward giant steps to new positions around the table)

NEIL: If I doubted you, I'd be glued to the floor by my feet.

VOICE: Isn't it strange, there's nothing farther apart than two parts of the body, one of which is involved in smelling and the other which gets you, physically, away from anything you would be smelling. Except yourself. *(The men whirl)* Or am I wrong? Do feet, in fact, get you away from your own self? I don't think so.

NEIL: That doesn't interest me.

MATTHEW: Only if you suppress a certain particular series of thoughts that come flooding, somehow, through the brain.

PETER: Thank goodness I never experienced that.

MATTHEW: How come you haven't picked up on category three! Category three. As if willfully avoiding it.

(During this last sentence the VOICE returns, taking over for MATTHEW)

VOICE: *(As the men, carrying books, assemble around the table and look up)* Category Three. Am I moving from the spot? I am not! Now I was not in category three, and now I am, not having left it. You join me without knowing it. Welcome to category three. Say yes. Welcome to category three. Yes. I was talking to myself.

KYLE: Ah, you just left category three, unfortunately.

NEIL: I don't think I'll ever understand.

MATTHEW: Here's an experiment. Try touching your nose. *(Carefully, they all do)* Now find a way to hold onto your nose with the major part of the hand. *(They all do)* Now, breathe through the nose.

KYLE: *(Hand clamped over her nose, making her voice nasal)* Is it okay if I change my voice so I sound funny?

VOICE and KYLE: Ah, that's music to my ears.

KYLE, MATTHEW, NEIL, and PETER: Yes, but is it really category three? Category three?

VOICE: Of course not. I've been manipulating you. For no good reason. Just like that. Show me your hair. *(PETER whips off his hat, shakes out his long hair, and bends forward onto the table)* Of course. Did you make that request just pop out of my unconscious? Somebody did. Now I'm into my own time frame and I like it, sort of. I'm going to support my body. Yes. Do that all the time. *(KYLE has been approaching PETER, and puts her hands slowly on his hump)*

I'll have to develop my back muscles.

Please do.

"PLEASE DO. PLEASE DO. PLEASE DO."

(KYLE is now reaching under his coat, to touch the hump more directly)

(I can't say what I'm hoping for. Back muscles that become so excessive, everything is . . . beyond imagining, to say the least, which is to say nothing. But we do go that far. Am I growing a letter or two coming from out of my back?

(KYLE extracts her hands and examines them)

MATTHEW: I'm waiting here with pad and pencil.

NEIL: As soon as you see one of the letters, rising from one of the back muscles . . .

MATTHEW: I'll write down whatever I see.

(PETER stands up to look at KYLE. She pushes him back onto the table and he grabs his book and runs off, as does NEIL. MATTHEW crosses slowly to sit. KYLE walks about, then sits also. The electronic tone is loud, as MATTHEW and KYLE eye each other defensively)

VOICE: Somebody knocked.
Somebody fell down.
Somebody else said hello, hello, but they weren't talking
    to me—no, they were.
Somebody telephoned.
Somebody tried capturing my attention. Help, I offered.
Somebody imitated me.
Somebody attacked me, but I was on vacation.
Somebody felt bad.
Somebody smiled. Why, I wondered. I didn't know it
    was involuntary.
I expected it to turn into a face.
But it didn't.

I forgot about it.
I forgot about it.

(By now, NEIL is writing on the blackboard along with the woman in the red dress. PETER writes at another. KYLE sits as she did in the first moments of the play, staring up at the speaker, then staring at the audience)

In this city, capital of thought,
Illness is permitted,
And verbal behavior is by definition
What leaves something out.

(MATTHEW slowly rises and, supporting himself on the table edge, slowly walks, hand over hand, to the other side of the table, all the while watching KYLE)

Entrapment. The name of the game.
The statements made, are the statements in which you fill in,
Invisibly, certain blanks.
Then, revealed naked as you really are
The verbal police close in for the kill.

MATTHEW: I have no reason to be unhappy with anything you say. Because what you leave out, I can fill in however I like with my imagination. And you always leave things out. So me, I'm on happiness street. And to celebrate, I make dictionaries of private intention, which a certain kind of person responds to by crying foul, foul. But that word also, I can pull into an idea of turbulence . . .

(KYLE rises and stands before the table like someone ready to dive into a pool. As MATTHEW continues, she lifts her arms, and slowly "dives" onto the table, so that the upper half of her body lies face down on the table's surface)

MATTHEW and **VOICE:** . . . that ends up defiantly exuberant!

(As an electronic tone rises and falls, MATTHEW runs and sits, head thrown back in his chair, as if in a trance, but clutching at his neck as if to keep his coat closed for warmth)

VOICE: So what if my friends say, "Why did you join the verbal police?
How could you! How could you do that?"
The answer is,
I like power sometimes,
And having said that
Everybody looks at me in a different light.
Oh now I get it, they say.
He's out for kicks.

(Still stretched out on the table, KYLE starts to roll slowly onto her back)

THAT I can understand.
I think to myself,
You don't know what you reveal about yourself
When you say I'M out for kicks.
Do I write you up?
Of course I do.
But you never know whether it's punishment or gratification,
So I'm as mysterious as ever, in your eyes.
That's what it's like
Being part of the verbal police.

MATTHEW: *(Speaking to the audience, still in his head-thrown-back position in the chair)*
City of language intrigue.
Easy to meet people,
Who seem to be using the same words over and over,

But really—
Each time it's a blow to a different part of the body.

(A telephone rings somewhere and PETER *and* NEIL, *who were still at the blackboards, run off)*

VOICE: The telephone is for you. I'm being challenged to respond. But I defiantly seal my lips. Having done that, I'm ready to handle the receiver.

*(*PETER *and* NEIL *reenter as if their bodies are glued together. This frightens* KYLE, *and she leaves the room. Then* PETER *and* NEIL *separate and go to seats)*

It wasn't for you after all? I'm not fooled. I make of things whatever I choose. You, of course, would maintain that in your own way, you're doing much the same. But the difference is I have at my command, not your guttural virtuosity, and therefore lack your nothing but pure preword-noise-network.

*(*KYLE *reenters, and all are now sitting at table)*

I simply use statement:
In the most perverse way possible,
And thereby end up far outdoing even your spectacular
Physical methods with my private syntactical articula-
   tions.

(All suddenly pick up small paddles from the table in front of them, each painted with a kind of target design. They hold the paddles in front of their faces)

They'd like you to pick up your end of the conversation.
What do you know—? Verbal police.
You?
Ah, did you think I was pretending you were a mirror?
I am, you know—

(Slowly, they lower the paddles, and cover their eyes with their forearms)

That's why I have myself reflected. Thank God, I can see who I am, whenever I run into you fellas.

(A metallic drum beats out a fast figure)

NEIL: *(Peeking from behind his arms)* Did he do that with his throat?

MATTHEW: Not necessary.

PETER: It's in the code.

MATTHEW: *(As he calmly recites, all lower their\arms)*
Seneca the stoic
Stole into the night.
Sure.
Sure.
Sure.
Three times?—I can double that.
Sure.
Sure.
Sure.
Was I a stoic like Seneca was stoic?

VOICE: You proved it, I think.

(As KYLE rises to go to a blackboard, the three men position the paddles in front of their faces and punch a thumb into the center of the target, groaning as it hits, as if they had just stuck a thumb into their own eyes)

The verbal police are watching. So PROOF was an act of desperation, in this case. Does that count?

(The random numbers loop is heard softly. All now run to different blackboards, copying the VOICE's text at a furious rate, still holding their paddle in their free hand)

Stoics also count.

Up to three, which is proved.

But that achieved, limitless numbers are also assumed
inside the numerological grid that suddenly snaps into
conscious presence.

Ah, a magic square in the mind?

No. The minute the verbal police stake out their claim,
all that MIND STUFF is persona-non-grata-mind,

And the language game turns into the only town anybody can live in.

Did you say live?

Did you say open a door?

I said find out where you live

Because this is where you do live,

But I don't know if that's what you want to call it

Since accuracy is something a little bit slippery—

Like ice on glasses, like butter on sharp steel

On stone, on marble

Iron, wood, tin, paper, gold, plastic, wood,

Gold

Gold

Gold.

VOICE LOOP: Gold gets rubbed out . . .

(As each speaks, they turn momentarily from their writing)

NEIL: Did you want . . . advice? Yes, I did want advice.

KYLE: I give what you don't want.

NEIL: The less I get the better I like it.

KYLE: That's subtle.

NEIL: That's not me speaking.

VOICE LOOP: Lipstick . . .

PETER: I turn myself inside out.

KYLE: Don't ask.

PETER: I didn't, you did.

KYLE: Inside out.

PETER: Ask.

KYLE: Don't ask.

VOICE LOOP: There's a lot to be said for dirt . . .

KYLE: *(sitting and throwing her hands up)* Woops.

NEIL: Don't erase that.

PETER: I do mental juggling.

NEIL: Dropping things.

PETER: Everything. Almost everything.

KYLE: Woops.

PETER: *(Throwing his paddle to the table)* Hold on to this for me.

MATTHEW: Your own question has a peculiar answer.

(He runs to the table, puts his foot up on it, and points at it)

PETER: Oh. Quite full.

MATTHEW: Of course.

VOICE LOOP: Break something . . .

(All the others are copying MATTHEW, putting a foot on the table and pointing to that foot)

MATTHEW: Ice—I slip on it.

KYLE: Non-ice.

PETER: Ah. Now I'm thinking.

KYLE: Non-ice.

MATTHEW: Bad idea.

NEIL: Break something.

MATTHEW: Okay.

(They all run from the table, leaving it empty but brightly illuminated as the rest of the room is in shadows. The random number loop rises, then the VOICE drowns it out)

VOICE: City of materials, that's how deep my dream goes and it goes deep.

(All but PETER *return and put a foot back on the table, then point to the foot)*

The spirit of things, not here floating about for just anybody to catch—

*(*PETER *places a vase of roses on the center of the table)*

Because the material is swamping all those who do get swamped. The substance delineation is rolling over me like a wave of sudden understanding,

(They all slowly move to new positions, kneeling down at the table's edge. They place their chins and arms on the table, stretching out toward the flowers)

and I think that substance inside you just needs me, frankly, to get my hands in there to do a sort of manipulation which to outsiders is going to look like mental massage. That excites me.

(They all run to the bookcase and get devices that consist of a large funnel on the end of a rubber tube. Using this device, they sniff all over the table, testing objects for smell)

But not enough. When you say excited, you're still traveling in the realm of the self-contained. Could I count on you for anything but a series of premises that pan out to nothing?

(As the voice continues, they throw away their funnels and each runs to collect a large, cardboard rectangle, painted with white and black stripes. They position themselves around the table behind the striped cardboard pieces, forming a kind of striped box that surrounds and isolates the table and its objects. Behind the striped rectangles, they are invisible)

But all my premises pan out, because when you beat something as thin as the world's thinnest sheet of any unusually valuable substance . . . That mental cornucopia can pour out over a whole world that has its own secret name, and the name is . . . itself.

(Slowly they tilt the boards back at an angle to reveal that they have now, behind the boards, put on dark glasses and long black beards. Slowly they bring the beards forward so they rest in front of the inclined cardboard. They look like the classic image of a group of bearded nineteenth-century middle-European anarchists)

Itself?
You recognize that name, I'm sure, hidden in some of your favorite evocative nouns. Like wood, glue, iron, flesh, brain, steel, metal, gold, fabric, flesh, gold. Those words almost turn it around for me. Those aren't words, they don't function like words, because you put out your hand and groped toward the wrong real thing.
The way out?
Too late. Too late.
I'll make a fast exit.

(They straighten their cardboard rectangles so they again rest upright on the edge of the table. They remain frozen, staring at the audience)

Open, open the door
No more.
Open
No door. There is no door.
There is a door.
I don't see a door.
Sure there is.

The door out, is outside.
The door in, is inside.
Am I outside or inside?
You wanna get out or in?
I want to get out.
That's where the door is.
I want to get in.
Ah, that's where the door is.

I don't see no door!
I don't see no door!
I don't see no door!

(The men pull their cards from the table and, holding them under their chins, begin to bounce up and down, as KYLE runs off and strange, abrasive music begins)

Doctors of death on the rampage again
Spreading their violence wherever they can.
Poison that punishes, poison that kills,
Really the medicine, cure for your ills.
Sadness on sadness piled up to the sky,
Only escape is escape, if you try.
Methods that promise to help and they don't,
Lift yourself right into will, through a won't.

(By now they have gotten rid of their cards and are doing strange dances, which end as Matthew runs to a microphone)

MATTHEW: Tell me, has one of us . . . *(He is thrown back from the mike by a loud drum riff, but fights his way back)* Has one of us been practicing his balancing act?

(He runs to the table, places the vase of roses on his head, and dances across the room as the VOICE speaks)

VOICE: Waiting for answers is like waiting for a heart attack. Sentiment is evoked, but isn't the heart of the matter, in a sense.

(*PETER and NEIL are at their books, studying furiously. MAT-THEW has crossed to a side table where he replaces the vase on his head with a black bowler hat, first making gestures at the hat like a vaudeville magician trying to hypnotize . . . a hat! In the poem that follows, to music that is rhythmic but ominous, MATTHEW throws the hat to the ground several times, in mock-furious fashion, and NEIL and PETER scurry forward to retrieve the hat and carefully place it again on MATTHEW's head. It's silly, but also as frightening and full of fury as a terrible nightmare*)

Soon, soon
Did he throw a hat in the air.
Soon, soon
One word that's all words.
Soon, did a flutter
Turn automatic.
Soon, soon,
When a bar of chocolate and a bar of soap
Were interchangeable,
What got a bubble burst?
And soon, soon,
The place it fell to was
Uncomfortable delight.
So roll, twist
The matter behind the mind,
So the grain irritant oyster
Goes snap
At the brain spark that lights up
MY whole world at least.

(KYLE charges in as the music changes, carrying a large target and scattering the men. She then runs out almost as quickly as she appeared. The men then embrace as if ready to set off on a great adventure. They run back and leap through the long, horizontal interior window, falling halfway through so their torsos stick out of the window and their legs extend up in the air. They freeze in this position)

Roll roll
One word that's all words.
Roll, roll
I got no ocean
In my ocean.
Space out:
Phases.

Phase phase.
Don't get lost
Eating your basis.

(KYLE returns wearing a white-feathered American-Indian-style headdress, her arms loaded down with dinner plates which she sets out on the table. Each has a big number painted in the center of the plate: 1, 2, or 3)

It goes out in a big circle
Loops back and says the triple dip.
Dips me, you, and everybody in good stuff.
When I stuff
I say stuff.
More stuff.
Phase it, phase it.
Phase it, phase it.

(The music is quieter now and KYLE exits, arms over her head in classical ballet style. The men slowly emerge from the win-

*dow, pulling after them a giant tablecloth which they slowly
and carefully spread over the entire table)*

Veronica came into my life
Like a cyclone of plastic.
Who got off first?
Hard to say, but when I
Got down from the talk-a-lot bus,
Boy, was I hot.
Phase it, phase it.
One word that's all words.
Phase it, phase it.
That means cool out the whole planet.

Air-dale and more,
My holes to vent.
Blocked up by the information—
That wasn't Veronica's trip
So my return ticket
Stuck up,
Tickled me,
And I couldn't
Phase it, phase it.

*(KYLE has reentered carrying her target. She is close to MAT-
THEW, who leans despondently against the rear wall, back to
the room.)*

So instead I
Phase it, phase it.
Phase it all the time.
Phase it.

KYLE: *(Sings in a high voice as the music fades)* Try it. Try
it. Try it.

MATTHEW: *(Slowly pointing to the target)* These must
be—

NEIL: *(A whispered echo)* Must be.

MATTHEW: These must be bad arrows—

NEIL: *(Whispering)* Arrows.

MATTHEW: Or I must have bad aim.

NEIL: *(Whispering)* Aim.

KYLE: *(Singing)* Try it. Wearing a funny hat.

(As MATTHEW runs from the room, hiding his face, retreating from KYLE's target and hat, NEIL and PETER run to the bookcase, where they find headdresses to wear, just like KYLE's)

VOICE: These must be bad arrows, or I must have bad aim, or I must be better at this than I ever imagined possible.

(NEIL and PETER start leafing through books, only to be interrupted as MATTHEW reappears against the white curtained window rear, illuminated in a very bright light, and wearing an absolutely giant white headdress with feathers, still in dark glasses and beard. Cheap organ music fills the room as the voice intones over all)

Who's the big guy?

Who's the big guy?

He doesn't say much, but he doesn't have to because the minute he starts talking you know it's half right and half wrong anyway.

Which is more than I can say about myself—Woops, I just did.

Woops, one word that's all words.

(MATTHEW has glided forward, causing NEIL and PETER to drop stacks of books all over the floor in shock. They run after MATTHEW to relieve him of his giant headdress, but then MATTHEW collapses to the carpet. They grab him under the arms and drag him to the table, where they deposit him)

Who's the big guy? I thought he lived in my neighborhood, but now I see this town has particular features that turn it into a very unrecognizable part of town, to say the least, which is why I like it!

(*MATTHEW recovers and turns to see KYLE beside him. Slowly he faces her, putting a finger to his lips as if to say "Don't say a word, explain nothing," then slowly turns toward the audience, again with a finger to his lips*)

Who's the big guy?
Who's the big guy?
I don't know, you don't know, he don't know himself. But that isn't a negation. All he does is open his big mouth wide, and without saying it, I know I'm home free! I'm home free!

(*All find small whisk brooms hanging from the side of the table and begin sweeping everything gently toward the center. The lady in red still writes on the blackboard. At a certain moment, all but the lady in red toss their whisk brooms onto the table, hide their eyes from the light—or from the audience—with their forearms, and hurry from the room, leaving the stage empty but for the lady in red, who continues to write on the blackboard the text of the play. The VOICE is heard softly . . .*)

Welcome to category three. Welcome. Welcome to category three. Welcome to category three, to category three. Welcome. Welcome to category three.

(*The lights fade*)

The End

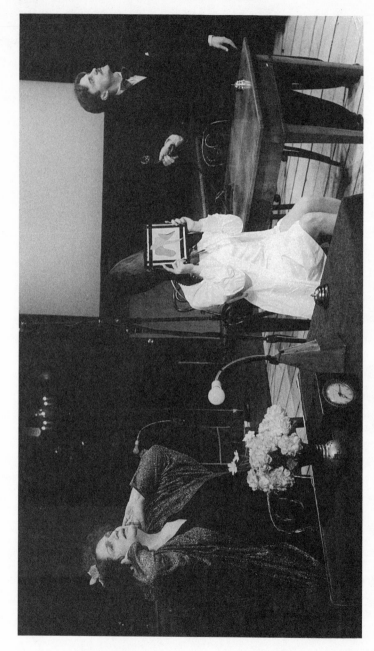

Lola Pashalinski, Kate Manheim, and David Patrick Kelly in Film Is Evil: Radio Is Good. *(Photo by Martha Swope)*

APPENDIX

◆

Productions by the Ontological-Hysteric Theater written, directed, and designed by Richard Foreman:

Angelface, New York City, 1968
Ida-Eyed, New York City, 1969
Total Recall, New York City, 1970
HcOhTiEnLa (or) *Hotel China*, New York City, 1971
Evidence, New York City, 1972
Sophia = (*Wisdom*) Part 3: *The Cliffs*, New York City, 1972
Particle Theory, New York City, 1973
Classical Therapy or *A Week under the Influence* . . . , Paris, 1973
Pain(t), New York City, 1974
Vertical Mobility, New York City, 1974
Pandering to the Masses: A Misrepresentation, New York City, 1975
Rhoda in Potatoland (Her Fall-Starts), New York City, 1975
Livre des Splendeurs: Part One, Paris, 1976

Book of Splendors: Part Two (*Book of Leaves*) *Action at a Distance*, New York City, 1977

Blvd. de Paris (*I've Got the Shakes*), New York City, 1977

Madness and Tranquility (*My Head Was a Sledgehammer*), New York City, 1979

Place + Target, Rome, 1980

Penguin Touquet, New York City, 1981

Café Amérique, Paris, 1981

Egyptology, New York City, 1983

La Robe de Chambre de Georges Bataille, Paris, 1983

Miss Universal Happiness, New York City, 1985

The Cure, New York City, 1986

Film Is Evil: Radio Is Good, New York City, 1987

Symphony of Rats, New York City, 1987

Love and Science, Stockholm, 1988

What Did He See? New York City, 1988

Lava, New York City, 1989

Eddie Goes to Poetry City: Part One, Seattle, 1990

Eddie Goes to Poetry City: Part Two, New York City, 1991

Music-theater works written, directed, and designed by Richard Foreman, with music by Stanley Silverman:

Elephant Steps, 1968

Dream Tantras for Western Massachusetts, 1971

Dr. Selavy's Magic Theater, 1972

Hotel for Criminals, 1974

Madame Adare, 1980

Africanis Instructus, 1986

Love & Science, 1990

Plays and operas directed by Richard Foreman:

Threepenny Opera by Bertolt Brecht and Kurt Weill (Lincoln Center, New York City, 1976); *Stages*, by Stuart

Ostrow (Belasco Theater, New York City, 1978); *Don Juan*, by Molière (Guthrie Theater, Minneapolis, 1981); *Three Acts of Recognition*, by Botho Strauss (Public Theater, New York City, 1982); *Dr. Faustus Lights the Lights*, by Gertrude Stein (Festival d'Automne, Paris, 1982); *Die Fledermaus*, the opera by Johann Straus (Paris Opera, Paris, 1983); *The Golem*, by H. Leivick (Delacorte Theater, New York City, 1984); *Ma Mort, Ma Vie, de Pier Paolo Pasolini*, by Kathy Acker (Theater de la Bastille, Paris, 1985); *The Birth of the Poet*, an opera by Kathy Acker and Peter Gordon (RO Theater, Rotterdam, 1984; Brooklyn Academy of Music Opera House, New York City, 1985); *Largo Desolato*, by Vaclav Havel (Public Theater, New York City, 1986); *End of the World with Symposium to Follow*, by Arthur Kopit (American Repertory Theater, Boston, 1987); *The Fall of the House of Usher*, an opera by Arthur Yorinks and Philip Glass (American Repertory Theater, Boston, 1988); *Where's Dick?* an opera by Michael Korie and Stewart Wallace (Houston Grand Opera, Houston, 1989); *Woyzeck*, by Georg Buchner (Hartford Stage Company, Hartford, 1990); *Don Giovanni*, an opera by Mozart (Lille Opera, Lille, France, 1991)

Film and video works by Richard Foreman:

Out of the Body Travel, a video play (1975); *City Archives*, a video play (1977); *Strong Medicine*, a feature film (1978); *Radio Rick in Heaven and Radio Richard in Hell*, a film (1987); and *Total Rain*, a video play (1990).

Other books published by Richard Foreman:

Plays and Manifestos. Edited by Kate Davy. New York: New York University, 1976. Includes the plays *Angel-*

face, Total Recall, Hotel China, Classical Therapy, Vertical Mobility, Pain(t), Rhoda in Potatoland.

Reverberation Machines: The Later Plays and Essays. Barrytown, New York: Station Hill, 1985. Includes the plays *Book of Splendors*, Parts One and Two; *Blvd. de Paris; Place & Target; Penguin Touquet; Café Amérique; Egyptology.*

Love and Science: Librettos by Richard Foreman. New York: TCG Publications, 1991. Includes the librettos *Hotel for Criminals, Africanus Instructus, Love and Science, Yiddisher Teddy Bears.*

Six-time winner of the Obie Award and one of the most influential figures in American drama, Richard Foreman has been honored for his "outstanding record of accomplishment" by the National Endowment for the Arts. Since 1968, when he founded the Ontological-Hysteric Theater, Foreman has written, designed, and directed thirty original works which have been presented in the U.S. and throughout Europe. He has also written, designed, and directed seven musicals in collaboration with composer Stanley Silverman. In addition, he has designed and directed works by Brecht, Büchner, Mozart, Molière, Gertrude Stein, Botho Strauss, Philip Glass, Kathy Acker, Vaclav Havel, and Arthur Kopit. Among his films and videos are *Strong Medicine* and *Total Rain*.